Education of a Princess

Marie, Grand Duchess of Russia

TO

THE MEMORY OF

MY FATHER

EDUCATION OF A PRINCESS

A MEMOIR

BY

MARIE, GRAND DUCHESS OF RUSSIA

Translated from the French & Russian

under the editorial supervision of

Russell Lord

NEW YORK

THE VIKING PRESS

MCMXXXI

PRINTED IN U. S. A.

MARIE, GRAND DUCHESS OF RUSSIA
From a drawing by E. Shoumatoff, 1930

CONTENTS

CONTENTS

ILLUSTRATIONS

EDUCATION OF A PRINCESS

A MEMOIR

IN MEMORY OF
ISABEL H. COHEN
1934

INTRODUCTION

SEMI-CYCLE

BORN in 1890, I have stepped through the ages. My earliest memories are of surroundings so remote, so unlike the world of swirling traffic and shining towers that I see from these windows, as to be, by comparison, mediæval.

When I try to think back to that time, I am persuaded that in calendars there is no reality, that time in itself has no meaning, and that the early events of my life are hardly anything more than a fairy tale.

My public entrance into the world was made, I am told, in a golden coach drawn by three pairs of white horses. The coach was surrounded with mounted hussars in scarlet uniforms. In this way I was taken to the Winter Palace for my christening. I was called Marie after my grandmother, wife of the Emperor Alexander II, and after my aunt and godmother, the consort of Alexander III, at the close of whose reign I came into the world.

The same fate that placed me in a setting so curious and magnificent deprived me of a normal upbringing. As a child I enjoyed no real family life and in consequence I have never been able to comprehend the meaning and true value of a home. I was cared for and brought up by strangers, and even had this not been so, even if my parents had both remained alive and at the head of our household, my education would have been about as it was—strictly in accord with standards and rules which prevailed in almost all the courts of Europe through the latter part of the nineteenth century.

Education, in the eyes of my teachers, was of little importance as compared with religious and moral instruction. Throughout all the long, slow years of my childhood, I was held—mentally, at least, and for the most part, actually—always within the four walls of our various palaces. They kept me purposely in ignorance of the importance of the situation into which I had been born. As an offset to the grandeur and luxury with which I was surrounded, I was treated with complete simplicity.

The same attitude was demanded of me in my relations to others, especially to inferiors. I was taught meekness and humility as Christian virtues; order, discipline, and restraint as civil ones. An exaggerated submission was required of me. I was deprived of all freedom of action; my every expression of will or of independence was at once suppressed. This, no doubt, was in order to counterbalance for the future the extreme independence which Russian royalty had in the past enjoyed and which had proven to involve many dangers. But it reflected also the tendency of that epoch towards the banal and conventional. I was shown the dangers of being royal but was never told how to shoulder efficiently the responsibilities which one day would be mine.

The insufficiency of such an education, and the results of this insufficiency in myself and in others far more powerful, will appear again and again in the course of my story. We in Russia were in the position to exert an enormous influence. But somehow the education that was given us atrophied our powers and limited our horizons. I soon knew of all the petty restrictions and disadvantages of my position, but remained until almost the end totally unaware of the grand possibilities it offered me to serve my country.

My studies were neglected or conducted from a point of view entirely superficial. I was moved so often from place to place that my teachers and professors changed constantly. And the change was seldom for the better; they were, with hardly an exception, beings of no personality, and with no ability to give life to facts.

A child learns by contacts; I had few. There was not even a library where I could curl up in a comfortable arm-chair with a book in my lap. The cases were always locked, or the books would be bound statistics which nobody had ever touched.

Royalty is destined by force of circumstance to dwell in a certain aloofness and, although constantly surrounded by people, to lead a lonely life. Absolutely nothing was given me as a compensating source of inner companionship. I was not equipped for the solitary hours, the hours when I would be off duty. By the time I was thrust out into life I was much more fit for a convent than for struggle, and I was endowed with an inferiority complex against which I have been obliged at times to put up a real fight.

But in spite of all the deficiencies of my upbringing and education, there was certainly something unique and altogether charming in that atmosphere. It called forth qualities removed from the requirements of a modern life; it was old-fashioned and narrow-minded; but there reigned over all its phases a patriarchal spirit that was profoundly real and moving.

The seclusion in which I had perforce to dwell, the very smallness of my orbit, constantly stimulated my interest in the outer world. Some curious instinct warned me at a very early age that the life we all were leading, the very principles by which it was governed, were somehow out of balance with life as a whole, and could not last. Outside, and all around us, I could feel brooding forces, and tendencies of which we knew nothing.

In spite of the apparent stability of our situation I somehow knew that all was not well with us. A year or so before the Russo-Japanese War, I remember sitting on the floor of the nursery and trying to button my own boots. In case of a revolution I had to know how to look after myself.

Subconsciously since that time, for many years after, I was

preparing for something to happen, and when it did happen I was still unprepared.

I faced the situation as well as I could. Something entirely new had now to be built up; there were even no ruins to serve as a foundation. Personal achievement had now to take the place of the old pedestal; I had now to build something of my own, something that no one would ever have the power to take away from me.

When my resources gave out I went to work. Work led me to business into which I threw myself with the energy of inexperience. But I was anxious to learn and the many disappointments I had to suffer did not kill my ardour. My horizon was widening prodigiously. I began to attain an individual outlook.

My curiosity as to life and all its manifestations was finally being gratified, beyond my utmost expectations.

Here in America, my education continues. I grieve for all of those who have been lost to me, but my own wounds and tribulations I cannot regret. They have taught me great lessons; I would never give up now what I have gained from them.

There is one thing, however, which comes to me from the past and which I treasure beyond anything else, present or to come, and that is my love for my country. This devotion was implanted in me by my family. In their great deeds and even in their failures, the Romanovs of all generations placed the interests and glory of Russia above any personal calculations. Russia was part of their soul and their body. To them the demanded sacrifice was never too great, and this they proved with their lives. I pray that their spirit may animate me to the end of my days.

New York City, 1930.

ROMANOV GENEALOGY

NOTE: The children and grandchildren of Emperors bear the hereditary title of Grand Duke or Grand Duchess. The great-grandchildren no longer bear this title.

Names in CAPITALS denote characters who appear in this narrative.

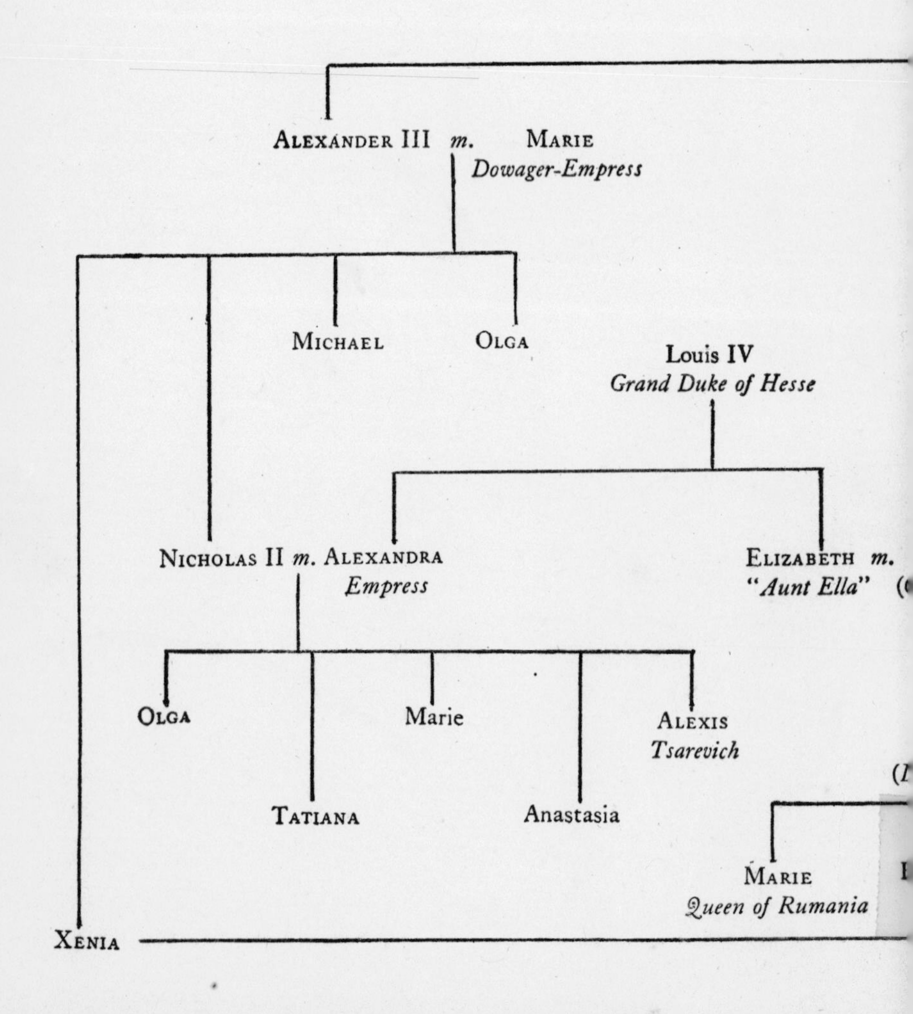

PART ONE

AUTOCRACY

CHAPTER I

EIGHTEEN NINETY-TWO

I DO not remember my mother. She died in giving birth to my brother Dmitri, who was born when I was one and a half years old. She was the Princess Alexandra of Greece, daughter of King George and of Queen Olga, who had been born a Grand Duchess of Russia.

In 1889, my mother, when only eighteen, was married to my father, the Grand Duke Paul of Russia. It proved a happy marriage, but brief. Towards the end of their third year together my parents were visiting at Ilinskoie, a country property of the Grand Duke Serge, my father's brother, when mother, seven months enceinte with her second child, fell gravely ill.

Her illness was so unexpected and it came upon her so suddenly that doctors could not be brought to her in time to help her. She was attended by the old midwife of the village. When the doctors finally arrived she was already in a state of coma from which she could never be recalled. She remained thus for six days, then gave birth and died.

Her death at the age of twenty-one prostrated the family and was mourned throughout Russia. The peasants of the region gathered in crowds; they raised her in her coffin to their shoulders and bore her to the railway station, a distance of some eight miles. It was a funeral march, but it seemed, rather, such a procession as welcomes to her home a young bride; everywhere she passed were flowers.

My mother was adored by all who knew her. From the photographs that remain of her, I can see that she was beautiful; the features are small and finely wrought; the outline of her face has a softness of contour almost infantile; her eyes are large and a little sad; and the whole of her person reflects a spirit of particular gentleness and charm.

My brother came into the world so small, so feeble, that no one thought he could live. His arrival went almost unnoticed amid the grief and disorder aroused by my mother's desperate condition. My old English nurse has told me of having found the newborn child bundled haphazardly among some blankets on a chair, as she came running to get news of my mother. It was only after my mother was dead that they began to pay attention to Dmitri.

At that time baby incubators were rare; they wrapped him in cotton-wool and kept him in a cradle heated with hot-water bottles. Uncle Serge, with his own hands, gave him the bouillon baths that the doctors prescribed, and the child gained in strength and began to grow.

He and I were left at Ilinskoie for several months, until he was judged strong enough to travel; we were then returned to our home in St. Petersburg, where our father awaited us.

All of this was, of course, in a past beyond my conscious recollection, and has been told me by other people. Of my own memories, the first, I am certain, goes back to a day in my fourth year when, standing on the seat of a black leather arm-chair, I was having my picture taken. I recall how the starched pleats of my little white dress scratched my arms and how the silk of my sash creaked. My head was of just the same height as the back of the chair on which the photographer had placed me; my feet, clad in pumps with silken pompons, rested on a leopard's skin.

We lived, Dmitri and I, in St. Petersburg with our father, in a palace on the Neva. Our palace was vast and rectangular, of no definite style or period, its diverse groups and wings drawn together around a spacious inner court. The front windows of the second floor opened to a sweeping view of the Neva, a wide river, in summer alive with ships.

Dmitri and I lived with our nurses and attendants in a series

THE PARENTS OF THE GRAND DUCHESS MARIE BEFORE THEIR MARRIAGE

The Grand Duke Paul, the Grand Duchess Alexandra, and her mother, Queen Olga of Greece

of rooms on the second floor. This nursery suite, the domain of our infancy, was entirely isolated from the rest of the palace. It was a little world of its own, a world ruled by our English nurse, Nannie Fry, and her assistant, Lizzie Grove.

Nannie Fry and Lizzie Grove had brought to Russia all the habits of their native country; they ruled the nursery according to their own ideas and principles, and enjoyed an absolute sovereignty not only over my brother and me but over an innumerable retinue of Russian chambermaids, valets, and assistant nurses.

Until I was six years old I spoke hardly a word of Russian. The immediate household and all of the family spoke English to us.

Father used to come upstairs twice a day to see us. His love for us was deep and fond, and we knew it, but he never displayed towards us a spontaneous tenderness, embracing us only when bidding us good-morning or good-night.

I adored him. Every moment that I could be with him was joyous and, if for any reason a day passed without our seeing him, it was a real disappointment.

He commanded at this time the Imperial Horse Guards. I recall him most distinctly in the dress uniform of that regiment. It was a truly magnificent uniform—all of white with gold braid. The gilded helmet was surmounted by the imperial eagle.

My father was tall and thin with wide shoulders. His head was small; his rounded forehead a little pinched at the temples. For so large a man his feet were remarkably small and his hands were of a beauty and delicacy that I have never since discovered in the hands of a human being.

He was uniquely charming. Every word, movement, gesture, bore the imprint of distinction. No one could approach him without feeling drawn to him; and this remained always true, for age could not dim his elegance, banish his gaiety, or embitter the goodness of his heart.

His humour ran sometimes to fantastic, enchanting lies which he maintained to the uttermost. He deftly slipped under our pet hare one Easter, for instance, an ordinary hen's egg and succeeded in making us believe that our tame hare had laid the egg.

At Christmas he was particularly joyous, and Christmas was the peak of our year. Days before, the trees would be brought out and set up. Then the doors of the great reception hall would be closed; then mysterious preparations, half sensed, would go forward all around us; then, and only then throughout all our year, would the brooding calm of that great palace be driven away and replaced by a delicious and joyous agitation.

As Christmas Eve approached our excitement became so intense that it required all the vigilance of our nurses to keep Dmitri and me from stealing a look behind those closed doors. To calm us they would take us driving, but Christmas lights and decorations and the gay holiday spirit of the crowds that thronged around our carriage in the streets only excited us the more.

Finally the great moment came. When we were dressed father came for us. He led us to the doors of the closed reception hall and made a sign. The electric lights within the large room were snapped off, the doors thrown open. Before our enchanted eyes appeared, in that immense dark room, the magic trees, ablaze with candles. Our hearts stopped beating, and tremblingly we entered after our father. He made another sign; darkness vanished; along the walls appeared tables covered with white cloths and on these tables were the gifts.

Our first glance at those tables, our first confused, rapturous attempt to see everything at once—no joy that I have experienced in all the years since can be compared to that!

After we had been permitted timidly to approach, greedily, rapturously, to examine our treasures, it became the turn of the others of the household to receive gifts. Those of my father's court who lived at the palace, his aides-de-camp, the chamberlain and his wife, our nurses, and the servants—they all came forward now for their Christmas presents, heaped on separate tables and marked by name.

Father had a gift table of his own, and that table bore the weirdest collection of love offerings imaginable. For months Dmitri and I had been occupied with needlework, creating with immense pains and incredibly bad taste such works of art as cushions, pen-wipers, clippers, and book covers to bestow upon him.

When we became a little older he besought us, for his sake, to give up needlework; thereafter we saved and bought in shops with great excitement such other useless and frightful objects as could not, for sentiment, be thrown away and so were doomed to accumulate, useless and hideous, year upon year in the darkness of wardrobes.

When the candles on the trees had lived out their brief life, that was the time ordained for my father to set off the fireworks in which he always took a great delight and interest. Once he exploded a fire-cracker so close to my legs that it set my dress afire. The flame was quickly put out but I was terribly frightened.

In the evening, worn by the day's emotions but completely happy, we would be put to bed, taking with us our chosen toy of the day's treasure. Only one thing would sadden me. At evening, every Christmas Eve, after our fête, father would leave us to pass the remaining days of the holiday with Uncle Serge and Aunt Ella at Moscow. His absence left in my heart a void that even the most beautiful of my presents could not fill.

Few persons were permitted to visit us. When there was company we were not allowed downstairs. Various members of the imperial family paid occasional dutiful calls to our nursery. They would watch us play, exchange a few remarks with Nannie Fry, and rapidly depart. Certain of my father's aides-de-camp would sometimes come to see us, particularly the

Baron Schilling; him we liked especially. When he died, very young, of galloping consumption, I remember vividly my sense of confusion and loss, for this was the first time that I was ever called upon to face the death, the mysterious dissolution and disappearance of a human being.

ii

ONCE when we were having our bread and milk our father, who had never before visited us at such a time, came into the nursery accompanying a giant with a light beard. I looked at him with open mouth as we were bidden to tell him good-bye. They explained that this was my Uncle Sasha (my father's eldest brother), the Emperor Alexander III. It was the first and last time that I ever saw him. Some time afterwards when the nurses were putting us into our red plush overcoats to go driving, someone came and told Nannie Fry that we must not wear those coats; that it would be unsuitable. Then we were told that Alexander III had died.

In the spring of the year following—1896—father took us to Moscow where members of our family from all of Europe were gathering for the coronation of my cousin Nicholas II. Although I was still very small, barely six, I recall perfectly some of the events of that time. Dmitri and I were taken first to Ilinskoie, our Uncle Serge's country place out from Moscow. Then father decided that I was old enough to attend the coronation ceremonies and that it would be a pity to deprive me of a spectacle that I would remember all my life—one which proved to be the last of its kind in our history.

So I was sent to Moscow with Nannie Fry and passed several days at the palace of the Governor General with my Uncle Serge.

On the day of the coronation I was taken to the Kremlin and from a window saw the royal procession come out of the Cathedral of the Assumption and cross the interior court.

TEA IN THE GARDENS

The Grand Duchess Marie and the Grand Duke Dmitri with the English nurses

Beside me the Grand Duchess Olga, the Emperor's eldest daughter, blinked at the brilliant spectacle from the arms of her nurse. She was only a few months old at the time and remarkably ugly, with a head too large for her small body.

I remember most distinctly the moment when the Emperor and the two Empresses, his mother and his consort, emerged from the church, each under a canopy decorated with ostrich plumes and carried by court dignitaries. It was magnificent. And there was my Uncle Serge behind the Emperor and my father behind the young Empress!

The numerous sovereigns and foreign princes representing their government or connected by marriage with our family had come on for the coronation; the palaces of Moscow were full of relatives. My Uncle Serge took me with him several times when he made calls.

One such call I particularly remember by reason of my villainous behaviour. It was at a tea given by my grandmother, Queen Olga of Greece. She put into my cup a drop of tea and filled it up with boiling milk covered with a skin-like scum. At that age, boiled milk had always been insupportable to me. Grandmother, seeing that I did not touch my "tea," asked why. I told her. Grandmother took the cup and tried to make me drink. I pushed the cup away so rudely as to splash milk on her dress, over mine, and all over the tablecloth. Uncle Serge was angry. Everyone else laughed, even my grandmother, but I was overcome with shame and left the house furious and humiliated.

After a few days I returned to Ilinskoie where my brother had remained with my young uncle, Prince Christopher of Greece, only two years my senior. After the final coronation ceremonies, the new Emperor and Empress removed to Ilinskoie to stay with my uncle and aunt. They came attended by the closest of their immediate relatives.

We were crowded out of Ilinskoie, we children, and spent that week at Usovo, Uncle Serge's other country place.

Magnificent preparation had been made for the fêtes attending the ascension of the young Emperor and Empress. All was blighted, however, by a frightful accident at Khodinsky Meadows where a distribution of gifts to the people was to take place. The crowd was far larger than had been expected and order could not be maintained by a carelessly organized police force. The crowd stormed the booths from which the gifts were to be distributed. Thousands of them were killed and maimed in the crush of the panic and stampede that followed.

In court circles the disaster was little mentioned, but I remember having heard it remarked that the Emperor and Empress and the other guests of Ilinskoie during the week following the coronation had seemed under a cloud of sadness and premonition. All, perhaps without saying so, regarded this catastrophe as a bad omen at the very beginning of the new reign.

CHAPTER II

ILINSKOIE

THE coronation guests departed. We settled again at Ilinskoie into the routine of country life. Dmitri and I always spent our summers there with Uncle Serge and Aunt Ella.

They had never had any children of their own. Their relations towards each other were distinguished by a strained fondness that rested on my aunt's serene acceptance of my uncle's decision in all matters great and small. Proud and timid, both of them, they seldom showed their true feelings and never offered confidences.

Converted after her marriage to the Orthodox religion, my aunt had become each year more devoutly attached to its forms and practices. Although himself pious and scrupulous in observance of all the rites of Orthodoxy, Uncle Serge regarded with anxiety his wife's increasing absorption in things spiritual, and ended by regarding it as immoderate.

He treated her rather as if she were a child. I believe that she was hurt by his attitude and longed to be better understood, but it was as if she were being driven deeper and deeper within herself for refuge. She and my uncle seemed never very intimate. They met for the most part only at meals and by day avoided being alone together. They slept, however, up to the last year of their life together, in the same great bed.

My uncle, the Grand Duke Serge, was possessed of a unique personality and of a character that remained to me, to the very day of his dreadful death, incomprehensible. The fourth son of the Emperor Alexander II, he was in 1891 appointed by his brother, Alexander III, as Governor General of Moscow, and he continued now in this post under the new reign. It was a position of great power and consequence, and his devotion to his duty was absolute. Even in the country, when he was supposed to be resting, he was constantly receiving couriers from Moscow and giving audiences.

From their early youth Uncle Serge and my father had been devoted to each other, and my uncle was also profoundly attached to my mother. The early death which came to her, as I have said, at Ilinskoie, left him with a sense of bereavement for which he could never be consoled. He ordered the rooms in which she had spent her last hours to be kept intact, exactly as they were when she died there. He had these rooms locked, and throughout the remainder of his life himself guarded the key, allowing no one else to enter.

He was as tall as my father. Like my father he had broad shoulders above a body excessively thin. He wore a small beard, closely trimmed. His hair, which was thick, was cut short and so brushed as to stand up briskly all over his head. In characteristic posture he stood erect, head up, chest out; his elbows would be drawn closely in towards his sides, and with the fingers of one hand he toyed with a jewelled ring that he habitually wore on the little finger of the other.

When he was vexed or surly, his lips would be compressed to one crisp straight line and his eyes became little hard points of light. Cold, inflexible, the world called him, and not without cause, but towards Dmitri and me he displayed a tenderness almost feminine. Despite which he demanded of us, as of all his household or following, exact and immediate obedience. The house, the farms, all business affairs, and the least personal detail of our separate lives he felt it incumbent upon him to direct himself, and to his least decision would permit not the slightest contradiction. Introspective, essentially diffident, his true spirit imprisoned within him, he hid private impulses of exceeding sensitiveness, and acted according to rigid conventions and to convictions altogether royalistic. Those few who knew him well were deeply devoted to him, but even his intimates feared him, and Dmitri and I feared him too.

In his fashion he loved us deeply. He liked to have us near him, and gave us a good deal of his time. But he was always jealous of us. If he had known the full extent of our devotion to our father it would have maddened him.

Aunt Ella was an elder sister of the young Empress and one of the most beautiful women I have ever seen in my life. She was tall and slight, of blonde colouring, with features of extraordinary fineness and purity. She had eyes of a grey-blue, on one of which was a spot of brown, and the effect of her glance was unusual.

Even when in the country my aunt gave a great deal of time and attention to her appearance. She designed most of her dresses herself, sketching and painting them in water-colours, planning them with care, and wearing them with art and distinction. My uncle, who had a passion for jewels, gave her many—so that she had a different set to harmonize with almost every costume that she wore.

Throughout our early childhood—throughout, indeed, our uncle's lifetime—Aunt Ella showed no interest in us or in anything that concerned us, and she saw as little of us as she could. She appeared to resent our presence in the household, and our uncle's evident affection for us. At times she said things to me that wounded me.

I recall one such time when she had dressed for an outing and seemed to me particularly beautiful. It was a simple dress of white muslin but she had her hair fixed a new way—gathered, unbound, at the back of her neck by a bow of black silk—and the effect was enchanting. I exclaimed:

"Oh! Auntie, you look like the picture of a little page in a fairy story."

She turned to my nurse without smiling and spoke in a dry, sharp tone:

"Fry, you really must teach her not to make personal remarks."

She swept away.

Of dressing for dinner she made a veritable ceremony and one that required much time. The maids, the mistress of the wardrobe, all were assembled. Cambric linen bordered with lace was made ready in a basket lined in rose satin. Wash basins were filled with hot water perfumed with verbena. Rose petals were floated in the bath.

Commercial cosmetics scarcely existed in Russia at the time. I believe that my aunt had never in her life seen rouge, and she used powder very rarely. Painting the face was an art almost unknown to Russian ladies of that day, and to princesses unknown entirely. Aunt Ella made her own face lotion, a mixture of cucumber juice and sour cream. She never permitted the summer sun to touch her skin, guarding it whenever she went out with a silk veil of thick mesh and a silk parasol lined in green.

After the maids and other attendants had taken off her outer dress of the afternoon, my aunt would shut herself in her dressing-room alone. With the chosen stockings, shoes, petticoats, and all the other complicated apparel of the period arrayed in orderly piles around them, the retinue waited. From the neighbouring room could be heard the splashing of water. Only when my aunt had bathed and put on her corset did she open the door. Then the maids would step briskly forward, each with her special task to perform.

While they were dressing her, my aunt would regard herself attentively, usually with pleasure, in a high triple mirror, so arranged that she saw herself from all sides. The final adjustments she made with her own hands. If the costume did not satisfy her in every particular, she had it taken off and demanded another which she adjusted with the same care and patience.

One of the maids dressed her hair. She did her nails herself.

They were curiously shaped, very flat and thin, curving forward over the ends of the fingers.

Manicuring accomplished, the dress of the evening donned —now came my part in the rites. My aunt would tell me the jewels she intended to wear, and I would go to her jewel cabinets—an array comparable almost to the show-cases at a jeweller's—and bring her her choice.

Soon my uncle, with habitual exactitude, would knock at the door to say that dinner was ready. Both of them would kiss me, then disappear; and Dmitri and I, having supped early, would be sent to bed.

One evening I remember, in those early days, I saw my aunt in court dress—majestic with her sweeping train of brocade, ablaze with jewels, and resplendently beautiful. Mute before the spectacle, I raised myself to the tips of my toes and placed a kiss full of devotion on the back of her white neck, directly under a magnificent necklace heavy with sapphires. She said nothing, but I could see her eyes, and the cold, hard look in them chilled me to the heart.

Only once in those early years did I see her face with her eyes unguarded. Taken with diphtheria, I lay desperately ill, with a fever of about 104 degrees, at Ilinskoie. I dwelt in a laughing world of phantasy, a world that distracted me from my sufferings and kept me occupied as in a story book. Always before my eyes were bright, charming pictures which I followed interestedly in my drowsy mind. Cracks and spots on the ceiling, after I watched them a while, turned into designs and cameos with soft grey backgrounds of an infinite variety. It was now a château with towers and drawbridges over a moat filled with water; a cavalcade left the gates; I saw the knights with falcons on their wrists, and Amazons in long dresses, their trains trailing on the ground in the dust. Then it would be a lake on which light barques floated. I saw the contour of islands with tall trees and clouds that passed across the sky. Once it seemed that I saw a high grille behind which was a magnificent palace in a beautiful garden of flowers. The cretonne of the curtains also presented fantastic subjects.

All that I saw was so lively and so lovely that I did not want anyone to come near me. At the approach of any human being, the visions disappeared. And after such delicious day-dreams my moments of lucidity were full of pain and sorrow. At night I slept little and badly. My head was heavy, my throat constricted, and there was a buzzing in my ears that seemed to come from a swarm of invisible flies. At one side, in the playroom, a night light burned, and from time to time a white shadow approached my bed.

Once, on hearing the sound of steps, I looked between half-opened lids and saw my aunt bent over me. Her expression astonished me; she was watching me with mingled curiosity and anxiety. It was the first time in my life that I had seen her face relaxed and natural. It was as if I had penetrated indiscreetly into the interior of her soul.

I moved. Her face was again as it had always been. It was years before I was again permitted to see her unmasked.

ii

I CAN say, nevertheless, that the most beautiful, the gayest memories of my childhood attach to Ilinskoie. It is to me the land in which Dmitri was born and where we grew up together; it is our little country in the immensity of all Russia, and it will always remain the strongest bond uniting me to our native soil.

It was a property of little more than 2400 acres, bordering the Moskva River, about forty miles from Moscow. It had nothing that belongs to those magnificent estates which so many great Russian families possessed before the disasters of the Revolution. It was modest, and perhaps on that account its charm was greater.

My uncle inherited Ilinskoie from his mother, the Empress

THE SUMMER HOUSE AT ILINSKOIE

Marie, who used it in her later years as a retreat from the fatigues and ceremonies of court life.

The house was square and of old oak. It was small, with few rooms, and had neither style nor pretension. Cottages were scattered throughout the park for guests and persons of the suite.

The park was the chief charm of the place. It bordered the river for some distance—cut by drives.

The place brought in nothing. Uncle Serge spent, on the contrary, a great deal of money to maintain it. Each year there was a new caprice. He would have prize cattle brought in—a special breed of a bright beige colour, from Switzerland, I believe; at any rate, I have never seen them anywhere else. He liked fine horses, and organized an Ardenne stud, the only one in Russia. He was always having something built—this year, a new school; the next, an extension of the greenhouses; and so on. The farm had a magnificent herd of Holstein cattle and elaborate poultry houses in which my uncle took a special interest. There were orchards and vegetable gardens and entire fields of flowers, cultivated for the house.

My uncle's suite and household were so numerous that each settling-down at Ilinskoie for the summer resembled the migration of an entire village. When we organized fêtes for the children of these people, we had always to plan for more than three hundred. My aunt had three women and one dressmaker, just for her personal service, without counting the maids. All these people were watched over by a mistress of the wardrobe. It was her duty to see that the apartments were kept in order, to engage servingwomen, to do the buying and shopping, to pay the bills of dressmakers and modistes, and to keep the keys of the jewel boxes.

My uncle had three or four valets who worked in relays of a week each. The male personnel, footmen, dishwashers, lamplighters, and so forth, were under the orders of a chief steward.

The stable, with its coachmen, grooms, ostlers, was entrusted to a man who did nothing else.

The railway station by which one came to Ilinskoie was called Odinzovo, and from the moment you stepped on to the small landing in front of the station, you were struck by the special air of the place. The coachman of our carriage, askew on the seat, would be there, gathering in one hand the numerous reins by which he drove his span of three horses; with the other lifting his little, round felt hat, gay with peacock feathers. Over his white silk shirt he wore a sleeveless garment of dark blue cloth pinched to his figure, and a wide belt of white wool, the ends of which floated over his knees. When we were seated in the carriage he replaced his hat. His hair was cut to the nape of his neck and carefully oiled.

He spread his arms, waved the reins. The horses started. They crossed the station enclosure and the little village at a walk, then our coachman, leaning forward a little, urged them into full speed. The horse in the middle trotted, balancing his great collar; the other two galloped at each side, head down, neck rounded. From the carriage you saw their shining rumps, their manes, and their long tails flying through the dust raised by their hoofs. Harness bells tinkled gaily. The straight, sandy road passed by the fields. The wheat, still green, was as high as the carriage. A warm breeze stirred the wheat in long waves.

After traversing a pine forest the carriage came out on to a vast meadow from which, beyond the river sunk between its banks and still invisible, you perceived the roof of Ilinskoie drowned in the crests of trees.

At the end of the meadow the coachman slowed down cautiously to cross a wooden bridge which was, because of frequent floods, a floating structure. Hoofs resounded on the planks and the horses breathed noisily.

Slowly now we traversed the village. Dirty children, in small shirts inadequately cut to their stature, played in the dust. Before the tavern stood peasant teams, tied to a trough hollowed out of a tree trunk. The short grass in front of the houses was matted with mud and trampled down by animals.

At the left there was a church with a green roof, and just beyond, the wide wooden gates of Ilinskoie, open to receive us.

The coachman now turned slowly in order not to lock the wheels with the posts of the entry, and we penetrated into a magnificent alley of four rows of immense lime trees. At its end was the house, bathed in the sunlight. My uncle, leaning on the balcony above the entrance, smiled at us. The coachman, with one movement of his elbows, sharply brought the three horses to a stop. Servants in white livery came down the steps to help us descend. They were all pleased to see us come again; they considered us the children of the house; and in the shadows of the vestibule, damp and close with the sweet smell of flowers, my uncle took us tenderly in his arms.

"At last you're here!" he said, giving his hand to our governess, who curtsied. "Come to your rooms."

Down a long corridor he led us into a large room, our playroom, which opened onto a little terrace. A sweet freshness reigned in this room protected from the rays of the sun by the large second-story balcony. I had the two rooms to the left of the playroom; Dmitri, the two rooms to the right.

As we chatted to Uncle Serge, trying to tell him everything at once, our aunt would appear and calmly lean to embrace us as we seized her hands to kiss them. Even towards her, at these moments of reunion, our hearts were overflowing; and we did not doubt that this house was as much ours as if it had been our own. Our uncle wished it so, and our aunt came in time to accustom herself to the idea.

iii

Every morning before breakfast we made a tour of the farm with my uncle. We would stop first at the stables and drink a glass of warm milk, fresh from the cow. Then we would go to see the chickens, gravely walking around their enclosed yards, and take with us fresh eggs which had been saved for us.

After the promenade, we generally took our coffee on the big balcony. Here our aunt came to join us after an hour of walking alone. My uncle read his newspaper; and my aunt, English pictorial reviews or French fashion magazines. She cut out of them whatever pleased her or caught her attention and collected these pictures in albums for use in designing her wardrobe.

After this, lessons began and lasted until eleven. Released, we generally sought the shade of trees or the banks of the water for our playing, and when we were bigger we frequently used to go bathing. On the river bank we had a little cabin of our own among the reeds; it only contained one room; worm-eaten and slippery steps led into the water. We undressed in turns and went down to the river, which was neither clear nor deep. At the right of the cabin there was a sort of beach of fine sand; here the village cattle stretched themselves out in the sun. From this beach came the lowing of cows, the bleating of sheep, and the cries of the village children who went in bathing with their beasts. In these cries heard afar, I find again all the atmosphere of Ilinskoie in summer. When I close my eyes on a hot day in July it seems to me that I can still hear them.

After the bath we made haste to return to the house to get ourselves ready for lunch, for my uncle held to a rigorous schedule in these matters, and the delay of a minute would bring remarks down upon us and even punishments. We ate a great deal; and moved for our coffee either on to the terrace adjoining the dining-room or to my aunt's balcony.

At the table I was seated beside my uncle, and Dmitri was placed near me. If there were guests, one of them was always my neighbour, and my uncle paid attention to my conversation. I was severely reprimanded and often punished if I did not find a subject to talk about. At our luncheons there were never fewer than fifteen or twenty persons; they were the most painful moments of the day for us.

The coffee finished, my uncle took himself off to his room for a siesta; he took his nap stretched out in an arm-chair, his legs upon another chair covered with a newspaper so that it might not be soiled by his boots. My aunt went down to the garden and established herself within the shadows of a covered terrace where it was always cool. Here she would do a little painting, or have someone read to her aloud while she and the ladies did embroidery. The things they read must have been childish, for I will never forget the difficulties my aunt had with *Recollections of a Dead-House*, her first attempt to appreciate Dostoievsky. She did not know enough Russian to read it herself; one of the ladies read it aloud to her. And so great was my aunt's fear of details too realistic that she would permit no one to attend these readings!

She had no admiration for French literature; once she said to me, apropos of a person whose life she found somewhat frivolous, that it was French novels with yellow covers that had corrupted her ideas. At this period she read only English books and chose her authors with great caution.

Before retiring to his room after luncheon, my uncle would have given orders as to how the afternoon should be employed; this he decided entirely by himself, never consulting my aunt. We children had at our disposal several pairs of ponies and mules. Uncle Serge always indicated exactly which animals should be harnessed and to which carriages. Occasionally it happened, for one reason or another, that his orders could not be executed at the last moment, and as no one dared disturb him during his nap, my aunt took it upon herself to alter the arrangements. When my uncle would find this out, he would be angry and make sharp remarks to my aunt.

During his sleep the house was plunged into a deep silence; only towards late afternoon did life begin to run its course again. Then one heard horses pawing the ground in front of the house, the wheels of carriages grating, and bells tinkling. Dmitri and I would go out with our mules in a small low carriage of pleated rushes, accompanied by a master of the stables. We disputed over the pleasure of holding the reins, and when we had them between our hands would not give them up easily. Occasionally my uncle went with us; then we had to behave. We sometimes drove to take tea and cakes with neighbours, especially with the Yusupovs, always great friends of our family. They had two sons, Nicholas and Felix, older than us by some years.

Such excursions were frequent in summer, but in autumn they often could not be made, because of the roads, which were impracticable for large carriages in bad weather. We always took the same routes; they grew so familiar that we could have described each peculiarity of them. The landscape was everywhere the same, plain but smiling; vast fields of wheat, meadows covered with a sweet, tufted grass, with bell-flowers and daisies; forests of pine, oak, birch; and a few villages always looking alike, with their wooden hovels.

When the berries were ripe in midsummer we went to pick them in the depths of the big park, and after rain we would go hunting for mushrooms. We knew every corner where they grew.

Mushrooms were so sought by the peasants that it was necessary to guard the parks as if they were private hunting-grounds. In spite of all threats the temptation was too strong; in the copses we would see the coloured handkerchiefs of the women and hear them run away at our approach.

The weather was nearly always the same, dry, calm, and beautiful. But terrible storms broke, sometimes followed by a day or two of almost tropical rain. These storms came upon us especially at night. The house would be shaken by terrific bursts of distant thunder. Terrified, unable to sleep, too proud to call the nurse who slept at my side, I would leave my bed, draw near the window, raise the blind, and peep out. Then lightning came, sharp and white, and rending a sky suddenly green; and immediately after, obscurity, intense and fearful. The darkness, the tense sense of waiting for the storm to break, became more and more agonizing. It was as if over all the earth catastrophe impended.

Finally the first drops of rain came, striking through the foliage, splashing loudly, heavily, to the ground. The air grew less heavy. Soon the rain was a deluge; in the dark, I could hear little brooks forming at the ends of rain-spouts. In the lightning flashes I saw against the greenish sky the tormented silhouettes of trees.

Next day, as a rule, the sky was again serene, and the air had a special flavour, light and delicious. The newly washed leaves shone, the grass was wet, the water in the river troubled, and the sand of the paths was streaked with small furrows.

iv

FROM time to time, there were fêtes to break the charming monotony of our existence. The fifth of July was my uncle's name day, Saint Serge's. That day he organized a lottery for the peasants and the personnel of the estate. Guests, arriving for the most part the night before, filled the little summer-houses in the park. In the morning, everyone went to mass. A luncheon followed, attended by the parish clergy, the district authorities, and the neighbours.

After lunch the lottery was drawn. This ceremony took place in a field; the heat was intense, great clouds of dust floated over the motley crowd. A military orchestra played waltzes and polkas. My uncle, elegant and fresh in his white summer tunic, went among the crowd, now talking with one, now another. No guest dared return to the house before my uncle gave them the signal. When the last lot was drawn, my uncle and my aunt, followed by their friends, took the path to go back. And it was with a sign of relief that the poor women let themselves fall into the wicker arm-chairs surrounding the tables where tea was served under the trees. It was a very fatiguing day for everybody.

Towards the end of July came Saint Elias's day, a parochial holiday and at the same time the festival of our village. Several days in advance, itinerant merchants built booths along the principal street. The fair lasted three days; they planted pike-staffs for the merry-go-rounds and swings, and put up tents for travelling shows and photographers. Peasants came from afar in their carts and wagons.

After mass, Uncle Serge opened the fair, and immediately after lunch we all went down to make purchases. My uncle and aunt felt obliged to buy from each merchant, even the most modest. They began their rounds, my uncle on one side, my aunt on the other, continued to the end, met, and began over again. Servants walked behind them carrying enormous baskets which filled rapidly. The merchandise was of no great variety, from year to year always the same: linens, printed calicoes, handkerchiefs and shawls, earthenware, glassware, ribbons, sweets. It was customary to make gifts, but difficult amid this confusion of perfectly useless objects. Sometimes, however, you chanced upon amusing things that you snatched away from the merchants' hands, now a carafe with a coloured bird blown inside, now an enormous lemon preserved in alcohol. There were tobacco boxes in enamelled papier-mâché, with portraits of the Emperor and Empress or of my uncle and aunt, and large cups decorated with droll paintings, charades, or caricatures.

Dmitri and I were given money to buy presents and souvenirs for everybody, including the servants, and we too had to visit the majority of the booths and all the attractions, which amused us much more.

Bands of curious children followed us from stall to stall. We bought enormous bags of caramels, sunflower seeds, and peanuts, throwing them to urchins who fought like small dogs to catch them.

In the evening after dinner we returned to the fair and rode on the merry-go-round by the light of the grease-pots and candles stuck in bottles. The crowd was as thick as by day; it became generally rowdy under the influence of drink, and we returned early to the house. The night air carried faintly up to us the sound of accordions, the sticky voices of peasants, and the strident laughter of women.

Towards the middle of August we always left Ilinskoie and moved across the river to Usovo, where the heating arrangements were more modern. The house at Usovo, built by my uncle, of brick and grey stone in the English manner, was not pretty. But it was spacious and comfortable, and there was a large winter garden forming all of one wing and filled with flowers and tropical plants. Moving into Usovo represented the last stage of our summer, the last weeks of vacation.

The days became shorter. The park trees lost their leaves and the birds flew away. The air turned sharp, and the grass was often covered with frost in the morning. Then we would go into the woods hunting nuts and bring them back in sacks; but soon there was nothing more for us to do; the fruits and the berries were all plucked, the mushrooms gathered; and all that remained was walking down damp paths, yellowed with dead leaves, under the almost naked trees. The evenings grew longer and we had to find things to do in the house.

CHAPTER III

DISCIPLINE

WHEREVER we were, Dmitri and I led a life entirely separated from that of the grown persons of the household. We had our own apartments, and were taken separately by our nurses on walks and rides. Into this small world, so carefully made for us and guarded, entered in my sixth year, a new and interesting influence.

My father decided that it was time to commence my education. He looked around and found a young woman of good family who seemed to meet all requirements. So one fine day he came into our playroom, just at our tea-time, and presented to us Mlle. Hélène, the governess who was to instruct, love, and torment me for the twelve years following, until my marriage.

After tea that day, she played with Dmitri and me, and was horrified to find that I spoke no Russian, and as to my English I dropped my *h's* right and left, just as my nurses did.

We could not help, Dmitri and I, from sharing the feeling of our nurses that this Mlle. Hélène was an intruder; we sensed their opposition, particularly that of Nannie Fry, who never ceased to defend her position and command. Finally, loaded with gifts, Nannie Fry capitulated and departed. For several days we lived in frightful mourning, weeping bitterly. (Old Nannie Fry is still living, I believe, in England. She has written and published reminiscences of the court of Russia that are absolutely unique.)

In 1897, the last year she was with us, she went with us on our first foreign travels. Our party occupied a private carriage, and needed all of it for our suite—Mlle. Hélène, two nurses, a doctor, three maids, and several footmen. We needed, moreover, the entire luggage van, which carried everywhere we went not only our own beds but also our own bathtubs and a great variety of other perfectly useless objects which our nurses judged absolutely indispensable for living in hotels—always, they said, "so dirty!"

At Birgenstoch, we were permitted to make the acquaintance of some young English girls. Our following impressed them prodigiously—especially the liveried male servants, whom they took to be Russian generals! They asked innumerable questions: Was it true that wolves still ran in the streets of St. Petersburg? Were we Christians? And how could that be, since in Russia the Tsar was adored as a God?

At St. Jean de Luz we had adventures. We saw the sea for the first time; we learned to ride bicycles; and father joined us for Dmitri's birthday, bringing with him Tom, his favourite French bulldog. Tom disappeared. Father was upset. We spent whole days tramping the highways and across open country, calling, "Tom! Tom! Here, Tom!" But we never found him.

It was also at St. Jean de Luz that I made my first experiment in independent action. Evading my multiple guardians, I went into the sea alone. The undertow swept me from my feet. I thought that my last hour had come. My screams attracted a middle-aged French gentleman, who plunged fully clad into the shallow water, brought me forth, led me, shamed and trembling, to the beach tent where our party was installed.

Father came forward inquiringly. My mud-stained rescuer spoke severely:

"Sir! You should not allow a little girl of this age to run alone on the beach."

(Years later, in Paris, Dmitri had need of an attorney, and was recommended to a young lawyer who proved to be the son of my rescuer!)

Late that September, we returned to Russia, and spent as

usual some weeks at Tsarskoie-Selo, before going on to St. Petersburg for the winter.

Our apartments at Tsarskoie-Selo were in the Great Palace of Catherine II. The young Empress would have us come often to the Alexander Palace to play with her daughters, of whom at the time there were but two. Their nursery apartments occupied an entire wing on the second floor of the Alexander Palace. These rooms, light and spacious, were hung with flowered cretonne and furnished throughout with polished lemonwood. The effect was luxurious, yet peaceful and comfortable. Through the windows you could see the palace gardens and guardhouses and a little beyond, through the grille of a high iron gate, a street corner.

The Emperor's daughters were governed as we were, by an English head nurse assisted by innumerable Russian nurses and chambermaids, and their nursery staff was uniformed as ours was, all in white, with small nurse-caps of white tulle. With this exception: two of their Russian nurses were peasants and wore the magnificent native peasant costumes.

Dmitri and I spent hours examining our young cousins' toys; one could never tire of them, they were so fine. Especially enchanting to me was the French President's gift to Olga at the time when she was taken with her parents on their first visit to France. In a trunk covered with soft leather was a doll with a complete trousseau: dresses, lingerie, hats, slippers, the entire equipment of a dressing-table, all reproduced with remarkable art and fidelity.

After an early supper with our cousins we would all be taken downstairs to see the Emperor and Empress. Sometimes my father and other members of the family would be there with them, too, at a round table, taking tea. We kissed the Empress's hand and received her embrace; then the Emperor would embrace us and the Empress would take from the nurse's arms her youngest daughter, keeping the baby beside her on the chaise-longue. We older children installed ourselves tranquilly in a

THE GRAND DUCHESS ELIZABETH

"Aunt Ella"

corner to look at pictures in the photograph albums, of which there was at least one on every table.

The Empress chatted with her visitors and played with her child. The Emperor drank his tea from a glass mounted in a gold frame, with a handle. Before his place at the table accumulated a pile of long white envelopes, each with a thread of orange-coloured silk passed under the seal to facilitate opening. These were dispatches from news agencies, scheduled on the morrow to appear in the press. When he had finished his tea he seated himself at the table and, drawing the silk cords, opened the dispatches, and read them. Occasionally he would pass one of them to the Empress, but almost always without comment, for it was not considered good taste to discuss politics *en famille.*

The room was the Empress's boudoir; she passed most of her time there, preferring it to all others, and attaching to everything in it a sentimental value. Later when she had the place redecorated, she kept this one room exactly as it was at the time of her marriage.

It was not large, but it was high, and had two great windows. Its curtains and hangings were of mauve silk, the arm-chairs completely covered with the same material; the woodwork was painted in cream colour. The effect was frankly ugly, but comfortable and gay. Flowers stood everywhere in vases, and grew in a large window-box between the two windows.

The Empress ordinarily sat lengthwise on the chaise-longue, half reclining against cushions covered with lace. Behind her there would be a sort of glass screen, protecting her from draughts, and her legs would be covered to the knees by a doubled shawl of lace lined with mauve muslin. When everyone had taken tea she rang for servants to clear the table. The Emperor, still holding in one hand dispatches, in the other a cigarette-holder formed like a small pipe, continued for a while to chat with his guests. Then, absently stroking with the back of his right hand his moustache and beard—a gesture habitual to him—he took leave of us all, embracing the children, and left the room. The Empress then, in her turn, would embrace and dismiss us and we would be taken back to our cousins' apartments and returned to our own home.

ii

This year, when we returned to St. Petersburg, it was found necessary to arrange my studies in a more systematic way. A young blonde person taught me Russian, another gave me piano lessons, and a priest came twice a week to instruct me in the catechism.

Children brought up in the Russian Orthodox religion take communion from their very birth, and towards the age of seven they are considered sufficiently developed to begin confessing their sins.

That spring, accordingly, I made confession. I clearly remember the emotion with which I entered the church, cold and empty, where the priest was waiting for me; and in confessing my chief crime, the theft of a few pieces of chocolate candy, I shed abundant tears.

The winter in St. Petersburg was interminable, dark, and dreary. Days came and went, always alike. We would get up about seven in the morning and have breakfast by electric light. Then I would prepare my lessons and at nine would come one of my teachers. At eleven we would go for a walk. At half-past twelve we would have lunch downstairs, a privilege never granted us before this year.

Besides my father, there would often be guests. We had the right to answer the questions addressed to us, but not to take part in the conversation. Between the courses we were supposed to place the tips of our fingers upon the edge of the table and sit very straight; if we forgot to do this, we were immediately reminded of it. It was: "Marie, your back," or "Dmitri, take your elbows from the table." The dining-room, which was somewhat dark, had carved Renaissance wainscots of almost black oak. The chairs, uncomfortable and high, covered with maroon-coloured leather, had large monograms on the backs.

After lunch, and coffee in the drawing-room, we often went for a drive. Since the time of the nurses this ceremony had been simplified. There was a carriage and several pairs of horses attached specially to our service, and we always drove with a footman sitting beside the enormous bearded coachman. Over his livery the footman wore a long scarlet coat with a cape and a bicorn hat. Nannie Fry would stop the carriage at the quay and alighting with us would have the footman follow us as we walked slowly along the sidewalk. It pleased her to have people turn around to stare at this procession, to see the soldiers and officers salute. Often at the end of the walk we would return to the carriage, surrounded by a crowd.

Mlle. Hélène found it unnecessary to attract all this attention; so now the footman remained beside the coachman while we took our walk. Upon our return from the drive, we took some light refreshments, and then went downstairs to our father for the most pleasant part of our day.

For two hours every evening, he read to us aloud, seated in his large leather arm-chair. A lamp with a green shade threw a peaceful light upon the pages of his book. The corners of the room and the outline of the objects were plunged in semi-darkness and the atmosphere was warm, soft, and intimate.

He read well and with pleasure. My imagination, always alert, illustrated better than could any artist the colourful and intense tales of my mother-tongue. As the story gradually unfolded, these pictures were enriched with a thousand details until the images became almost a reality. When father stopped reading, thus breaking the thread of the tale, I seemed to awake from a dream and the return to actual life was painful. The reading finished, he rose, but I did not yet dare to move, afraid of chasing away the beautiful images with which my mind was dancing.

Father often dined at home alone and, now that we no longer went to bed at six o'clock, he allowed us to follow him to the dining-room and be with him as he ate. During the meal he questioned us about the way we spent our day, our lessons, our games. Then he would look at his watch, kiss us, and send us to bed.

We watched with impatience for the coming of spring. Each new sign filled us with joy. The days became longer, the sparrows chirped with more ado, and the snow acquired a glitter. Labourers removed the boards that had served as sidewalks to cross the ice-bound Neva. When that happened it meant that spring was really coming, for the great river was the last to shed its winter cloak.

Buds would be appearing upon the bare tree branches, and birds singing uproariously, before the Neva yielded. Dull cracking noises rose from the depths of the ice; rifts appeared here and there, disclosing black water. Soon the river was furrowed by gaps which kept widening. Immense pieces of ice broke away with a crash and whirled downstream, obstructing the current. They smashed against each other with a dry sound, turned, climbed one upon another. The river swelled, the turbulent water, muddy and yellowish, swept its burden at full speed towards the sea. The air was filled with a continual sound—plaintive, grating.

When the Neva was altogether cleared, navigation was opened by a ceremony instituted in the time of Peter the Great and faithfully maintained ever since. The Chief Commissioner of the river police boarded a large yawl manned by numerous oarsmen who belonged, according to tradition, not to the Navy, but to the First Regiment of the Infantry Guards. The passage of the Commissioner was saluted by cannonades; banners and flags floated in the air and the quays were thronged with crowds always avid of spectacles. Immediately after the ceremony thousands of craft of all sorts were launched upon the water and furrowed the stream, raising oily waves. It was spring!

iii

We would pack then and move with our suite to our apartments in the Great Palace at Tsarskoie-Selo. How we loved it there, after the long winter months in town! The Great Palace had a private garden which was for children an enchanting playground. This garden sloped gently towards a pond with many small islands. On these islands summer-houses, kiosks, and temples had been built. One of these playhouses was a farmstead in the so-called Russian style. It had been built by Emperor Alexander for my father's sister, the Duchess of Edinburgh, later Duchess of Saxe-Coburg. The little house had two rooms, a kitchen and a dining-room, completely equipped with plates, dishes, and kitchen utensils. Barberry and syringa bushes grew all over the small veranda and stretched their branches across the windows. Toy railway tracks, with tunnels and posts, were set in front of the house, and a little farther along, my uncles had amused themselves, as children, by building a fortress of red bricks with a small bridge in the middle.

This year, instead of proceeding from Tsarskoie-Selo to Ilinskoie, we again went abroad, but with a changed itinerary that took us first to Kreuznach. At Kreuznach began my first serious misunderstandings with my governess. I do not think that I was particularly mischievous or difficult to manage. But Mlle. Hélène not only submitted me to a strict discipline; she demanded that I tell her my most secret thoughts. Instead of observing me, and trying to follow on her own accord the movements of my mind, she submitted me to lengthy questionnaires. I was asked to explain my every gesture, my slightest movement. If unfortunately I had no explanation to give her, or had nothing to say, my governess flew into a passion, accusing me of a lack of frankness and even of deceit.

Often, unable to understand what she wanted of me, or being out of patience and nervous, I would answer her rudely. This resulted in scenes, tears, punishments. I developed defences, acquired cunning. Knowing what sort of confidences she expected from me, I learned in time to invent all sorts of things to appease her suspicions.

She still found, however, many ways in which to "discipline" me. An old beggar stood at the gate in Kreuznach, jingling pennies in a tin bowl. For some inexplicable reason the sight of this man frightened me. Mlle. Hélène noticed this; so she sent me one day alone to place alms in his hand. Trembling, I obeyed, but the following day I refused to do so. She took me home and kept me locked in a room alone all that afternoon. In the evening she sought me out, accused me of hardness, denounced me as cruel, upbraided me for my lack of sensibility in general, and towards her in particular.

I spent a sleepless night. From this day on my confidence in her was shaken. I saw that it was not of the beggar she was thinking, but of herself. I knew now that she could be unjust.

IV

On returning from St. Petersburg, I left the nursery on the second floor to move into my mother's apartments on the first. I had two spacious rooms now, separated by a large dressing-room. Dmitri remained upstairs. On the same floor with me Mlle. Hélène occupied her own apartment, at the end of a long corridor. Following the wishes of my father, she proceeded to make an inventory of toilet articles and all other objects left by my mother; no one had touched them since her death.

They opened cupboards and immense wardrobes with rusty locks, and in their musty-smelling depths, hung from rods,

FAMILY GROUP

"Aunt Ella" and the Grand Duchess Marie are seated; the Grand Duke Serge sits on the floor with his back turned; the other men belong to his staff; one of the English nurses is holding the Grand Duke Dmitri

appeared the poor dresses, outmoded and stiff, rows of little shoes whose cracked satin time had already begun to nibble away. From chests of drawers they drew muslins of many colours, pairs of gloves by the dozen in boxes lined in white satin, laces, flowers, and feathers, handkerchiefs in sachets that had lost their odour. There were little stores of everything—hairpins, soap, perfumes, eau-de-Cologne.

Mlle. Hélène, assisted by Tania, my Russian chambermaid, sorted, catalogued, classified. Heaps of garments accumulated on the floor. Between lessons I came to watch their work. In spite of me, a vague sadness took hold of my heart. These old things—how pretty and fresh they must have been when my mother wore them! In my imagination I saw her before me in her youth, clad in this gay attire, her pretty face animated by the joy of living. Had she been truly happy? Had she, in dying, really regretted her life? She seemed to me already to belong to another century, although it was only seven years since she had died.

They made priestly vestments out of silks that could still be used. Clothes and other effects were distributed to the poor, the laces and linen kept for me, and the remainder, worn out and useless, was burned in order not to collect dust.

V

THAT winter we commenced to take dancing lessons once a week, and other children were invited in to take part. The professor, a former ballet dancer, was a thin, old man with Gladstone whiskers. He was very severe; if we made an error or lacked grace, he addressed us with observations full of sarcasm.

My father, who had often seen him dance in his youth, liked to attend the lessons, and he laughed until he cried at observing our clumsiness and hearing the stinging remarks of the old professor.

Sometimes on Sundays, other playmates came; but their presence added nothing to our existence. No real intimacy was permitted. We had to behave like grown persons receiving visitors. No one was allowed to *tutoie* us or call us by our names. All games took place under the vigilant gaze of our guardians, and the children who became too noisy were not invited again.

I could not help envying the lot of these children, nor could Dmitri. We discussed the matter thoroughly. Accustomed to being always among grown persons, our intellectual development was precocious enough; and our elders would have been shocked if they had been able to hear our conversations. We were thoroughly obedient, but we were part of a new generation, a generation which carried within itself the germs of revolt.

We always went about together, Dmitri and I, whenever we were free, and played together. Girls' games never had any interest for me; I hated dolls; the congealed expression on their porcelain faces provoked me. It was with lead soldiers that we played, without ever growing tired. Dmitri took charge of military operations, and I of the work at the rear. Our armies, our constructions of pasteboard bricks, covered entire tables; and as we became older, our war games grew in a mass of technical complications until they offered a large field for the imagination. I played at this game with pleasure until even the year of my marriage.

When not leaning over our lead soldiers, we played other games less tranquil. In one of the large reception rooms they had erected for us a slide of waxed boards, several yards high; you slid down it seated on squares of cloth. Our father often came to join us at this sport. We also had gymnasium apparatus that we could climb like monkeys.

My governess ended by resigning herself to seeing me grow up a boy and stopped following us about even into the playroom. But she revenged herself elsewhere and unremittingly pushed her lessons in good manners, deportment, and humility —especially humility. She repeatedly dinned in my ears a phrase attributed to my great-grandfather, Emperor Nicholas the First, who would say to his children: "Always act so that you will be forgiven for being born Grand Dukes."

It happened once that she saw me, in the excitement of a noisy game, make a face at a footman, and not only did she remonstrate with me severely—and deservedly—but demanded that I apologize to him and tormented me for several days until I did so. I will never forget the poor man's face, for he didn't know what it was all about; nor my humiliation. Afterwards I avoided meeting him, and as for him, he hardly dared lift his eyes to me.

She accused me of possessing a ferocious egoism, and loved to force me to ask her pardon. She was tireless in what she conceived to be her duty, but her instruction was formless and for the most part useless. In other work, especially that of the Red Cross, in which she held an important position, her capacities were apparently highly valued.

She took me sometimes with her on her visits to hospitals, and taught me to gaze on suffering humanity and not be afraid —a lesson for which I had cause to thank her later. She was, moreover, good and charitable, and excessively attached to religion. Every morning, after having said her prayers, she read a chapter in her Bible, which was worn out and filled with signatures and the yellowed photographs of dead members of her family. The sight of this book never failed to soften me, even in those moments when I was most unkindly disposed towards her. She had lost her parents and an older brother, and in spite of our quarrels, I had much sympathy for her loneliness.

In 1901 my father found that it was time to give my brother a tutor, in order to remove him from the exclusive influence of women. His choice fell on General Laiming, who had already educated one of our cousins and whom my governess knew very well. In the spring he came with his wife and little boy, and settled in an apartment connected with my brother's rooms.

At the beginning this was a great blow to me, but my separation from Dmitri proved not to be so complete, under the new arrangement, as I had feared it would be.

My brother and I continued between lessons to play and to amuse ourselves together, and the General, who took part in our distractions, soon gained the entire confidence of both of us. (This led, incidentally, to further scenes with poor Mlle. Hélène, who tortured me—and was herself tortured—by her jealousy.)

In the Laiming apartment, where we seemed always welcome, Dmitri and I found the first real family life we had ever known. The relations between the General and his pretty, dark-eyed wife, and the atmosphere that their happiness created around them, were to us a revelation. Often in the evening, after lessons, we sat in their little dining-room around the table covered with a very white tablecloth, on which the light flooded with a gay clearness. Before us there was a fruit dish filled with nuts and dried fruits which we ate while talking tranquilly of one thing and another. You could talk of everything without fear of offending too susceptible sentiments. Our questions found clear answers, patient explanations; never were they met in that brusque tone which my aunt and my governess so often took: "That's none of your business; go and play; don't ask such questions." At my bedtime, when Mlle. Hélène climbed the stairs to get me, I would get to my feet in sudden discomfiture, as if I had been caught in a fault, and silently follow her down to my own rooms.

CHAPTER IV

BANISHMENT

THE year previous, shortly after our return to St. Petersburg for the winter, Dmitri and I had noticed on father's desk a new photograph in a small, gold frame. It was of a boy, four or five years old—a beautiful little boy with long curls and a dress that came down to his ankles. At our first chance, we asked father who it was. He turned the talk to other matters, avoiding response.

Later that year, we once went downstairs at tea-time and opened his study door, as we always did, without knocking. He was seated in his arm-chair, and in front of him, with her back to us, stood a woman. At our entrance she turned, and we recognized her. We did not know her name but had seen her. One day, at Tsarskoie-Selo, we were in a boat on the lake when she had passed near us along the shore, dressed in a white skirt and a red jacket with golden buttons. She was very pretty and had sent us smiles and amicable signs which we did not return.

I do not know what instinct now drove us to it, but we closed that door at once and fled in haste, despite my father's appeals. In the anteroom a footman was holding a sable pelisse; in the air floated an unfamiliar perfume.

A vague jealousy gripped our hearts; we did not like this stranger penetrating into our personal sanctuary, our father's study. But he treated us always with the same tenderness; he seemed, indeed, now to wish to hold us more closely than ever to him.

The summer of 1902, which was the last year of my childhood, we were not sent to Ilinskoie, but were kept at Tsarskoie-Selo. Father, now a General, commanded a cavalry division garrisoned at Krasnoie-Selo, some thirty miles away. We drove often to Krasnoie to see him, in a carriage drawn by four horses. The camp, the proximity of the military life, enchanted us.

Tsarskoie, where we were installed in our regular apartments, was alive with preparations for a great ceremony that was to take place in the month of August—the marriage of my cousin Helen with my uncle, Prince Nicholas of Greece—and numerous princely guests were expected. The King of Greece, my grandfather, and the Emperor, were to preside at the fêtes.

Dmitri and I were told we might attend the religious part of the ceremony, and for this occasion I was to wear my first court dress. The cut was discussed at great length and finally decided upon. It was a short dress in pale blue satin, tailored in the Russian manner. I was terrifically proud of it, and impatiently awaited the great day.

The guests began to arrive; we greeted our grandfather, King George of Greece, who had not been in Russia since our mother's death. He was very kind to us but we saw that he and my father avoided each other scrupulously.

Throughout all the marriage festivities, in fact, my father was so nervous and preoccupied that I was moved to ask Mlle. Hélène, to whom I rarely expressed my real concerns, what, in her opinion, was worrying him so. It must, she replied, be the sad memories aroused in him by this family reunion.

My uncle and aunt had also arrived. At a family dinner some dispute arose between Uncle Serge and father that made a strong impression on me, although I cannot recall the subject of it. My uncle, wishing to put an end to the discussion, said with a forced smile as he rose from the table: "My boy, you are simply in a very bad mood; you ought to take better care of yourself." My aunt said nothing, casting anxious looks at us. We sensed a tension in the air which had never existed before. Without knowing why, I felt sorry for my father; and never experienced greater tenderness towards him than I did during those days.

We attended the marriage in the choir of the palace church. I retain a very vague memory of it; all that happened afterwards was too tragic and important. Before the marriage we were conducted into the room where the fiancée dressed herself in ceremony, and, according to an old Russian practice, I slipped a gold piece into her shoe. After the marriage, when the family was congratulating the young couple, we too approached, and I kissed my cousin's hand with the immense respect inspired by her new state of wife.

The day after the marriage my father went away. We went to the railway station with him, and when I saw him carried off by the train I thought that my heart was going to break. I do not know why, but I felt as if I would never see him again.

Dmitri and I stayed on at Tsarskoie to be with our grandparents. We stayed there until all the fêtes were over, then followed the court to Peterhof, where our grandparents were installed in the house of the Emperor's mother, the Dowager Empress Marie. Every morning on bicycles we went to see them; and our days were gay, for my uncles, the princes of Greece, were all young and full of high spirits. Mlle. Hélène did not like that; she complained that the Greek princes had bad manners and would teach us nothing good.

But when they had departed, and we found ourselves back at Tsarskoie, it seemed by comparison that our life was sad and empty. Autumn had come. Dead leaves floated on the ponds; the little boats were shut up in their houses; and the statues were all covered with planks to protect them against the frosts.

Uncle Serge and Aunt Ella came to see us for a few days before departing for abroad. They too seemed sad, cast down; there was that in their attitude towards us—my aunt's particularly—which aroused in us a vague presentiment.

One evening I was seated before my desk doing my lessons when Mlle. Hélène came into the room and handed me an envelope on which I recognized my father's handwriting. I tore it open quickly, spread out the letter, and started to read.

From the very first sentence I understood that my father was about to announce something terrible. At first I could not understand what it was; then, as I read, I knew. Mlle. Hélène, hovering near, came close and wanted to take me in her arms. I lifted an empty gaze towards her, and re-read the letter.

My father announced his marriage to a person he called Olga Valerianovna Pistolkors. He wrote of how much he had suffered from loneliness and how great his love was for this woman, who would make him happy. He added that nothing could ever lessen his affection for us and that he hoped to keep ours. He asked us to think of his wife without ill feeling.

The sheet of paper fell to the floor, and I hid my head in my hands and broke into sobs. My governess drew me over to the couch and took me on her knee.

My dominating impression was that my father was dead to me. My sobs became a kind of nervous hiccupping which nothing could stop for hours. I didn't think; I didn't move.

Then little by little my ideas became clearer. Thoughts began to run rapidly in my mind. Egotism: how could my father do this, he who lacked nothing, who led so agreeable a life; who had us, both of us, alone to himself? So! We possessed no importance in his life? How could this person dare to take him from us; she knew, she ought to know, how much we loved him.

"I'll *show* her how I detest her!" I told Mlle. Hélène.

"My dear," she said, "you ought not to talk that way about your father's wife. It would cause him much pain if he heard you."

"Do you think—will he come back for Christmas?" I asked.

"Perhaps, my dear," said Mlle. Hélène, with a slight hesitation which I was quick to observe.

"Oh, say 'yes,' say 'yes'; he *must* come back for Christmas!" I insisted passionately. And poor Mlle. Hélène did not know what to say.

Meanwhile Dmitri was reading a letter similar to mine in his

THE GRAND DUCHESS MARIE WITH HER UNCLE, THE GRAND DUKE SERGE

own room. We saw each other, hours afterwards, through eyes swollen with weeping, and sought to speak with lips still trembling; only, at the first attempt, to burst out crying anew. The long, sorrowful days that followed left a lasting trace on my heart. It was my first real sorrow, the first wound that life dealt me.

I devoted a great deal of time to composing a reply to my father's letter, covering numberless sheets of paper, only to throw them away; nothing that I could write satisfied me. It was too sentimental, or too cold.

I must finally have decided on the sentimental version; for, although I don't remember the text, I recall having been moved to tears in re-reading what I had written. Mlle. Hélène approved it, but reproached me for not having put in a kind word to my father's wife. I refused to change anything in the letter. She preached to me a long time. Then, to give her satisfaction, at the bottom of the letter I added a sentence, obscure enough, which meant that I harboured no ill feeling against my stepmother. I remember having added these words in a different handwriting, even a little hesitant; and my father ought certainly to have perceived the difference.

A little later, we learned the worst. Since my father had married morganatically and without the Emperor's permission, he was from that moment banished from Russia, and deprived of all his rights. All his official revenues were, moreover, confiscated.

Our aunt and uncle's trip abroad, it now appeared, had been to Rome to meet our banished father; they would soon come back, and we would see them, we were told.

We found both of them overcome with sorrow; they cried over us a long time. My uncle sharply denounced Mme. Pistolkors; he accused her of having divorced a suitable husband to ruin my father's life and future, and of having taken him from his children, who needed him.

The marriage, it seemed, had taken place secretly in Italy,

and it was at Rome that my father learned from my uncle the Emperor's verdict. They had discussed our future—which future was now revealed to us, there in my uncle's gloomy study, that painful afternoon, over a tea that nobody touched.

By the Emperor's order my uncle had been made our guardian. Our palace in St. Petersburg would be closed and in the spring we must move definitely to Moscow, to live always with my aunt and uncle, now our foster-parents. And in spite of the great sorrow that my uncle felt at his brother's mésalliance, he could not conceal the joy he felt at the fact that from now on he would be able to keep us entirely to himself. He kept saying: "It is I who am now your father, and you are *my* children!"

We sat there, Dmitri and I, blankly staring at him, saying nothing.

ii

THAT year, for the first time in our lives, we did not hold our Christmas festivities at our palace on the Neva. It was the first sign of the change. My uncle and aunt, who inhabited the Governor General's palace at Moscow, spent the holidays in a little palace belonging to the Crown, called Neskuchnoie, situated outside of the city on the banks of the Moskva.

We returned to St. Petersburg several days after the new year. Already in our palace things began to take on an aspect of ruin and neglect. Everybody had a sad face; servants without enough work to do trailed aimlessly through the big empty rooms, awaiting the moment when they would not be needed at all. Some of the older ones had already departed; little by little the stables emptied. We saw each of these changes with a sort of tightening of the heart, and each face disappearing from the home reminded us that soon we too would be leaving it.

The family did what they could to divert us. My mother's sister, married to a cousin of my father's, had us come often to her house, and my great-uncle, the Grand Duke Michael, younger son of the Emperor Nicholas I, came from time to time to pay us visits. He was an old gentleman of great height and of unforgettable elegance; he fascinated us by the perfection and harmony of his gestures, by his affability and his air of a grand seigneur of an epoch already vanished. He was the last of the Grand Dukes who, according to the custom of my grandfather's time, *tutoi*-ed the men, and in spite of his age he bowed with touching grace before the women as he kssed their hands.

We often went to the Winter Palace to play with the little Grand Duchesses. Then we were happiest, for there we sensed ourselves in a real family atmosphere, tender, simple, and calm. The Emperor and his wife held for each other and for their children a deep and unswerving devotion, and their conjugal happiness was beautiful to see.

The Dowager Empress Marie, widow of the Emperor Alexander III, also asked us to visit her, and we liked to go to the Gachina Palace, her preferred residence, some forty miles from St. Petersburg. Gachina had been built by the Emperor Paul I. There he had dwelt in that retirement from active dominion which was forced upon him by his vigorous mother, the Empress Catherine. The château still wore the imprint of this unhappily demented, taciturn, but chivalrous monarch. In one of the towers his room had been kept intact; they had brought here from St. Petersburg the camp bed covered with bloodstained sheets on which he had been stretched after his tragic death. The servants said that the soul of Paul I haunted this habitation, and they had many other stories that would make you shiver.

The palace was surrounded by vast domains. The rivers and the lakes swarmed with fish. Near the palace, with its park, were the Emperor's kennels and hunting-stables, a little world by itself. All breeds of dogs were found there, from graceful borzois with silky hair to the colossi with bulldog heads, called Medeliane, and employed for bear hunting. In the stables were horses, reserved for coursing, attended by a small army of grooms, trainers, and professional huntsmen. But since the death of Alexander III all this array had become useless. The Emperor Nicholas II did not like hunting.

The Empress Marie led a retired and peaceful life at Gachina. At that time she had with her her younger children, the Grand Duchess Olga and the Grand Duke Michael. The Empress, who was my godmother, always was very kind to both my brother and me; and—despite our difference in age—we found our cousins charming. My cousin Olga, light and supple, was remarkably gifted in sports; she was gay, of a child-like and disarming simplicity, and had a generous heart. She loved to surround herself with simple people; peasants, in particular, fascinated her; and she knew how to talk with such people and win their confidence.

The last winter that we were ever to spend in our own home passed us by, day by day, and came to an end. They began to pack trunks; packing-boxes were brought out; familiar things disappeared. The stripped rooms became suddenly immense, altered, almost alien.

Finally the day of departure arrived. In the morning we went to mass in the palace chapel, and after the service the members of the house personnel assembled in one of the reception halls to present their farewells to us and to offer Dmitri and me an ikon. The old butler, who had seen us born, made a little speech, but his voice shook and the tears kept him from finishing it. Dmitri and I wept torrents, both of us.

We went to the fortress cathedral of SS. Peter and Paul, containing our family vault, and placed flowers on my mother's tomb. Then, after a whole day of painful good-byes and tears, we entrained for Moscow. We were followed—myself by Mlle. Hélène, Dmitri by General Laiming. A new era began in our lives. My childhood lay behind me—in St. Petersburg, in that great palace on the Neva, now empty and silent.

CHAPTER V

MOSCOW

EARLY in 1902, as Dmitri and I were preparing to leave St. Petersburg and became part of our uncle's household, the Emperor Nicholas II decided that it would be expedient to renew a custom which for some fifty years had been permitted to lapse; he decided to go to Moscow at Holy Week, there to perform his paschal duties.

Dmitri and I reached Moscow several days before his arrival. We found my uncle and aunt and everyone at the Governor General's palace very busy making arrangements.

The sovereigns arrived a few days before Easter. Morning and evening thereafter we attended religious services in the different churches of the Kremlin. Holy Week services, ordinarily long and tiring, seemed to me now to take on a special charm and interest. Old ikons, darkened by time, lit with innumerable candles reflecting themselves in the goldwork, seemed suddenly to live again mysteriously. Beautiful chants, soft and plaintive, floated in air heavy with incense.

The ancient part of the Kremlin enclosed small, vaulted chambers, chapels and oratories of all dimensions. There was one in particular that I loved. It was very small; scarcely ten persons could get in. The holy images of the altar-screens had all been embroidered in needlework in the seventeenth century by the daughters of Tsar Alexis Mikhailovich. The sight of this patient, meticulous work evoked in my imagination the picture of the princesses cloistered in Oriental fashion in their apartments, and bent over their labours. I saw them in high, jewelled head-dresses and in brocades of burnished gold; their fingers, blending the silks, were loaded with rings.

After this week, spent entirely in church, came Easter Sunday with all its festive rites, official felicitations, and Receptions. The population of Moscow, which rarely saw its sovereign, was enthusiastic. All streets along which the Emperor passed were thronged, and a crowd surrounded the Kremlin all day long, hoping to catch a glimpse of him.

One day the Emperor decided to make a tour of the Kremlin, going afoot along the height of the ramparts that enclosed the old citadel. My brother and I received permission to join the party. We set forth.

From the height of the walls an impressive panorama presented itself. Here, at our feet, lay the city; and beyond, open country, spotted with snow. Bright sunlight made the river sparkle, and glittered on the domes and spires of the numerous churches.

An increasing crowd, massed at the foot of the wall, watched our little group advancing slowly, and surged to follow us. Looking down, we saw them, dense as ants, hurrying, gathering, milling in groups and eddies after our procession.

Soon the crowd became enormous. Its cries mounted to our ears. The tour ended. We descended by the stairway of one of the towers and started back to the palace. Then real trouble began.

No system of keeping order having been established, the crowd hurled itself through the gates and surrounded us. We found ourselves completely hemmed in, almost carried away, by great masses of people shouting hurrahs and deafening cries.

Frantic policemen tried to force a way for the sovereigns, but the mob pressed compactly about us on all sides and closed behind us immediately after our passage.

By sheer mass pressure Dmitri and I were lifted from our feet and swept away from our party. We were thrown this way and that by the uncontrolled surge of the crowd, which might have trampled us down, had not my uncle, seeing that we had disappeared, stopped the whole party and sent police agents to find us. They found and restored us from the surging tide of humankind.

My jacket was torn and I had some bruises, but was not really hurt. The Emperor was visibly moved by the homage and signs of loyalty with which the Muscovites surrounded him.

I remember having myself been stirred by the general exaltation, and I dreamed secretly of an occasion when I could prove my devotion to my sovereign in a truly striking fashion. My uncle was happy; all had gone well; the city, for which he was wholly responsible, had shown itself worthy of the occasion; there had been every evidence of an impulsive, expansive loyalty on the part of the people; and the political horizon appeared in all ways serene.

ii

After the departure of the Emperor and Empress we went to Ilinskoie. We had lessons now at Ilinskoie, as elsewhere, and our summer there seemed less idyllic than in the past. I grieved for my father and frequently spoke to my uncle about him. He gave me patient but unsympathetic answers, speaking of my father without open criticism, but in a manner half jealous, half condescending, that hurt me deeply.

It was a year since the day father had been banished. His marriage had not been recognized. His wife had neither name nor title. One day, however, towards the end of summer, after what parleys I am not aware, Uncle Serge told us that we could go to see him. The interview was to take place in Bavaria in the villa of my aunt Marie, Duchess of Saxe-Coburg.

Dmitri and I left Ilinskoie with my uncle, my aunt, and several others, among them Mlle. Hélène and General Laiming.

My father, as was previously understood, kept the rendezvous alone. He talked a great deal and treated me almost as a confidential equal, but his distrait, preoccupied air went to my heart. I had determined to ask him news of his wife but a kind of inexplicable timidity held me back. Finally one day I screwed up my courage, and with eyes lowered, uttered in a small trembling voice a sentence which I had prepared in advance.

Father, who had not until then pronounced his wife's name in my presence, was surprised and visibly touched. He rose, came over to me, and took me in his arms. This little scene bound us together for ever. From that moment, in spite of my age, we became allies, almost accomplices, and my uncle's efforts to attach me to him, to separate me in spirit as well as in fact from my own father, could not but fail.

The two brothers had some words on this subject during our stay—words which ended when my uncle shrugged his shoulders and announced that he considered himself as possessing all the rights which my father had given up. This was no idle boast; he did have the full rights of guardian over us, and exercised these rights without consulting my father's wishes on any point; and father, though he suffered a great deal from this state of things, was utterly powerless to act or protest.

Our sojourn was charming at Tegernsee, a fascinating place. My aunt, Marie of Saxe-Coburg, in spite of brusque ways which intimidated certain of those who approached her, was a person of high spirits and of a sense of humour a little ironic. She never hid her opinions and always spoke what she thought, a rare thing among us. Even though they teased her about her grand airs, her brothers had a great deal of respect for her. I can still see her installed in a large arm-chair with an interminable piece of knitting in her hands, looking over her big spectacles at the bustling and plotting of the people who moved around her; seeing everything, judging everything with a kind of serene mockery.

At the beginning of winter as we were settling down in the Governor General's palace in Moscow, my father announced

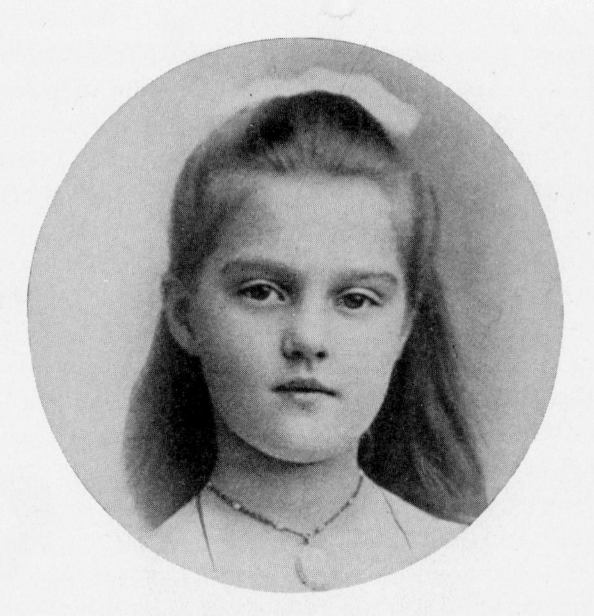

THE GRAND DUCHESS MARIE

At the age of eight

THE GRAND DUCHESS ELIZABETH AS A NUN

by letter the birth of his daughter Irene; later I learned that my father wanted me to be the godmother of my little step-sister, but my uncle, whom he was obliged to consult, would not hear of it.

iii

Upon our settling in Moscow that winter a new existence began for us. For my brother and me, my uncle gathered in a whole staff of pedagogues. Also—since religious instruction played an important part in the education of every Grand Duke—a priest. This priest was old. He had a yellow beard and his robes exhaled a peculiar musty odour. His principles were exactly those of my uncle; he was an extreme monarchist, representing God as absolute monarch of the universe, and identifying the idea of religion with a kind of rigorous bureaucracy, controlling every detail of life.

Dmitri and I took a dislike to him at once. His dry and mawkish appearance, his interminable, monotonous lessons, uttered in a nasal voice, set us on edge, and after several months, became unendurable.

We complained to our uncle. He reproached us soundly for our lack of respect. The lessons continued. At last I was pushed to the extremity of writing a letter of complaint to my father. The outcome of this correspondence was not happy for me; my uncle called me into his study, complained that I had gone behind his back, and remonstrated with me severely. It was not until my uncle's death that we were at last rid of this poor priest, whose only power over us was to irritate us with droning instruction narrowly bound to a political hierarchy.

My uncle followed, or thought he followed, our education. He concerned himself with the smallest detail of our daily life. His love for us, his desire to help us, was undeniable; but alas, his touching efforts often produced in me effects precisely opposite from the effects intended. He was a man limited in his affections and extremely jealous.

That isolation in which Dmitri and I had always lived was now intensified. Once or twice Madame Laiming came herself to ask my uncle to let us come to her house to dinner, but he granted this permission with such bad grace that she did not dare renew the request. So, little by little, we became more and more cut off from the world, and more lonely.

CHAPTER VI

NINETEEN HUNDRED AND FIVE

I SUPPOSE that the world at that moment must have been occupied with the political situation in the Far East, and the probabilities of war with Japan. If we were permitted to hear such conversations, I have no remembrance of it. When, however, at the close of January 1904, war was actually declared, we went with my uncle to the Church of the Assumption in the Kremlin, where there was a Te Deum, and I can still hear the archdeacon's voice, deep and trembling with emotion, reading the manifesto in the church at the end of the service.

At first, the war went well. Every afternoon a crowd of Muscovites came to make loyal, patriotic demonstrations in the square in front of our palace. The men in the front ranks carried flags and portraits of the Emperor and Empress. With heads uncovered, the throng sang the national anthem, then cheered and quietly went its way. The people took a liking to this distraction. Their enthusiasm grew more and more noisy, and, noting that the authorities were loath to quiet their expressions of patriotism, they ended by refusing to leave the square and disperse. Their last assemblage degenerated into a kind of popular orgy, with a good deal of drunkenness, and ended with their hurling bottles and stones at our windows. Police had to be called out and posted along the sidewalk to protect the entrance to our palace. Disquieting roars and mutters of the crowd penetrated to our rooms for the better part of that night.

From the very start something had seemed to tell me that these demonstrations could only end badly, and in spite of my thirteen years I stated my opinion to a friend of my uncle's. I added that the crowd was using its patriotic emotions only as an excuse for brawling and that in my opinion the authorities were wrong not to intervene. I understood, even then, that a crowd is ruled by an obscure instinct entirely its own, and is always dangerous. But my listener in no way appreciated my reflections; he was shocked by them, and reported them immediately to my uncle, who spoke to me severely.

He said to me, in effect, and quite seriously, that the voice of the people is the voice of God. A crowd manifesting royalistic sentiments appeared in his eyes, and in the eyes of his entourage, in some sort a religious procession. In my mistrust of the crowd's temper I was guilty, he told me, of lack of respect for traditions.

This incident gave me much to think about. In my young mind ideas began to form which had never come to me before, and I looked around me with greater attention. An uneasiness crept into my consciousness and left an imprint.

ii

THE war excited new activities around me. My aunt organized hospitals in Moscow. She sent ambulances and nursing units to the front, created committees for widows and war orphans, and established a workroom at the Kremlin palace where ladies from the city made up linen and bandages for the hospitals. This workshop took on gigantic proportions; its various sections soon occupied all the palace halls. To go there to work was one of my ways of escape on Sunday. After the wounded began to arrive my aunt visited them frequently. Sometimes she took me with her. We spent whole afternoons in the hospitals talking with the sick.

The war was at first taken lightly by a public that refused to believe the Orientals could muster a capable military force. But when months passed without our troops achieving a victory, the war quickly became unpopular, and discontent was general. My uncle's duties doubled and redoubled, and we could see that he was greatly worried. We were guarded, as always, however, against knowledge of the outer world. Political differences did not penetrate to our study-room, and in our presence no serious discussion was permitted. We felt a certain disquietude and nervousness in the air; that was all. And this we felt only vaguely, for we were kept very busy. That winter of 1904 was the last in which my schooling and occupations were directed with any semblance of method.

The summer of 1904 was marked by a happy event, the birth of the poor little Tsarevich. But Russia had waited so long for the arrival of an heir, and this waiting had been so many times rewarded with disappointment, that the newborn heir was received without enthusiasm, and joy was of short duration.

Even in our house a certain melancholy reigned. My uncle and aunt undoubtedly knew already that the child was born suffering and that from his birth he carried in him the seeds of an incurable illness, hæmophilia—a tendency to bleed easily, an inability of the blood to clot quickly. There is no doubt that the parents were quickly advised as to the nature of their son's illness. Nobody ever knew what emotions were aroused in them by this horrible certainty, but from that moment, troubled and apprehensive, the Empress's character underwent a change, and her health, physical as well as moral, altered.

We accompanied my uncle and aunt to Peterhof to attend the little Tsarevich's baptism. A gilded coach followed by a cavalry troop bore the newly born son to the church. He was accompanied by his nurse and the Mistress of the Robes. Since dawn regiments had been drawn up along the route the cortège would take, with its numerous gala carriages drawn by horses gay with plumes.

At eleven o'clock in the morning the imperial family and the court were ready, the men in their full-dress uniforms, the ladies adorned with jewels in gowns of gold and silver cloth with long trains. The Emperor, the Grand Dukes and Duchesses, the ambassadors, and the high dignitaries formed in procession; they reached the palace church by crossing halls filled with guests. The little Tsarevich was carried at the head of the procession on a cushion of silver cloth by the Mistress of the Robes. The church glistened with light. At the entrance numerous members of the clergy, presided over by the Archbishop of St. Petersburg, greeted the Emperor. The religious service ended, the child was brought back to the house with the same ceremonial. Felicitations and a banquet brought the day to an end.

In honour of the Army, then fighting on the distant plains of Manchuria, all the combatants were inscribed as godfathers to the young prince.

That summer at Ilinskoie was long—almost tedious; it was not until after the autumn removal to Usovo that anything memorable occurred; and this incident, though perhaps trivial, made a deep impression on me. On a Sunday morning when the servants went down to begin their housework, they found that burglars had carried off a large part of the silver. Chills ran up and down my spine when I saw the traces left by the thieves. They had even eaten in the very room where we had spent the evening, and, their hunger satisfied, had calmly smoked; here were crumbs of tobacco and some forgotten cigarette papers. Here they had calmly broken a window to leave; there, from the window, lay their tracks in the snow!

It wasn't the amount or value of their booty that impressed me; it was the ease with which they had penetrated into our house, our accessibility to invasion.

iii

Returning to Moscow, we found the city on the verge of what historians now call the Revolution of 1905. Strikes and student disorders, in some degree prevalent throughout Russia, were in Moscow especially severe.

My uncle was not in accord with the government as to measures of control. He felt that only the utmost severity could put an end to the revolutionary ferment. St. Petersburg vacillated between consent to such a policy and talk of evasions, delay. All such talk appeared to my uncle little less than monstrous.

One evening when Dmitri and I came to him in his room for the reading hour, we found him greatly agitated. He took long strides around the room, saying nothing. We too kept silent, fearing to question him. After a while he began to speak.

In terms that he sought to make clear, even to us, he outlined the political situation, and then announced that he had tendered his resignation to the Emperor, who had accepted it.

He added, however, that he had no intention of leaving Moscow; that he had retained command of its military forces.

Before dismissing us, he spoke, with a certain dignity and great depth of feeling of his deep sorrow for the state of affairs in Russia, of the necessity for serious measures, and of the criminal weakness of the Emperor's ministers and councillors.

The seriousness of his tone impressed us; we felt that events must, indeed, be grave. But children receive impressions mainly in terms of external happenings, and we could not yet understand the implications of our uncle's deep uneasiness. All it really meant to us was that soon we must leave the Governor General's house to move into the Neskuchnoie Palace in the suburbs of Moscow, where, as in previous years, we spent the Christmas holidays.

That was a sad time. Strikes and disorders continued; our holiday was overshadowed by anxiety, and we did not dare venture outside the park gates. A squadron of cavalry was camped in the palace stableyard, and the guard was increased. The city was in a state of excitement. At any moment a general uprising was expected, the consequences of which nobody could predict. There was doubt as to the loyalty of the Moscow garrison, and in several regiments revolt broke forth.

One evening a few days after Christmas, when we had already gone to bed, we were awakened at my uncle's order and told to dress quickly in order to leave the Neskuchnoie Palace at once. "We are going to the Kremlin," he said brusquely when we joined him in the hall.

At the door the big closed carriage was already waiting with its two black horses. We climbed in with my uncle and aunt and were driven at full speed into the night. The curtains of the carriage were drawn. We saw nothing that passed by. No one spoke and we did not dare break the silence to ask questions. The night was cold, the snow creaked under the wheels and the horses' shoes. We were well acquainted with the way to the Kremlin and could tell, although nothing could be seen, that we were taking numerous detours to reach it. Behind us in the silence of the streets resounded the galloping hoofbeats of an escort.

I was not afraid. Excitement and curiosity left no room for other feelings. We reached the Kremlin safely; the coachman drove at an easier pace under the arcade of one of its gates to the Nicholas Palace. A few sleepy servants awaited us; doors were opened and we entered. I had never had occasion to visit this palace, which was only used to shelter foreign princes during court ceremonies, and little did I think that I was destined never to leave it until the moment of my marriage.

We went up to the first floor, where we settled ourselves in a reception room to await the arrival of the persons who were to follow us.

The palace had not been heated or aired for a long time; a damp and glacial chill enveloped its badly lighted apartments. Soon my governess, a lady-in-waiting, and an aide-de-camp arrived, followed shortly by our servants who brought us the things necessary for passing the night.

We were given tea; then my uncle selected the rooms and

THE GRAND DUKE SERGE

In old Russian court costume

we spent the night well enough in improvised beds, buried under mountains of blankets.

I never knew what incited our departure from Neskuchnoie so precipitately, but they told us the next day that our stay at the Kremlin was only temporary and as soon as events permitted we would return there. We did not need any explanations to comprehend that under the present circumstances we were better protected within the walls of the Kremlin than in suburbs inhabited by workers and where numerous factories were situated.

The days passed, however, and nothing was said about the return to Neskuchnoie.

Little by little a routine established itself, habits were taken up again, and we recommenced the lessons that had been interrupted for several days by the disturbance in our household. The Nicholas Palace, so cold and so uncomfortable at the start, ended by being very pleasant to us, as we got used to it.

But the news from outside became more and more ominous, and I sensed acutely that we were living on a volcano that was ready to belch fire and swallow us up at any instant.

CHAPTER VII

MURDER

MOSCOW was torn with turmoil and uncertainty, but within the walls of the Kremlin, our life was peaceful. My aunt and uncle rarely went out, and at home received only their closest friends.

During the second fortnight in February, however, we all went to the Moscow Opera House to attend a war benefit. The big, old-fashioned closed carriage, cushioned inside in white silk, carried us to the theatre. It was not until some days later that we learned how close we were to death.

A band of terrorists who followed all my uncle's movements had been warned of our going out and knew the route we would take. One of the group, armed with bombs, was posted to destroy us, at a signal from an accomplice. But when this man saw that Dmitri and I were in the carriage he had not the courage to wave his handkerchief, the signal agreed upon.

It was all a matter of a second; the carriage passed; we were saved. Many years later I learned the name of the man who spared our lives. It was Boris Savinkov, who played a prominent part in the revolution of 1917.

The performance that evening was magnificent; one of the artists was Chaliapin, already at the height of his glory. The hall glittered with jewels and uniforms, and there was no thought of any such catastrophe as the one that we had just escaped.

Two days passed. The eighteenth of February began like all the previous days. In the course of each afternoon, invariably at the same hour, my uncle would go in a closed brougham to the Governor General's house to supervise the removal of his belongings. On this particular afternoon he insisted, as he had for some time, on going alone. When lunch ended he kissed us good-bye as usual. I went to my lessons.

My thoughts were not on my work. As the charming old gentleman who taught me mathematics began his instruction, my mind kept turning perversely, I remember, to a mandolin which I wanted to ask my uncle for, and which I was afraid he would refuse me.

The whole scene comes back to me; my instructor speaking, myself pretending to listen; Fräulein Hase, my German teacher, placidly reading a book in a corner. The windows of the schoolroom gave onto a wide square of the Kremlin; through the windows, I could see across the way the big steeple of St. John's.

A beautiful winter's day was ending; everything was calm, and the noises of the city came to us muffled by the snow. Suddenly a frightful detonation shook the air and rattled the window-panes.

The silence that followed was so crushing that for some seconds we did not stir or look at each other. Fräulein Hase was the first to recover. She dashed to the window. The old professor and I followed. Quick! quick! my thoughts buzzed; ideas hastened, pell-mell, one upon another, through my mind.

One of the old towers of the Kremlin collapsed? . . . Sliding snow had crashed into an avalanche, carrying a roof with it? And my uncle . . . where was he? Dmitri came running from his own study. We looked at each other, not daring to express our thoughts.

A flock of crows, frightened by the explosion, wheeled madly around the steeple and disappeared. The square began to show signs of life. People came running, all from the same direction.

A servant came into the room. I bade him go at once and see if my uncle had gone out. He returned in a few seconds and told us evasively that he thought my uncle was still in the house.

Now the square was filled with people. Two sleighs appeared, going in a direction contrary to the current of the crowd. In these sleighs were men roughly dressed; and with them were policemen. The men in plain clothes appeared to be struggling and haranguing the crowd. They were hatless, their hair blowing in the wind, their clothing in disorder, and it seemed to me I saw blood on their hands and faces.

At this moment we saw that my aunt's sleigh, which waited below to take her to the workshop, had been brought near to the steps. My aunt ran out of the house, a cloak thrown over her shoulders, loosely. She was followed by Mlle. Hélène in a man's overcoat. Both were without hats. They clambered into the sleigh, which started immediately, at top speed, and was lost to our sight behind the angle of the square.

Indescribable moments of anguish crept by. The square was black with people. But no one had yet come up to us to announce the news that we trembled to learn and could no longer doubt.

Finally we saw our aunt's sleigh slowly coming back, forcing its way through the crowd massed before the house. Aunt Ella was not in it; only Mlle. Hélène. She set foot on the ground and climbed the steps heavily, without looking up.

A movement occurred among the people, as if from afar they saw something following the sleigh. Several minutes later my governess entered the room. Her face, habitually high in colour, was now blue; her breathing was laboured; her lips were violet, and her countenance frightful to behold. We threw ourselves upon her and pressed her with questions. The poor woman could not pronounce a word; she pressed trembling hands to her heart; only inarticulate sounds escaped her lips. But she finally succeeded in making us understand that we must put on our coats and follow her. By this time my legs were trembling. No one had as yet told us a single detail; but horrible pictures of what had happened assailed my imagination. We were just putting on our coats when General Laiming came into the room.

"The Grand Duchess does not wish the children to come. She sent me ahead to tell you," he told Mlle. Hélène, breathlessly. "She doesn't even want them to stay at the window."

We were hurried from the window, and we hovered at refuge in the room at the side, terrified and shaking with sobs.

I do not know how long it was before we were told what had happened; I cannot remember; but the facts were these. Our uncle had been assassinated, blown to death by a bomb, as he drove to the Governor General's palace.

General Laiming was the last one who had talked with him. After lunch he had asked him for a few minutes' interview to speak with my uncle about my mandolin, and had obtained permission to buy it for me.

My aunt had hurried, as we had seen, to the corpse in the snow. She had gathered together the fragments of mangled flesh and placed them on an ordinary army stretcher, hastily brought from her workshop near by. Soldiers from the barracks opposite had covered the body with their coats; then, hoisting the litter to their shoulders, they had carried the body to the shelter of the Monastery of the Miracle, and placed it in the church, directly next door to the palace in which we were staying.

It was only when this had been done that we were fetched. We went down to the first floor and by a little corridor gained the inside door which led to the monastery. The church was thronged; all were kneeling; many were weeping. Close to the altar steps, low on the stones, the stretcher had been placed. It could not have contained very much, for the coats covering it formed only a very small pile. At one end a boot protruded casually from the coverings. Drops of blood fell on the floor, slowly forming a small dark pool.

My aunt was on her knees beside the litter. Her bright dress shone forth grotesquely amid the humble garments surrounding her. I did not dare look at her.

A frightened priest said the service in a trembling voice. There was no choir. From the semi-darkness in which all the church was plunged, the congregation chanted the responses. Candles burned here and there in people's hands.

The service ended. The congregation rose and I saw my aunt advancing towards us. Her face was white, her features terrible in their stricken rigidity. She did not weep, but the expression of her eyes made an impression on me I will never forget as long as I live.

In time she lost this strained expression of hallucination, but the depths of her eyes retained for ever an infinite sadness.

Leaning on the arm of the Governor of the city, my aunt drew near the door slowly, and when she perceived us she stretched out her arms to us. We ran to her.

"He loved you so, he loved you," she repeated endlessly, pressing our heads against her. We drew her by slow degrees out into the corridor to escape the glances of the curious, who grew in numbers around us. I noticed that, low on her right arm the sleeve of her gay blue dress was stained with blood. There was blood on her hand, too, and under the nails of her fingers, in which she gripped tightly the medals that my uncle always wore on a chain at his neck.

Dmitri and I succeeded in leading her back towards her rooms. She let herself fall weakly into an arm-chair. Her eyes dry and with the same peculiar fixity of gaze, she looked straight into space, and said nothing.

After a time, she arose and, with feverish need of activity, demanded paper and wrote telegrams to all the family, beginning with the Emperor. Her face while writing did not change expression. Now and then she got up, walked tensely about the room, then sat down to her desk again. People came and went. She looked at them without seeming to see them.

Throughout the palace people moved with muffled steps and

spoke in whispers. Evening came, but no light was lit. The half-light of dusk crept into the rooms.

My aunt had several times demanded news of my uncle's coachman. He lay in the hospital, his life despaired of, his body torn by the same bomb that had killed my uncle. Towards six in the evening Aunt Ella went herself to visit the wounded man; and, in order not to dismay him by signs of mourning, she wore to the hospital the same gay blue dress she had worn all afternoon.

She went farther! When the coachman asked news of my uncle she had the courage to reply to him with a smile that it was the Grand Duke himself who had sent her to him. The poor man died peacefully during the night.

During all these sad days my aunt gave proof of an almost incomprehensible heroism; no one could understand whence came the strength so to bear her misfortune. Always shut up in herself, she became more so. Only her eyes and sometimes the beaten look on her face betrayed her suffering; and with an energy that, following long years of almost complete passivity, was astonishing, she took charge herself of all the grisly details.

On that first evening of our mourning Dmitri and I, completely exhausted, still felt the need to talk, to exchange impressions. We lingered there in the schoolroom, conversing in whispers. The room was dark; outside night had fallen; the tall steeple of St. John's made a black bar against the sky. Snow made the ramparts and roofs blue. On all sides arose the heavy masses of cupolas. Upon the ancient walls of the Kremlin had again descended the calm of centuries.

Silence fell between us. Without saying a word, Dmitri and I gazed from the same window at the impassive town. Nothing was altered; the most terrible events in people's lives—what did they matter? Things went on to their destined end. What of our own future? It would be different, but how? . . .

"What do you think?" said Dmitri's voice in the darkness. "Will we be . . . happier?"

ii

DINNER was announced. I felt the same astonishment at finding the old order of things renewed. In the sight of the table set with the usual array of objects, there was something shocking.

Aunt Ella did not eat, but she entered the room before the end of the repast and sat with us at the table. She still wore the same blue dress. Facing her white, worn face, we were ashamed to eat.

She said that she wanted to spend the night in my room; she did not want to be alone in her apartment on the first floor. Before sending Dmitri to bed, she had asked us to say our prayers before her, and we knelt down together, all three.

We remained a long while awake, my aunt and I, talking of my uncle. Little by little she softened. The pose of rigidity which had so long enclosed her yielded. She ended by relaxing completely, and wept.

I fell quickly into a dead sleep; I do not know whether she slept or not, but when I awakened she was not in my room.

During the night my uncle's remains were placed in a coffin that rested on a platform draped in black. According to the Orthodox practice, this coffin had to remain open until burial, but my uncle's shattered face and hands were veiled from view, and the rest of his body was covered with a large square of brocade bordered with gold braid.

Sentinels stood at attention at all four corners of the platform, and all day long services were held. We went morning and evening to join in the prayers, and our aunt went often during the day to pass hours on her knees near the bier. She spoke seldom now, and seemed lost in a sort of dolorous dream.

Occasionally it happened that, the service ended, she remained in the same spot without realizing it, without seeing what went on around her. Then, as gently as possible, I would

IN "AUNT ELLA'S" ROOM, 1904

The Grand Duchess Marie with her brother

take her by the arm. At this she would wince as if from a blow, and fix upon me a blind look tragic in its tormented simplicity.

She found strength, none the less, to think of everything and particularly of Dmitri and me. She came to seek us out at every moment of the day and kept us near her as much as she could. Her manner towards us changed completely; it was as if for the first time she had looked into our souls. Those weeks of sorrow brought us closer together and we had long conversations full of an intimacy we had never known before.

In one of these talks she confessed to me that she had suffered a great deal because of the affection which my uncle had shown us so completely, especially since Dmitri and I had come to be part of his household in Moscow. She acknowledged herself guilty of brusqueness and injustice, born of that jealousy; and set herself now to make amends, attaching herself particularly to my brother, who was my uncle's favourite. They were bound together by a bond of real affection until the day when events separated them for ever.

As for me, I remained always a little apart; and whether that was my fault or my aunt's, I cannot say.

My aunt dwelt, in those days, above all earthly considerations; she was remote, and except in the performance of what she deemed her duty, she appeared indifferent to all happenings around her. Some of the things that she did were so divorced from earthly considerations as to appear all but incalculable and—in the view of those who did not know her well—insane.

The day after the murder, she drove off in a carriage draped with black cloth and crape, and remained away a long time. She had gone to the prison to see the murderer! This struck the administration into utter confusion; nothing like it had ever happened before.

No one knows to this day exactly what passed between my aunt and her husband's assassin. She insisted on speaking with the prisoner alone. Her impulses, I have reason to know, were wholly those of Christian abnegation, but countless other versions of the interview circulated in town. Echoes of these tales reached the prisoner. Hurt by the words attributed to him, he wrote an insulting letter to my aunt; naturally it was never delivered to her.

In spite of a certain admiration for an act so exalted, my brother and I belonged to a generation entirely too practical to believe in the utility of such a gesture. The anarchists of this period were madmen and fanatics; they were fully persuaded of the justice and legitimacy of their crimes; in playing the hero, they needed no help, certainly not from the wives of their victims.

In the evening when my aunt came to her room we tried to question her but she would tell us nothing.

My uncle was buried on the morning of the twenty-third of February. My uncle's brothers as well as his sister-in-law, the Dowager Empress, expressed a desire to attend but found at the last moment that they could not do so. Disorders were feared; strikes were breaking out one after another, in all the great industrial centres. Any gathering of royal persons would only invite new catastrophes. A cousin of my uncle, the Grand Duke Constantine, took the risk; and so did the Duchess of Saxe-Coburg, her daughter, Beatrice, and the Grand Duke of Hesse and his wife. Finally, my father, in his banishment now installed in Paris, asked the Emperor's permission to come. It was granted.

Dmitri and I went to see him at the railway station and received him with sobs which could not lessen the joy we had at seeing him again. We took him back to the house. The meeting between him and his sister-in-law was painful.

My aunt had conceived the idea of building a chapel in the crypt of the Miracle monastery to shelter the remains of my uncle. While waiting for the chapel to be built, she obtained permission to place the coffin in one of the convent churches.

The funeral service was celebrated with great solemnity; officers with drawn swords and sentinels were stationed around the bier. The Archbishop and the high clergy of Moscow celebrated the mass, a service so long and tiring that I almost fainted, and father had to take me out. The church was full of people; wreaths and flowers were heaped around the coffin and on the steps of the catafalque. By this time I had reached such a degree of physical lassitude that I could hardly think or feel anything. We had lived for six days in a state of nervous tension that never relaxed. At the end of the service the coffin was carried to one of the little churches of the monastery, and here for forty days and nights prayers were said. We attended them every evening.

iii

Some days later my father and other members of the family departed. Little by little life took up its normal course. Normal is an expression only relatively exact, for my aunt never left off her mourning and rarely went out. Laughter or a sudden shout seemed shocking in her presence, and the house was an abode of heavy memories. I could not feel, even at the time, that all of my aunt's rapt preoccupation was for the memory of my uncle. She seemed to me as one obsessed with griefs and perplexities as yet unresolved. But I had at the time barely an intimation of the full scope of her character and intent.

Always very devout, she now turned entirely to religion and sought her comfort there. Her life from that time seemed dedicated solely to pious works. Never worldly, her mourning gave her an excuse to turn from social life, and she gave herself over entirely to the performance of her duties as she saw them—mystic as well as concrete. The last she found trying; for more than twenty years she had never given an order in her own house. Now she had to decide everything. She had to re-educate herself. One could not but feel sorry for her, with her air of suffering and detachment, trying to take an interest in all the perplexing, practical questions of household management.

My father made overtures to have us with him. They failed. My aunt held us to her, dutifully, in memory of her husband.

We resumed our occupations and soon a new routine founded itself on the ruins of the past. My aunt wished to follow the traditions established by my uncle. At each new circumstance she evoked his name. Her constant effort was to regulate our existence by the formula: What would *he* have done?

But new necessities greatly modified our life; our uncle was dead; we had to adapt ourselves to that condition; and we were on the whole, it must be admitted, the happier for the change.

And so the winter passed, and at the first breath of spring we went to Tsarskoie-Selo to spend the Easter holidays. There, too, the atmosphere was far from joyous. The imperial family lived in the shadow of threatened death and political upheaval. The war with Japan continued, unpromisingly; the situation at home became more and more complicated and acute. Weak, indecisive, timorous, the government, unable to agree upon any energetic action, stood shakily aloof and let events precipitate themselves. The reign of assassinations and assaults had begun.

Established now completely at Tsarskoie-Selo, the sovereigns since the war lived in comparative retirement made sadder by anxiety. The Empress did not know a peaceful moment, neither on her husband's account nor on that of her son, whose illness became more and more disquieting. The dangers that threatened the Emperor had led to the organization of a curiously complicated system of spying and tattling; spies were set to watch spies; the air was filled with whisperings, cross-currents of fear and mistrust.

On the eve of Easter, while we were still at Tsarskoie, a serious conspiracy came to light. Two members of the terrorist organization made themselves up as singers, intending to enter as such into the choir that sang in religious services at the court.

They planned, apparently, to bring in bombs under their vestments, and to hurl those bombs in the church as they chanted during Easter mass. The Emperor, although knowing of the plot, went to church with his family as usual. A number of persons were arrested that day. Nothing further happened; but that mass was the saddest that I have ever attended.

CHAPTER VIII

DEBUT

MOURNING did not prevent our going to Ilinskoie at the beginning of summer. It was a pleasant summer; and our pleasure was increased, if anything, by the company of soldiers that was sent to guard us, and by a new automobile, bought in case we had to flee.

Every day I rode horseback with Dmitri. We were permitted playmates; ran with them, sang with them, went with them to choir rehearsals. Life's aspect changed. Even my aunt lifted her head and gave proofs of initiative.

She organized a hospital for wounded on the estate, a thing which would have been impossible in my uncle's day. This hospital was a great consolation to her, and she spent most of her time there, busying herself with the smallest details. It was the first time in her life she had come near the people.

But her inexperience and her slight acquaintance with their language and customs often led her too far. The soldiers soon saw that they were dealing with a woman who was too good to be altogether wise, and they took advantage of the familiar way she dealt with them. Soon they became unbearable. General Laiming shook his head, troubled by the slackening of discipline.

I, myself, at first was diligent in visiting the sick, but I soon got tired of it. Impatiently I heard them holding forth on subjects with which their undeveloped mentalities could only fumble; and I saw them in all ways being spoiled.

My aunt was saddened by my attitude. She reproached me. I felt myself too young, too inarticulate, to explain my reasons to her, and thought it more reasonable to keep quiet.

My grandmother, Queen Olga of Greece, accompanied by her son, Christopher, came to pass several weeks with us. She was a delicious old lady, charming to look at and full of kindness. Her charm had a candid softness, and her soul was serene as a child's. The vulgar or equivocal sides of life had never come close to her; she had passed them without seeing them. She was the only being in the world who gave me a clear idea of what love and maternal tenderness could be; but such was my timidity, and such that inner rigidity with which I protected my sensibilities, over-developed in isolation, that I was prevented from going towards her in all simplicity. Her caresses and her radiant, affectionate eyes made me want to go to her arms for refuge; but I was so little used to caresses that I did not know how to begin.

My grandmother had led a long life full of trials; she had lived through wars and revolutions, and lost people dear to her. Sustained by a simple, boundless faith, she endured everything with the same patience and resignation. During her stay at Ilinskoie she passionately seconded my aunt in working among the wounded at the hospital; their happy absorption in this pious indulgence left Christopher, Dmitri, and me free to run wild and raise mischief. We did crazy things and Christopher was ringleader. He involved us in the wreck of a cart; the horse, fortunately wise, stopped in his tracks, and we ourselves got out without a scratch, covered with mud, our clothes in tatters, shaking with mad laughter. He played pranks on the governesses and teased my little friends, but all in such a droll way that nobody minded it. My grandmother, who adored him, read him a gentle sermon, but he made a face at her or gave her a kiss, and all was forgiven.

My aunt, I must say, had a great deal of patience with us, far more than formerly; and certainly more trust existed in our relations to each other. But I could never free myself of a kind of stiffness before her. I felt my ideas growing in a direction contrary to hers and did not want to have it otherwise. I admired her but I did not wish to be like her. She was escaping life, it seemed to me. For my part, I wanted to know everything.

She found me too modern in my manners, lacking that blushing timidity which, according to her, was a young girl's principal charm. She desired that in everything my education should be like hers and like that of all the young princesses of her time; she imagined that the years between our two generations could not and ought not to make any difference.

I bowed to her demands, on the surface, and executed her wishes, but often smiled inwardly, persuaded that the old rules did not amount to much.

Even in my toilet I had to follow her sense of tradition. She made me do up my hair when I was not yet fifteen, and my coiffure was copied after that of the Austrian Archduchesses of her time. My hair thus was drawn back from my brow, and my large plait, ashy blonde, coiled basket-like on the top of my head.

In spite of my taste for sports I was clumsy, and my aunt thought me unrefined.

My brother never went through this transient, awkward period of long-leggedness. He was always slender, straight, and well built; much more gay, more high-spirited than I. My aunt yielded to his charm as did all others around him. He was more mischievous than I; where he got fun out of something, I found food for reflection beyond my years—which won a reproving glance from my aunt.

My childhood had, in fact, ended. I observed and noted everything that went on around me; I debated with myself in a troubled world of ideas and of thoughts half-formed, all of which came to me at the same time. This tendency my aunt combated, even as my uncle had; he often warned us that to him we must always remain little children. My aunt imitated this principle. She discussed with us no family or political subject, and never confided in us her personal projects and

YOUNG MATRON, 1912

The Grand Duchess Marie in the fashion of the hour

THE GRAND DUCHESS MARIE, IN SWEDISH PEASANT DRESS, 1909

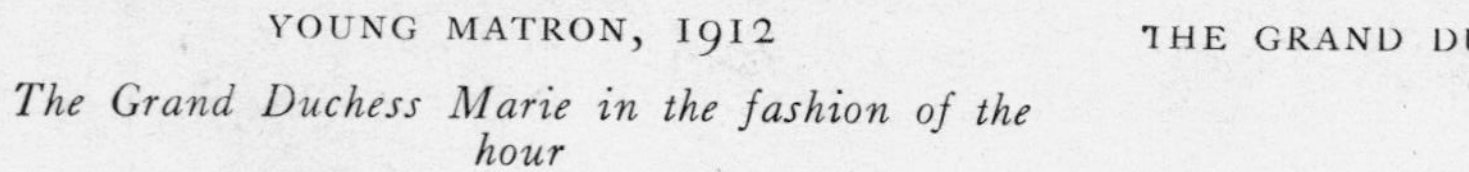

intentions. We were always the last to be advised of a change. Usually it was from the entourage that we learned a piece of news, and, when finally she decided to announce it and saw that we already knew it, she was very much displeased.

The ignorance in which she kept us was part of her educational system, but it exasperated us and made us curious and prying. Besides, we knew very well how to humour her, and generally we pretended to be *au courant* in nothing. The equilibrium of our contacts was thus conserved, and her tranquillity assured. Besides, it rather amused us—her idea that by seeing us to bed at nine o'clock she would preserve in us all the illusions of childhood as well as our rosy cheeks.

ii

In autumn we returned to the Nicholas Palace to occupy new quarters, furnished according to my aunt's tastes. On the first floor I had two bright, spacious rooms. Dmitri's rooms, on the second, opened to a splendid view over the Kremlin and Moscow.

My aunt arranged her bedroom like a nun's cell, all white, hung with ikons and pictures of the saints. In one of the corners she placed a large wooden cross in which were enclosed what remained of the clothes worn by my uncle on the day of his death.

Not wishing to give up her wounded soldiers, she rented a house in the city near the Kremlin and turned it into a hospital. She continued her visits to the sick. I scarcely went any more. My brother and I found her infatuation with the wounded a little ridiculous.

Political tension was now at its height, and the situation caused serious unrest. Strikes, riots, troubles, broke out everywhere; revolution was impending.

The decree of October 17th, by which the Emperor, granting certain liberties to the people, instituted the Duma, did not suffice to calm the gathering storm. Moscow was struck that autumn by a wave of madness. One after another strikes broke out, and we found ourselves one fine day completely isolated in the Kremlin, cut off from the rest of the world, protected only by a guard of soldiers whose loyalty was uncertain.

All means of communication, the post, the telegraph, the telephone, had ceased to function, and our home was lighted only because the Kremlin had an electric plant of its own. We lacked food and water. The gates of the Kremlin were closed. No one could enter except by day, and then only if he had a pass. In the evening they did not dare light the lamps in the Kremlin, nor the chandeliers in the Nicholas Palace; all lights in rooms were placed under tables in order not to attract attention outside.

We were besieged within the walls of the old fortress; riots sounded all around us. Disquieting news came—threat of a night attack, a revolutionary project to penetrate as far as our rooms and to take us children as hostages.

The house was filled with soldiers, the doors were guarded, and we could not go out except to walk inside the walls.

My aunt maintained her habitual air of preoccupation, communicating no fears to us, quietly arranging with General Laiming to conceal us in case of danger. Several times she went out into the city, unwilling to abide by the precautions set down by the prefect of police. One evening she insisted on going to the hospital to assist at an urgent operation, and General Laiming, though disapproving this rashness, was naturally obliged to accompany her.

Usually, they went in a carriage, but this time they had to make the trip afoot in order not to attract attention. She had hoped, I believe, to hide this escapade from us, but, finding by chance what she had done, we were most uneasy, and sat up to wait for her.

It was late when she returned. Not having dined, she went up to the dining-room where a cold supper had been kept for her. We joined her as she ate. I was so angry that my vexation overcame my timidity, and after long years of holding my tongue I spoke up and told her what I thought.

I told her first that her exaggerated fondness for her wounded, long ridiculous, was now worse than that. This late visit to the hospital was dangerous and would be talked about the next day by everybody. And at the end, hardly knowing any longer what I said, I added that my uncle would have severely criticized her present actions.

I do not know where I found the courage to speak in this way. I expected every minute to be sent to my room. But to my astonishment my aunt listened meekly, without replying, to all I had to say. When I uttered my uncle's name she lowered her head and began to cry. Her tears melted my anger; immediately, I was sorry for all I had said; I stood silent.

Then, without resentment, she replied. She said she knew my words were just, that the hospital and the wounded had perhaps become too important in her life, and that probably my uncle would have disapproved.

But she found herself so lonely, so desolate, that she had to do something, to forget her grief at the sight of others' suffering.

We talked a long while. Before it was over, I asked her to pardon me for my outburst. Fortunately, this was our first and last scene of this kind. The next day we assumed our respective attitudes as if nothing had happened. But my aunt widened the intervals of her visits to the hospital, and no longer went there after dark.

iii

WHEN the strikes ceased, after several reprisals, my aunt thought it would be wiser to remove to Tsarskoie-Selo. There we remained until the end of winter. At first we lived with the Emperor and Empress; later in apartments at the Great Palace.

After our departure from Moscow new disorders occurred, but this time the government adopted severe measures; a regiment of the Guards was sent from St. Petersburg; blood ran in the gutters; order was re-established. My aunt returned to Moscow alone.

In April, we attended the opening of the Duma in the Winter Palace at St. Petersburg. This was supposed to mark a new era, with the will of the Crown more responsive, and responsible, to the voice of the people. But in thus limiting his power, the Emperor had no intention of making such concessions final. The institution of the Duma was a half-measure lacking depth or sincerity.

On the day of the assembly the Winter Palace looked more like a fortress, so greatly did they fear an attack or hostile demonstrations. The court went out in gala formation, the men in full-dress uniforms, the women in gowns with trains and diadems. I wore a train of regulation length and took my place in the procession like a grown-up person. No ceremony of this kind ever having taken place before, it was all a little vague, and many of the actors were not sure of their parts. The majority of them wore a lugubrious aspect; and it was easy to believe yourself at a funeral. Even the Emperor, ordinarily able to hide his feelings, was sad and nervous.

Life at Tsarskoie-Selo was very pleasant. We were surrounded by a numerous family, happy in the close intimacy of their isolation. The relations between the sovereigns and their children, in spite of all the luxury, were candid and simple.

This particular winter, the Emperor wished personally to inspect all the regiments camped in St. Petersburg and its suburbs, and for this reason he had them come in turn to Tsarskoie-Selo. Once or twice a week there would be a parade in the morning and in the afternoon a dinner for the officers at the palace. As for the women, there were only the Empress, myself, sometimes the Grand Duchess Olga, the Emperor's sister, and the two ladies-in-waiting. I enjoyed those dinners immensely.

The events of the previous year had completely upset our studies, and for months we had paid them no attention at all. At the Alexander Palace it was impossible to organize serious, sustained activities, so it was decided that we should go to the Great Palace to live in my father's old apartments.

The two palaces were only a short distance apart. . . . It was arranged that we take our repasts with the sovereigns. Once more new professors were engaged, and they did their best to make up for the lost time; but all sorts of distractions arose continually—and I did not complain.

These distractions were pleasant and various. Often I went to visit my cousins, the Grand Duke Constantine's children, who lived in the palace at Pavlovsk three miles away. It was a large family, with the eldest children older than I, and a new member added each year. At that moment there were, I believe, six boys and one daughter, with whom I took a course in Russian history twice a week. We went sleigh riding with the boys, and as we were much more enterprising than our cousins, our animation added to the occasion. One of the parties was marked by an accident; I cut my lip against a stone mile-post and returned to the house covered with blood. In the evening there was a court dinner and I went with a swollen face and twisted mouth. The Emperor laughed a great deal at me.

Mlle. Hélène began to grow jealous again; but I did not brood on that fact as of old. She had been accustomed to follow me everywhere, but now that she was excluded from visits to the Alexander Palace, she resented it bitterly, and ended by driving me to the wall with a direct accusation of premeditated lying. First she put it in a note to me in due form; then, her face flaming, continued her reproaches in a loud voice in the presence of servants.

I kept silent until we were alone; and then let go. I cannot remember what I said to her, but it must have been striking, for at my first word she was muted. At the end of my explosion a breathless moment passed before she could find words; and when she did they were in a tone almost obsequious. Her spiritless attitude was painful to me. I was robbed of all sense of triumph at my first successful revolt; but from that day our disagreements grew rarer, peace reigned between us, and we became better friends.

In the spring of the year 1906, I was sixteen years old and my aunt and the sovereigns planned to give this anniversary a certain solemnity. I received presents from everybody, and was very happy that day, for from then on I was considered officially no longer a child, but a *jeune fille.*

Our mourning had ended in February, and the Grand Duke Constantine and his wife gave a ball for me and for their daughter, who was also just sixteen years old.

This ball was a great event. I made preparations long in advance. My aunt herself took charge of my toilet. She had a dress made for me. It was of slightly transparent voile over rose. I was to wear lilies-of-the-valley with it. Secretly, I remember, I thought the dress too heavy, too complicated for the debutante that I was; I would have preferred a very simple white silk, but my aunt did not ask my opinion.

My brother accompanied me to the ball. He wore a little sub-lieutenant's uniform. The Emperor and Empress conducted us to the festivities which began about six o'clock in the evening and lasted until one in the morning. First there was a dinner and later a supper.

The evening was long, very long, but not long enough for me; it was all such fun! We returned home with Mlle. Hélène and the General. I was worn out, the hem of my dress in tatters, and my coiffure completely disarranged, but the flowers and the cotillion favours filling my arms were tangible proofs of my success. Dmitri, still too young, did not know how to dance; truly a boy, he looked askance on this form of exercise and complained that he had spent a very dull evening. But I dreamed only of starting it all over again.

But many months passed before a new holiday came along. My aunt did not find it proper to let me go out in the world accompanied only by Mlle. Hélène. It was necessary also, my aunt felt, to have a member of my family chaperon me. She herself could not do so on account of her mourning and as there was no one else to go with me I never went out.

We had hoped to see father that year, but Aunt Ella would not hear of our travelling abroad in the company of General Laiming and Mlle. Hélène.

We spent that summer partly at Peterhof, partly at Ilinskoie. Autumn found us again settled in the Nicholas Palace at Moscow. I noticed for some time that my aunt had acquired a new vitality. All her energy seemed now concentrated upon some goal that, so far as we were concerned, she shielded in mystery. Two new figures made their appearance in our little world of retainers and attendants: a widow, Mme. Uzlov, whose husband had been assassinated during the recent disorders; and Father Alexander, a priest. Father Alexander had been to war with the armies in the Orient and had distinguished himself by his courage, his moral qualities, and his eloquence.

Mme. Uzlov inspired me with sympathy; she was not used to courts and bore herself with great simplicity. But I took a dislike to Father Alexander from the very beginning. He was remarkably handsome and thoroughly conscious of it. He had a soft voice which he did not modulate. I never came to know him well; perhaps that is why I never liked him. My aunt spent all her time with these two new-comers, and they were the only ones to whom she confided her plans.

On her return to Moscow she purchased a house and some land on the far side of the river. She told us that she intended it for war cripples. Her interest in her former hospital had by this time waned; she seldom went there any more.

The house on the Moskva was carefully fitted for its

new purpose, and my aunt personally supervised all the arrangements.

Dmitri and I were sent back to our studies. Joylessly we saw our former professors reappear and resume their droning discourses. My aunt thought that I had now studied long enough; the women of her time, she said, did not burden their brains with so many useless subjects. I was almost ready to agree with her. But General Laiming held his ground and insisted that my education should be continued. He won his point but I did not learn anything; all continuity and order of instruction had been broken and the methods of teaching were profitless and dull.

iv

RUSSIA still writhed and stumbled. The wave of revolts and uprisings, the constant agitations, the incessant inflammatory orations of men possessed with little political competence, had by this time cowed the Emperor and the ruling class into bewildered and sullen inertia. They had long since lost contact with the true thought and interests of the country. The government had become more and more centralized, more and more rigid; it no longer had the discernment and the elasticity that were necessary to meet changing demands.

On the other hand, the mouthpieces of the so-called public opinion; those men, who by high sounding formulas had so impressed the densely ignorant masses—they too lacked competence and initiative. They had neither sufficient moral force nor experience necessary to build up a new system. Their mental store was limited to theories, often excellent but inapplicable to reality. A noisy and threatening minority, they readily and easily overcame such resistance as was offered by the weak and cowardly councillors of the Emperor; and launched the country upon a programme of social liberties and political reforms for which it was not ripe.

In establishing the Duma, the Emperor ostensibly had

limited his power; actually he held intact the greater part of his prerogatives; but neither he nor his councillors knew how to take advantage of the leeway thus gained. They had the power but they did not know how to apply it; the Emperor scowled impotently at the young liberal institution, refusing frankly to recognize it, remembering always that it represented a concession extorted from him.

A certain tolerance might have quieted the spirit of the representatives of the nation, awakened a feeling of political responsibility, created a respect for tradition. But the Emperor's constant and apparent ill-will had upon the Duma and upon the people an exasperating effect. The people and their representatives in the Duma had somehow awakened to a definite understanding of their rights. They saw their suggestions for the benefit of the country granted in principle, only, when it came to practical application, to be smothered at birth with obstacles, many of them transparently unreal. The errors and the weaknesses of the regime were thus emphasized; the prestige of the Throne attacked at every new occasion.

Parties of every orientation took form. Of these, perhaps the most harmful to the monarchy was the extreme right, flattering the Emperor with vain illusions.

Under such conditions co-operation between the Tsar and the Duma was impossible; and from the very beginning, the effort peacefully to liberalize Russian absolutism was doomed to failure.

Within the walls of the Kremlin, life went on much as ever. We went often that winter to the theatre.

Our theatre-going was quite an event. In the back of the imperial box we had a large drawing-room in which to drink tea in the intervals. The cups, the plates, the silver, and provisions were brought by the personnel of our palace. The Chief Commissioner of the police customarily took tea with us; we invited those of our intimates who happened to be at the performance. Besides, we had permission to ask the actors, singers, or dancers to come into the box, but we could not offer them tea; they had to remain standing during the few minutes of conversation that convention allowed. Thus we met all the prominent Moscow artists who played at the Imperial Theatre at that time. Unfortunately, my aunt would not let me attend the performances at the Moscow Art Theatre, then famous.

I often spent my Sundays in the company of my friends, the sisters Kleinmichel. They lived with their parents in a spacious old house situated between the courtyard and the gardens in a quiet, bourgeois street. I preferred going to see them to inviting them to Nicholas Palace. The simplicity of their family life attracted me greatly. The Countess Kleinmichel, intelligent and still young, was a real friend to her daughters; she gave them a happy home and knew how to make herself indispensable to all our joys. Knowing my loneliness, she did everything in her power to make me feel at home in her house. I experienced a feeling of depression and of something like jealousy each time, my call ended, I had to go back to grandeur.

CHAPTER IX

BETROTHAL

THAT air of mystery with which my aunt surrounded her every project was something of a family trait. Most of my relatives made secrets of things of no consequence. Dmitri and I became, therefore, accustomed to gathering our own information, and sometimes did not hesitate to resort to indelicate means.

My aunt had the habit of strewing all her correspondence everywhere, and I must confess that often Dmitri and I threw indiscreet glances upon letters and telegrams that lay open.

We came thus one day into knowledge of a telegram, the contents of which rather startled me.

It was signed by Princess Irene, wife of Prince Henry of Prussia, my aunt's sister. It said that the then Crown Princess of Sweden wished for my latest photographs; they should be sent to Stockholm without delay.

Dismayed, we looked at each other; we knew at once what it meant. The royal family of Sweden was but slightly allied to ours by marriage and maintained no familiar relations with us. This request could only indicate a project of marriage.

The first moment of surprise over, this discovery did not, for some reason, especially impress me. I knew that some day I was destined to marry a foreigner; I had always known that only by a stroke of extraordinary luck would I be able to make a choice according to the dictates of my heart. In all times, the marriages of princes have been prearranged; I had been brought up to accept the idea.

I suppose that the photograph was forwarded; no reference

was made to the matter; and as the days went by, I all but forgot it.

We went to Tsarskoie-Selo for Easter. As soon as the festivities were over my aunt announced that we must return to Moscow. Urgent business, she said, recalled us; and my request for a longer stay at Tsarskoie could not be considered.

Back in Moscow, she asked me to keep my afternoon free of engagements, as she was expecting a guest for tea. It would be well, she added, for me to put on a more suitable dress.

At four, the hour appointed, I descended without any great enthusiasm, to the drawing-room and found my aunt still alone. While filling the teapot she remarked casually, avoiding my glance, that her guest was the young Prince William of Sweden, the second son of her old childhood friend, the Crown Princess of Sweden. He was travelling, she said, incognito, to see the country.

I smiled to myself. Her announcement awakened no further emotion in me and when, a few moments later, the doors opened and the young Prince made his appearance, I looked him over with calm curiosity.

He was personable, even distinguished looking, with beautiful grey eyes veiled by thick eyelashes. His shoulders were somewhat narrow, and his height so marked that he sought to modify it, it seemed, by a slight stoop. We sat around a table, politely chatting. Most of the conversation was between my aunt and the Prince. As no one spoke to me, I kept silent. Dmitri was out of the house. But before leaving my room I had written a note telling him to join me in the drawing-room upon his return. When he finally appeared, a handsome small boy, in his blue sailor blouse, his hair dishevelled, his surprise was great. He and the Prince examined each other attentively and shook hands. The conversation between the Prince and my aunt continued. As he left, my aunt asked him to come back to dinner and he accepted.

When we were alone my aunt sought to discover my impression of the Prince. I pretended not to understand what she wanted. Dmitri followed me to my room and plied me with questions:

"Do you think that was the Prince for whom your photos were intended? Did he come especially to see you? And are you going to marry him?"

"Don't be tiresome," I told him. "Who else do you suppose he would come to see if it were not me? But he has not yet spoken to me," I added, laughing.

I dressed for dinner but had not yet, at sixteen, attained the age of true coquetry, and threw only preoccupied and troubled glances at the mirror while Tania fixed my braids. At dinner, the Prince sat beside me. I could feel the attention of the entire table centred upon us. Yet I overcame my timidity and we talked with great ease. My aunt sent Dmitri and me to bed about ten o'clock, our usual hour, and kept the Prince by her side, after having dismissed her attendants.

Next morning she summoned me into her drawing-room. I kissed her hand and waited for her to speak; we sat facing each other.

"Listen to me," she began, looking away from me and crumpling nervously in her hand a handkerchief edged with black, "I must speak to you of a very serious matter and I want you to think carefully before answering."

Her face was flushed with suppressed emotion and she chose her words with difficulty.

"Prince William came here to make your acquaintance. He likes you, and wants to know whether you would consent to marry him. . . ."

The shock of her words was violent and painful. Although I had been brought up in the idea that I must make a political marriage, I had never expected such abruptness. The rush of my aunt's words, her haste to have me married, and the complete absence of any thought as to the sentimental side of such a compact, revolted me, seemed to me indecent. Noting my stupefaction, she took me by the hand and sought to draw me towards her.

"Darling, you must not let yourself be disturbed. I repeat I do not want your immediate answer; you must think it over. . . . Don't you know that I only want your happiness? . . ."

"But, Auntie," I stammered, "I do not know him at all. He has just arrived. How can I give you an answer?"

Somewhat troubled by the pain that her words had caused, she tried now to soften their bluntness, but I listened in silence, heavy-hearted. When she thought that I was calmer, she let me go, but only upon my promise to say nothing of our conversation.

Mlle. Hélène was there when I got back to my room. She noticed my agitation and pressed me with questions. I ended by telling her everything. Her sense of shock was almost as great as mine.

"Don't let yourself be influenced. Above all, take your time in answering," she advised me.

That afternoon Dmitri and I went driving with the Prince. I had returned from Tsarskoie-Selo with a cold and was feverish and out of sorts. At dinner, in the presence of the Prince, I felt so ill that I had to leave the table, and weakly made my way to my room, pressing against walls, holding to the furniture.

Put to bed, I fell into a sleep haunted with nightmares. Towards morning, I awoke with a severe pain in my cheek and slept no more that night. My fever increased, and my suffering. A specialist, summoned in haste, announced that it was sinus and that he would be obliged to operate if the fever persisted.

The situation was ridiculous and painful, and my aunt was beside herself. For me, I was indifferent to everything but my pain and my fear of an operation. The events of the previous day, the Prince, the answer that I must give him—all these were mixed up in my fretful nightmares.

My aunt went back and forth from my bed to the drawing-room where the Prince was waiting for news. Her elder sister, the Princess Victoria of Battenberg, arrived in Moscow and relieved her at my bedside. That evening my temperature fell; next morning an operation was deemed no longer necessary. I spent that day in bed and on the next was permitted to recline on a chaise-longue.

My aunt expressed great worry as to the Prince; she was afraid that he might grow tired of waiting. She came into my room and said:

"I cannot keep this young man waiting any longer. He is in a hurry to return to Sweden, and he must be given an answer one way or another." She sat down on the edge of the chaise-longue. "What do you want me to tell him?"

I had spent the previous day thinking. My disappointment was now somewhat attenuated. I was beginning to be resigned to my fate. I did not dislike the Prince. Until then only Dmitri counted in my life; the only great drawback of the new situation, as I saw it, would be the necessity of leaving him. Yet our separation was imminent, anyway, for one reason or another. Soon he would be sent to military school. After his departure there would really be nothing to hold me in Moscow. After all, I would be free to organize my life; I would have my home, a family; children perhaps . . .

I said to my aunt:

"I accept, but with one condition: I don't want to be married before I am eighteen; I am much too young. Have you informed my father of this project; and what does he say?"

"I have the consent and approval of the Emperor, as you are under his guardianship. Your father is abroad. You shall write him yourself very soon," replied my aunt somewhat vaguely, following her own thoughts. Then she added: "I shall say to the Prince that he may see you tomorrow, and ask for your hand."

"Yes," I said.

She embraced me and went away, her mind, so far as I was able to judge, completely at ease.

In the afternoon of the same day I was dressed and taken into the parlour of my suite. My weakness and agitation were such that I could scarcely stand, so I was placed on the sofa. A tea table was brought in. My aunt, followed by her sister and the Prince, joined me. The two women hastened through their tea and left us. The Prince, who was visibly ill at ease, asked several questions as to my health; then suddenly he took me by the hand, and demanded if I liked him.

I said that I did.

He hesitated a second; then he said: "Do you want to come to Sweden . . . with me?"

Again I answered: "Yes."

He lifted my hand to his lips and kissed it. The situation was as trying for him as it was for me. At that moment, I heard my dog scratching at the door and, happy to find a new topic of conversation, I asked the Prince if he would please let my dog in. He arose and did so; then came again towards me. "You are tired," he said. "I will go now, and let you rest."

Bending, he placed a kiss on my forehead, and left me. It was done.

Some moments after, my aunts returned and congratulated me upon my engagement. Then I was put back to bed. I had not yet recovered from my illness; the fever returned.

It was agreed that no one be told of my engagement until it had first been announced to the sovereigns of the two countries, and to my father. I could not, however, keep myself from telling Dmitri and Mlle. Hélène and the Laimings. They all received the news without enthusiasm, my brother especially; he refused to take it seriously.

My old maid, Tania, from whom I was able to hide nothing, was brushing my hair when I told her about it. Reflected in the glass, I saw her eyes fill with tears, as she bent to kiss the top of my head. The rapidity with which it had all been done disconcerted all my intimates; but all except Dmitri guarded their lips and would not tell me what they thought.

It would be insincere to pretend that, at this stage of the proceedings, I was unhappy. My sense of shock had vanished; I accepted the situation calmly, even with a certain pleasure. It flattered my pride to be the centre of everyone's attention. I was too young to look into the future and foresee the heavy responsibilities that had been laid upon my slender shoulders.

And then I wished to believe in happiness; it seemed a thing that life owed to me, and would pay as a sort of recompense for a childhood so empty and sad. I was tired of the ordered existence, dull and tranquil, which we then were undergoing in that great house. I longed for movement, noise, excitement, release, for any change.

In two or three days the Prince left Moscow. By this time I was well again, and the last afternoons and evenings before his departure we spent together. The usage of the times did not permit engaged couples to remain for a moment alone; but my aunt made a concession which she thought immense. If the Prince and I were together in a room, she would establish herself in the room adjoining, leaving the door open. But a chill timidity seized me in his presence, and so far as was possible I avoided *tête-à-têtes*.

My chief worry was how to break the news to my father. My heart was heavy with remorse at not having sought his counsel. I took my problem to my aunt. She seemed unable to understand my scruples, and could only repeat those phrases which we had heard so often from her and, in days prior, from our uncle.

Our father had abandoned us. He had left his responsibilities to others. It was now the duty of those others to make such decisions as would provide for my happiness. . . .

The word, "happiness," in her mouth, had the ring of a verdict. I heard her pronounce this word so many times, and in so many tones, during the months that followed, that I came thoroughly to detest it. "Your happiness requires . . . For your happiness . . . In the interests of your happiness . . ." And so on, interminably.

My father had nothing to say as to all this happiness; he was not able to change anything; it was decided. And now all that I had to do was to write him and tell him about it.

Since I did not know what to write, or what to say, my aunt dictated to me a letter of which I have never since been able to think without blushing. Upon that occasion, as throughout the period of my engagement, I most assuredly did honour to my princely education. Now I humbled myself entirely to my aunt's judgment, and wrote exactly as she dictated.

My letter did not deceive my father. It was as sentimental as could be wished, but the words of love and of happiness were set down with too great ease, and with too great emphasis; he knew that they could not be sincere.

By the text of that letter I at last understood exactly the sentiments I was supposed to entertain towards my fiancé. I understood that I was "madly in love" with him, and that this love had come upon me like a thunder-clap.

"A rather official thunder-clap," I thought to myself, disgustedly, but I docilely copied the letter, word for word.

The answer that I received from Paris was pained and sad. My aunt's attitude towards my father throughout all these happenings hurt him profoundly; he held it against her always. The haste with which they had disposed of my future seemed to him incomprehensible. I was too young, he said, to marry, too young to have developed independence of judgment. And he deeply resented the fact that all arrangements had been made without his having been consulted, or even notified.

Nor was my father the only one unfavourably impressed by so rushed and abrupt an engagement. My grandfather, the King of Greece, likewise protested. He wrote my aunt, pointing out that I was barely seventeen, and asked that the marriage be postponed until my eighteenth year.

My aunt announced that in this she would submit to his wish, my father's, and mine. The marriage was set for the spring of 1908.

ii

My aunt annoyed me at first with the little teasings customary to the approach of holy matrimony; but I soon became insensitive on this score, and commenced to enter quite easily into the spirit of the situation. My obedience to her pleasure was such that I finally persuaded myself that my affection for the Prince was real. It was easier to take that view than to try to resist the inevitable.

Early in June we went to Peterhof where the Prince joined us for the official declaration of the engagement. His arrival entailed a certain amount of ceremony. The Emperor sent Dmitri at the head of a guard of honour to meet him at the station. We never knew exactly how it happened, but to the general consternation, Dmitri arrived late and missed the Prince, catching up with him only after he had reached the palace. The Emperor thought that very funny, and teased us a great deal about it.

The day of the official announcement, a Te Deum was chanted in the Emperor's private chapel. This church was in a park surrounded by masses of lilies and hydrangeas. During the service rain fell softly. Through the great open doors, the air carried the perfume of flowers, and the singing of nightingales in the brushwood mingled with the voices of the choir.

After the service we all went to one of the Emperor's villas. Champagne was served and we received congratulations.

We left Peterhof and all went to Ilinskoie. The life of the country and the greater liberty it allowed drew me closer to my fiancé. Shortly after we became engaged I had been set to studying Swedish. Now, after some two months with a governess, I was beginning to speak it, a little. The Prince, himself very young, took part with pleasure in our simple amusements. We became, in a sense, good comrades but, in spite of these amicable relations, there were always differences of race and education that raised between us barriers, shadowy but impassable. I could feel growing up between my brother and the Prince a vague antipathy that disturbed me.

My aunt was often closeted with my fiancé to discuss the material side of the union. I was not included in these conferences. I thought that a little strange.

The Prince was an officer in the Swedish Navy. Soon he left for a cruise to America. Shortly after his departure I developed measles, and had to stay for several weeks in bed. He wrote me regularly, and I dictated replies to my governess; I was forbidden to write, because of my eyes.

Dmitri caught my measles and was far more sick than I. The doctors suggested that to promote his convalescence we both be taken to the Crimea. My aunt made the trip with us. It was in autumn. We stayed in the villa at Koreiz, a Tatar village near Yalta, returning in two months to Moscow where my fiancé was soon to arrive.

He brought with him plans for the house which my aunt was having built for us at Stockholm. We discussed these plans, my fiancé and I, timidly expressing puerile differences of opinion, which, slight as they were, reflected wide differences in our temperament and point of view. The several months of our separation had given me time more clearly to judge my situation; and a stir of inquietude took me by the heart each time when, my future husband there before me, I attempted to look forward into our future.

CHAPTER X

WEDLOCK

FOR a long time my father had wanted to bring his wife to Russia, even if it were only for a short visit, but the court had always forbidden it. Now at last permission was given. My father and his wife arrived in St. Petersburg and settled for fifteen days at our old palace on the Neva.

By this time his situation had been somewhat regulated. His wife now bore the Bavarian title of Countess Hohenfelsen; and their marriage had been recognized by the Crown. The Countess's eldest daughter by her first marriage was expecting a child. This was the reason given in the appeal to the Emperor—a mother's desire to be with her daughter at such a time.

My father wished, moreover, that we should meet and know his wife and also that she should re-establish her contact with the society of the capital.

My aunt opposed the whole idea, but the Emperor could not find it in his heart to withhold permission. Consequently we went one day to St. Petersburg, accompanied by my aunt, who was glum. My uncle, she felt, would have known how to prevent this useless, almost unseemly meeting.

My heart beat hard and rapidly as I stepped through the large glass doors of the vestibule. Nothing seemed changed during the few years of our absence, not even the smell; only the dimensions of the rooms—they seemed to me to have become smaller. My father smiled at us gaily from the top of the stairway.

We ascended. As father bent over Aunt Ella's hand and turned to kiss us, I caught, reflected in the mirror from the next room, a glimpse of Countess Hohenfelsen's profile. Her face was rigid and pale from emotion.

My father preceded us; a few more steps and I faced his wife.

She was beautiful, very beautiful. An intelligent face, with features irregular but fine; a skin remarkably white, contrasting strikingly with the dark violet of a velvet dress trimmed at the neck and sleeves with flounces of old lace. All this I took in at a glance, and I can still see her as she stood there.

Father made the introductions. The Countess greeted my aunt with a profound curtsy, and turned to me. We were both embarrassed. I did not know how to greet her; finally I timidly put forth my cheek.

Tea was served in my father's study. The Countess did the honours. Her bejewelled hands passed adroitly above the white cups bordered with red and marked with my father's monogram. But in spite of all her efforts and those of my father, the conversation languished. My aunt had decided to lend to this interview a purely official character, and she was succeeding

Finally having exhausted all possible topics, we passed into the large English drawing-room. Here, upon the billiard table, were spread the jewels, the furs, and the laces of my mother. My father wanted to divide them between Dmitri and myself before my marriage.

In silence my father and aunt bent over the dusty jewel cases containing the old-fashioned settings and the tarnished precious stones, uncleaned, neglected now for almost twenty years. How many memories—of which they no longer dared to speak—these objects brought to light! This fortune without lustre, spread out in front of me, half of it soon to be mine, did not impress me at all. Jewels were a part of our attire, they represented to me no more than a customary ornament. I saw no material value in them.

While my father and my aunt discussed the way of dividing the jewels, the Countess and I examined the furs. Twenty

THE GRAND DUCHESS MARIE AND PRINCE WILLIAM OF SWEDEN

Dressed for their marriage ceremony

years of naphthaline had not beautified them; the Countess offered to take them to Paris and have them restored. We spoke of my trousseau and of the Paris dressmaking houses. Before we parted she said that she would like to give me something in memory of our first meeting; what did I wish? I did not know what to answer, but my glance fell upon the necklace of amethyst balls she was wearing and I replied that I would like to have such a necklace as that. She sent it to me. I wear it still.

My father had hoped that this first meeting would be followed by others more intimate. But my aunt would not hear of this. We went once more to St. Petersburg, but again escorted by my aunt; and the second conference was as chill and formal as the first. Father, seeing the uselessness of such efforts, did not persevere. Only one thing about the meeting comforted me; I felt that in his new life he was at peace, and happy.

And I determined to find in marriage at least one advantage; no one then, I thought, would be able to prevent me from seeing my father.

ii

THE Prince came to Moscow for Christmas. The holidays, spent from morning till night side by side, proved difficult. We really had nothing to say to each other. It seemed that my fiancé had become to me a stranger—a stranger, however, to whom I was bound. Soon I regarded him almost with hostility. His rare caresses were disagreeable to me. The situation was becoming intolerable. I shivered to contemplate this impasse into which I had been led.

Preparations for the marriage took their course without my being able to feel any pleasure or interest in them. Mlle. Hélène assumed entire charge of everything. It was she who ordered my lingerie, the house linens and kitchen utensils, the shoes and the stockings matching my dresses, the gloves which were made to order, the corsets, the flowers, and the innumerable details which composed the somewhat complicated toilet of the women of those days. The automobiles, the table services, and the glasses had been ordered abroad, and I was to take with me the silver left to me by my uncle.

Every day a great dressmaker of Moscow, widely known for her art and her prices, came to my apartment, attended by her staff carrying cartons and boxes with models and materials. My aunt sometimes took part in these important conferences, and remembered then her former taste for finery. I spent long hours in front of a mirror, while the fitters, their mouths full of pins, crawled on all fours around me. But all this animation and bustle did not succeed in diverting me from my preoccupation. What must I do?

It seemed to me that in spite of his more liberal education, the Prince lacked initiative almost in the same measure as I. Others thought and decided for him, just as they did for me. What would come of that when we were married? How would we use our new independence? I was moved to the point of remorse because of this man, so young and apparently so confident, hoping to create a home with me and find happiness in it. I was offering him a heart almost empty, and was using him, in a sense, only to obtain my freedom.

Shortly after Christmas I made a trip to St. Petersburg with Mlle. Hélène to see the dentist. It was the first trip that I had ever made without my brother; and even this short separation was so painful that it finally aroused me to action. I decided to ask to be released from my promise.

When we returned to Moscow, I was met at the station by Mme. Laiming who handed me a note from my aunt.

My aunt wrote that, even as I read her note, she would be submitting to an operation, and that during the time of her illness she was going to live in the house that she had prepared as a hospital.

It was quite a serious operation. The result was not known until many hours later. Anxiety and confusion reigned in the house.

My aunt's absence made the execution of my project easier. I wrote the Prince and gave him the reasons for wishing to break the engagement. A few days later I received a charming reply; he begged me to think carefully before making a decision which would cause him great pain. The genuine sincerity of feeling that animated his letter moved me deeply but failed to alter my decision, and I was just on the point of more decisive action when, one morning, the Princess Irene of Prussia, who had come to nurse her sister, burst into my room. It was she who had taken the preliminary steps; consequently it was she who first had been informed from Sweden of my bid for independence.

Very gently, yet with great firmness, she explained to me that it was impossible at present to reverse an agreement the execution of which was of political importance. All arrangements had been made; actual preparations begun; the date was set. The scandal, she said, gently, would be too great.

Weeping, I tried to explain to her my reasons and my fears; patiently, she argued to show me their absurdity. As a final argument she told me that my decision would kill my aunt, and if I persisted in it I must shoulder the entire responsibility.

This assertion confounded me. Seeing that I was beginning to weaken, the Princess made me promise to do nothing rashly; and left me in an indescribable state of mind. The whole thing was too much for me, and I had no one competent to help me. My aunt, whose condition was satisfactory, was nevertheless still weak; the shock, for all I knew, might really have proved fatal. What could I do? I gave in.

The Princess attached so little importance to the whole incident that she did not think it necessary, apparently, to speak of it to my aunt even when the latter was out of danger. When, years later, I spoke to my aunt about it, her astonishment was great, and she assured me earnestly that had she known at the time of my doubts and scruples, her advice and conduct would have been quite different from that of her sister. Perhaps.

Meanwhile, my resistance had been broken. There seemed nothing left for me to do but to submit. The Prince returned to Moscow at the end of the winter and we met as if nothing had happened. Pride so urged me to maintain appearances that people who saw us together without knowing us intimately were persuaded that I was making a marriage of inclination. Even of my friends, few knew otherwise; only the Laimings and Mlle. Hélène trembled for my future, and they never spoke to me about it.

My aunt, completely recovered, had now left the hospital to return to the Nicholas Palace. She herself helped adorn me for a ball that was given me by the Countess Kleinmichel just before the return of the Prince to Sweden. That evening I wore a very beautiful Russian costume, with a head-dress all embroidered with pearls and precious stones. I danced alone —a solo dance. My knees shook, my heart beat wildly; I do not know how I mustered enough courage to set myself in movement to the sound of the music. But how I enjoyed it; I was applauded for the first time in my life, and I had to repeat the dance!

This was the second and last ball in my life of a young girl.

iii

SPRING advanced with giant strides towards my marriage day. The city of Moscow, which considered me in a way its own, chose the nineteenth of April, my eighteenth birthday, to bid me official good-bye. From morning till evening I received deputations which presented me with addresses and gifts, some of which were magnificent. Oh, dear old Moscow, with its Kremlin, its churches with many-coloured cupolas, its streets rugged and badly paved, how many memories of it I cherish and how much, oh, how much, I would like to see it again some day.

I left a few days before Easter. I shall never forget the evening when just before our departure we went into the little Byzantine church where my uncle was buried. Hand in hand my brother and I knelt on the marble floor. It seemed to me as if I were there to ask the benediction of my dead uncle. I felt vague presentiments of what life had in store for me, and was gripped with a profound despair.

I held tightly to my brother's hand. Fate, which already had tried us sorely, was now going to separate us. I must leave him, this brother of mine, the only true affection of my life. It was monstrous.

Minutes passed; we were both so upset that time had for us no longer any importance. My aunt, herself moved, had to remind us of the hour and take us away.

We arrived in Tsarskoie-Selo where we were soon joined by my father. It did not take him long to discover my state of mind. Without much questioning, he clearly understood. But it was too late. Nevertheless, he sternly blamed my aunt for having too easily disposed of me and told her so. The reverberation of such charges and counter-charges reached me only through closed doors. My father told me later that my aunt had exasperated him beyond measure by her complete lack of common sense and humane feelings; that she was distant and so different from her former self, he could not make her out.

For some time she had been going through a crisis; no one could know the inner workings of her soul. Her detachment, her lack of interest in the things of this life, were then at their height. Later, when she had become readjusted, she returned to reality. Possessing a great soul, she came victorious out of her crisis; returned to life stronger, more capable, and far more wise and tolerant than she had ever been. Unfortunately, my future had to be settled during this transitional period; in a way, I was sacrificed, but I can bear her no ill-will.

A few days before the marriage King Gustave, who had just succeeded his father, arrived in Tsarskoie-Selo with his brother Charles and Charles's wife Ingeborg, my fiancé, and a numerous suite. The Emperor, the Empress, and all the imperial family went to the station to greet them.

I trembled with emotion as the blue cars of the special train moved slowly down the platform and stopped. The King and his family alighted, and, as soon as they had stepped upon the red carpet of the station, the imperial party came forward to meet them. After the first greetings the Emperor made a sign for me to approach. I was presented to my future father-in-law who kissed me. Then the Emperor presented to the King the guard of honour formed in line along the platform.

A band was playing the national anthems of the two countries; drums were beating; introductions multiplied. In the waiting-room I made the acquaintance of Prince Charles and his wife and of their suite. The Swedish ladies-in-waiting confused me very much by wanting to kiss my hand.

Then the sovereigns entered the carriage and took the King to the Great Palace where an apartment was reserved for him. That evening there was a gala dinner with an exchange of toasts and speeches prepared in advance. As I now spoke Swedish quite easily, I was able rather to astonish our visitors by addressing them in their mother-tongue.

One of the ladies, the Baroness Falkenberg, had been sent by the Queen to be in attendance on my person until my own court was formed. A charming woman, she inspired me with confidence from the first. When she was brought to me, after dinner, she made me a deep curtsy. I hid my two hands behind my back. She has never forgotten this gesture of a small, shy girl.

The great day arrived. In the morning I went to mass and communion, then had a quiet lunch with the Emperor, the

Empress, and the children. The Russian custom is that on the day of marriage the betrothed should not see each other until they meet to go to the church.

After lunch I went to my room and began to dress. My cambric underwear edged with valenciennes, the wide, starched petticoats, my shoes and stockings, were laid out on the bed. After having put them on one after the other, I slipped on a gown of silver cloth, so thick that it seemed to be of cardboard. The hairdresser waved my hair.

Thus, with the first part of my toilet completed, I went to the drawing-room, where my father was waiting to bless me. My aunt left us alone. Over my bent head my father made a large sign of the cross with the ikon he held with both hands. My aunt came into the room and in her turn blessed me.

She wore that day a long gown of white crêpe and the widow's bonnet which she had adopted since her husband's death. This bonnet was also white, with a long veil that floated around her head like a cloud and fell lightly to the bottom of her dress. She was not going to participate in the court reception, but would assist at the ceremony in the church. My father and my aunt shook hands, then kissed; the tension between them yielded before my distressed expression at seeing them estranged.

I was to continue my toilet at the Great Palace where the marriage was to be celebrated. It was time to go; the carriage awaiting us was drawn up before the door. The day was dull; large flakes of wet snow splashed against the carriage windows.

At the Great Palace two gentlemen in the service of my aunt waited to help me up the stairway. We entered one of the large drawing-rooms of the palace where several other people awaited us. In the centre of the room was a dressing-table decorated with lace and ribbons and furnished with a gold set, dating from the days of the Empress Elizabeth, the daughter of Peter the Great.

On the table were disposed the Crown jewels that the

Grand Duchesses had to wear on the day of their marriage.

These were, first, the diadem of the Empress Catherine, with a pink diamond of extraordinary beauty in the centre and the small crimson velvet crown all covered with diamonds. Then came the diamond necklace of large stones, the bracelets, and the earrings in the shape of cherries, so heavy that they had to be attached to gold hoops and ringed over the ears.

The attendants began by draping around my waist an immense train of silver cloth embroidered with embossed silver lilies and roses. Then I had to sit in front of the mirror while the old court hairdresser, a Frenchman by name Delcroix, attached on both sides of my face two long curls which fell upon my bare shoulders. Next he set the diadem.

Then the "ladies of the Palace," the wives of high officials, led by the Mistress of the Court, placed on my head the lace veil and the small crown, and fastened sprigs of orange blossoms amidst the folds. Finally, they laid upon my shoulders the crimson mantle of velvet, with cape and edges of ermine, fastened by an immense silver buckle. Someone helped me to rise. I was ready.

The sovereigns arrived, the doors were thrown wide open, and my fiancé appeared on the threshold of the drawing-room. He held a bouquet of white lilies and roses, and he advanced haltingly into the room. Turning, I caught sight of his profile silhouetted against the window, and shuddered. My destiny was being fulfilled at this moment.

I was now adorned like an idol; the weight of all I wore seemed to crush me. I could scarcely move.

The Emperor approached the table on which stood the two large ikons with which he was going to bless me. He took one of them. I approached, and with the help of my father and of one of my cousins, knelt before him. He traced in the air the sign of the cross.

I could not rise. The Emperor, replacing the ikon upon the

table, took me under the elbows and stood me up. Then the wedding procession was formed.

The Prince, who was to precede me at the church, went ahead. I followed on the arm of the Emperor. Two chamberlains, two pages, and General Mengden, my aunt's chamberlain, carried my train and my court mantle, yet in spite of all this help I could hardly walk. We passed through halls, large and small, filled with people in uniforms and court gowns and finally arrived at the church.

There the Prince was awaiting me. We were placed in the centre of the nave, he on the right, I on the left. The bridesmen stood in two files behind each of us. The service began.

Priests in their stiff chasubles of gold cloth moved around us performing the various rites of the Russian Orthodox marriage. Indifferent now to everything, I followed them with my eyes. I felt cold in spite of the heat of the church, and I must have been very pale for Christo, one of my bridesmen, bent towards me and asked if I felt well; he took from one of the pages a bottle of smelling-salts and pushed it into my hand.

The service ended and a Te Deum was sung. The Archbishop of St. Petersburg took part, surrounded by the clergy of the city. Magnificent hymns of gladness filled the church. Outside, cannon saluting made the windows rattle.

Hearing the deacon announce for the first time my title of married Grand Duchess I lifted my eyes and saw the Emperor and my father smiling at me. The Archbishop and the clergy, before retiring in a body, bowed to me profoundly. The Emperor, the two Empresses, the King, and my father came towards us to congratulate my husband and me.

On his arm, this time, and at the head of the procession, we went into a room of the palace where a Protestant chapel had been arranged. Here the second marriage was celebrated. We sat in arm-chairs placed before two *prie-Dieu*, our rings were removed and replaced again by a bishop who had come expressly from Sweden. The Emperor's choir sang Swedish hymns. Tired, the congregation behind us whispered and stirred.

The service finally ended. We rose to pass into still another drawing-room and receive steadily for an hour and a half the congratulations of the members of the court. After that, my aunt took me into one of the private apartments to rest before the banquet. I was relieved of the mantle and the crown, which eased me somewhat. Tea was served. While my aunt and I wrote replies to the telegrams of congratulation I placed my weary feet upon a chair. The stiff folds of my dress still weighed upon me and I still wore the diadem and the lace veil.

iv

At seven o'clock the Prince and I took places side by side at the head of an immense table in the shape of a horseshoe.

At my left was the Emperor. The Empress sat at the right of the Prince. The other side of the table, inside the horseshoe, was not occupied, so that the guests could see us at their ease. The banquet was served by pupils of the Corps of Pages. At each of the toasts, followed by a cannonade, the chamberlains presented tall champagne glasses upon golden plates. Behind each of the princely guests stood the pages and dignitaries assigned to their personal service.

My earrings hurt me so that in the middle of the banquet I took them off and hung them, to the great amusement of the Emperor, on the edge of the glass of water before me. My napkin kept slipping upon the smooth surface of my dress and falling to the floor. Each time the page behind my chair disappeared under the table and retrieved it. Amused, I recovered my habitual good humour, and the Emperor and I talked gaily throughout the meal.

At the end of the banquet we returned to the drawing-room and sat awaiting the completion of all arrangements for the gala reception that was to close the programme of this day.

When all the guests had arrived and been placed, the Grand Chamberlain of the court came and made the announcement. We entered the immense ballroom, carpeted for this occasion entirely in red.

Then began a fête the ceremonial of which had not been modified since the time of Catherine the Great. To the slow notes of an old polonaise the sovereigns, the princely guests, and the imperial family, divided into pairs. Each couple made three turns of the ballroom, at each round changing partners. They held each other by the hand as in a ballet, and each time they separated or began a new round the lady curtsied and the gentleman bowed deeply. Court etiquette had even preserved tradition to the extent of placing at one end of the ballroom a card table with lighted candles and packs of cards. This was in memory of the Empress Catherine, who at the ceremony played at cards with guests of note.

I made my first round with the Emperor, the second with the Grand Duke of Hesse and the third with the Crown Prince of Rumania, who later became King Ferdinand. Waves of bowing followed our passage down the tight rows of the guests. My curtsy, in leaving the Emperor, was particularly low, a veritable feat of exact balancing of diadem, lace veil, and dress of silver cloth.

The reception over, we found ourselves in a carriage drawn by four horses in which the Emperor was taking us to his palace. It was already dark and the crowds that filled the streets could not see inside the vehicle. At the threshold of the Alexander Palace, the Empress, assisted by the King of Sweden, met us, again by custom, with bread and salt on a large silver platter. The Empress still wore her large diadem of pearls and diamonds and her court gown of white moire trimmed with heavy gold embroidery. We alighted and took the platter from her hands. That ended the ceremonies of my marriage.

I went into the apartment which only this morning had been

so full of life and movement. Now it was empty and deserted. My governess came to help me to undress. She took off my jewels, my veil, my garments of pomp. My head ached and the weight of my marriage gown had bruised my shoulders, leaving deep bluish marks.

I put on a suit of pearl-grey cloth and a small hat trimmed with hyacinths with a bow of cerise velvet on the side. The Prince was waiting for me in the next room.

Mlle. Hélène dressed me in silence; it was a hard moment for both of us. After twelve years of shared joys and sorrows, we were now to part. All our misunderstandings were long since forgotten; they were a part of my childhood, dear memories, good or bad, part of the past.

I tore myself from her embrace and joined the Prince. Together, we went to take leave of the sovereigns. The Empress, always maternal, was very tender to me that evening. She put on my finger a beautiful sapphire ring, her parting gift.

We were driven to the station and went to St. Petersburg. There we were to spend several days at my uncle's old palace. Accompanied by both the Russian and Swedish escorts of honour, we reached the palace that night to find my aunt awaiting us, again with bread and salt, by way of welcome. She stayed with us for a late supper. Then everybody went away and we were left alone.

Next day our bridesmen, who were all uncles and cousins, came with my brother in the lead, to bring me a bouquet and remain for lunch. In the afternoon we made calls and in the evening went back to Tsarskoie-Selo for a gala concert given by Moscow artists. A day or so later we went to the Winter Palace for a ceremony called "The Great Diplomatic Circle" and the "*Baisemain.*" Although it was a morning affair, everybody had to wear court gowns and diadems. I wore a train of sky-blue velvet embroidered with gold and a set of turquoises which had belonged to my mother.

First we received the ambassadors. They came one by one

HONEYMOON

The Grand Duchess Marie with her husband, Prince William of Sweden, 1908

into the room where we stood. The first one was the Turkish Ambassador, at that time the doyen of the diplomatic corps. Our conversation did not vary; a few words of congratulation, a few compliments, bows and thanks.

Having received the ambassadors we passed into the next room where, along the walls, were standing in groups the heads of legations with their secretaries and the personnel of the embassies. To my left the ladies stood in line; first the ambassadresses, then the wives of the ministers and of the secretaries. Having never gone out into society, I knew almost no one; and the sight of that immense room filled with strangers, their eyes fixed on us, following our every movement, was truly frightening.

I began with the ladies. The Prince, leaving me, started in the opposite direction. After I had spoken to all the ladies, I passed over to the gentlemen, stopping at each group. The introductions made, I proffered my hand to be kissed, said a word or so and continued on my way. Throughout, I was followed by a page who carried my train and by an escort of honour. At the end, the Prince and I stood side by side for more than two hours while the people of the city who had admission to court filed before us. All, both men and women, kissed my hand.

We stayed for eight days in St. Petersburg, in a whirl of dinners, parties, receptions, the making of calls and the giving of audiences. It was all strange to me, and it rather amused me.

The day set for our departure arrived, its sadness attenuated by the fact that my father was coming part of the way with us; also, I had, in a sense, said my good-byes to Russia when I left Moscow; again, I was to see Dmitri in Paris at the end of my honeymoon. Yet, when I saw him on the platform, staying behind all alone with my aunt, when I thought of his melancholy return into those empty apartments, my heart contracted painfully.

Life was separating us at present, each had to follow his

own way, fight his own battles. The sorrows and the joys of our solitary childhood had bound us closely together and the tenderness and the affection which united us had never been impaired. And now, the machinations, doubtless well intended, of my aunt, were thrusting us apart. My destiny was to be fulfilled alone, in a new and unknown world.

All had been done for me; I was helpless. The protected and restricted existence of a Grand Duchess had rendered in me, thus far, all ideas of independence or initiative useless, even dangerous. I had been cast in the bourgeois ideals then current in royal circles, and levelled to my kind. This levelling had penetrated into our circle long before the equalizing of the masses; a Princess who distinguished herself by her intelligence or by a desire for intellectual activity, if this activity should go beyond the commonplace domain of charity, attracted the envy of her equals, and was spared neither criticism nor irony. An intellectual mediocrity was both a refuge and a protection; and this was true not only in Russia, but in princely circles everywhere.

In changing my country I was not changing my milieu. My aunt would be replaced by other aunts, my governess by a lady-in-waiting. This lack of essential change would be in itself only vaguely painful because I knew so little of all that I was missing—so little of simple unaffected friendship; so little of Russia, her life, her grandeur, her vast expanses, her infinitely varied beauties.

With the exception of my brother I left nothing behind me, neither family, home, nor attachments. Yet, in spite of the sad memories of my childhood, in spite of the life barren of any interest that I had led, in spite of a lack of tangible ties with my motherland, I conserved, somehow, a passionate cult of my vast, mysterious country. Without knowing her I understood her through instinct; I felt her weaknesses, her infinite possibilities, her madness and her wisdom, and always in my mind, as long as I live, I shall identify myself with Russia.

PART TWO

AWAKENING

CHAPTER XI

SWEDEN

OUR wedding journey began with a visit to the Queen of Sweden, my husband's mother, whose ill health had prevented her from attending the wedding. Born a Princess of Baden, she was then staying in Germany, at Karlsruhe, with her mother, the Grand Duchess Louise.

At Karlsruhe an official reception awaited us. It was necessary for me to alight from the train in an elaborate afternoon dress, with decorations; you can imagine the difficulties of so adorning oneself within the limits of an ordinary first-class compartment! At Karlsruhe we found the court in mourning for my husband's grandfather. All the princesses and maids of honour wore black dresses and veils, and the favourite chairs of the deceased Grand Duke were marked with funeral wreaths resting on the seat.

The Grand Duchess Louise, daughter of the Emperor William I, was one of the last representatives of a generation of princesses now vanished. She was an old lady who combined strict principles and an iron will with great intelligence and an extraordinarily wide range of interests. Despite my extreme youth she treated me always with a consideration which astonished me. From eight o'clock in the morning, when she used to send her first chambermaid to inquire how I had slept, her courtesies were unceasing. Often she would come into our apartment while my husband and I were still at breakfast. Even at that hour she would be formally dressed in her black crape mourning with a long train, and would carry a fan in her black-gloved hand.

Her devotion to the family was remarkable, and so was

her insatiable interest in all that concerned it. For hours at a time she would question me about distant relatives in Russia, known to her only by name. The least detail of their lives interested her. This solicitude extended also to the dead, who seemed still to hold the same place in her life as they had done before. Her bedroom, which she invited me to visit one day, was hung with photographs of kings, queens, princes, and princesses, on their death beds. Some of the frames were decorated with wreaths of immortelles, or bows of crape.

The strictest of etiquette prevailed at the Court of Baden. Even family gatherings were stamped with a solemnity which seemed to me to be a form of play-acting indulged in by great personages bereft of other amusements. My new family took itself very seriously.

The day after we arrived at Karlsruhe, the Emperor William II came to pay an official visit. In the evening, after parades and ceremonies, the family assembled for an informal dinner, with only seven or eight at table. I sat next to Prince Max, still a young man then, and more lively than the others. Some pleasantry of his caused me to laugh.

There was silence. The whole party turned to regard me with shocked astonishment. I subsided, blushing. At home in Russia, where everything was on a so much larger scale, personal relations were far simpler. Etiquette existed only for ceremonies.

We went next to Venice, where we were alone, the King of Sweden having decided that we should not be attended by a following during our honeymoon. Venice, which I had longed from childhood to visit, proved disappointing; I did not find it in any way charming; it was only in later years that I came to appreciate it. Then to Nice, where a car was awaiting us, in which we were to tour France, and finally reach Paris.

At Marseilles the Prince had to go to bed with a slight cold. Escorted by our chauffeur, I went on a small excursion boat to see the Château d'If. The boat also carried a Sunday crowd of labourers and soldiers on leave, all more or less drunk, and singing at the top of their voices.

At Biarritz I saw again my cousin, the Grand Duchess Xenia, and her children, who were living in a big villa by the sea. We went once to St. Sebastian to see a bull fight, but we had to sit out in the sun, and a headache forced me to leave before the end. From Biarritz we drove to Tours, from Tours to see the châteaux of the Loire.

By this time I hated it. Motoring tired me; breakdowns were frequent, and the clothes of that period were ill adapted to such a trip. I was not at the time accustomed to being my own dressing-maid. My hat, perched on the top of a high coiffure, would not stay on; in order not to lose it I had to lash it down firmly to my head with a thick veil that got full of dust and prevented me from moving my neck freely. Skirts were too long and full for sport. Each time I cast a glance in the mirror on the way, it showed me the same disconsolate image; the wind had flattened my hair down on one side and my hat was set at an angle above a chignon much disarranged. I was miserable.

At last we had only one more stop to make before reaching Paris, where my father awaited me, and Dmitri! But five tires blew out in succession, that last day; and it required at least three-quarters of an hour to change each tire. My patience was sorely tried. I paced desperately up and down the roadside, exasperated by each new delay.

It was late in the evening when we reached Paris. As the car drew up to the hotel the first person I saw was Zhdanov, my brother's old valet. I threw my arms around his neck trembling with joy.

Having given up hope of seeing us that night, Dmitri was spending the evening at my father's house at Boulogne-sur-Seine. But he soon arrived, and we saw each other again, after a separation that had seemed to both of us interminable. We had so much to say to each other that for a few moments we could think of nothing at all to say, and were silent, overcome by emotion.

Although my husband sought manfully to hide it, I could not help seeing that my impatience to see Dmitri, my joy when we met, really hurt him. I said to myself that I must be discreet, but despite my good intentions, I could not help, as soon as the Prince was in bed, stealing into my brother's room. He would have had me return at once; but we had still so much to say to each other that time passed unnoticed, and we spent a good half of the night sitting side by side on the stairs, exchanging confidences in whispers.

The next day we had lunch with my father. I saw at last the home to which for years my thoughts had flown, and met for the first time my half-brother and my two little half-sisters, the eldest of whom was six years old. The house at Boulogne was comfortable, peaceful, and simple. It was a home. My father could have no possible regret for the great palace, cold and bare, that he had left at St. Petersburg. He and his wife were ideally happy.

Seeing them thus side by side in the home they had made together, there passed from my heart the last trace of all ill feeling that I had harboured towards my stepmother. Thereafter we called each other by name as friends do, and employed the familiar "*tu*" and "*toi*" in addressing each other. This made my father very happy.

I had not been to Paris since I was seven years old. Everything I saw excited me. The shops were full of wonders; choice was so difficult that so far as I can remember I made only two purchases, and those were curious enough. One was what was called by the Parisian coiffeur a "false front," more commonly a "rat," but a glorified one. It consisted of a long tress of waved hair, mounted on a horsehair pad, that was added to one's own hair so as to make it stand up as high as possible over the forehead. After the hairdresser had once put it on for me, I never knew how to use it again, my own hair being much too thick. It must have been a queer idea of coquetry that made me so adorn myself, and my new lady-in-waiting, Baroness Falkenberg, laughed about it till she cried.

My other purchase was an enormous boa of yellow and blue ostrich feathers, the Swedish colours. I intended to wear it when I made my official entrance into Stockholm.

Dmitri left Paris a few days before me—to visit, so he made me believe, the Grand Duke of Hesse. My husband and I crossed Germany, then the Baltic, and entered Sweden. All the way to Stockholm cheering crowds thronged to greet us. I was vastly pleased by all this curiosity, all this attention. Without any instruction I seemed to know what to do. I found myself replying to speeches, kissing little girls who tendered me flowers, talking to strangers, smiling at acclamations, tossing my handkerchief to the crowd. My knowledge of Swedish was helpful; and in all sincerity I tried to please. I longed ardently to be loved by the people of my new country, and the feeling that I was succeeding intoxicated me.

We entered Stockholm by water, crossing between the islands on a warship. It was a gorgeous day. I was dressed entirely in white, with a lace coat and a big hat surmounted by ostrich plumes. Round my neck I wore the famous boa.

A decorated boat took us to the landing-stage from which we were to make our entry into the town. There we transferred to an open carriage followed by an escort of cavalry in sky-blue uniforms and silver helmets.

Slowly we started. A procession of carriages followed us. The streets, decorated with the Swedish and Russian colours, surged with people. Children waved flags, women threw flowers—they soon filled the carriage—everyone shouted.

At the palace, which dominates the town, and is visible a long way off, a guard of honour was posted, dressed in uniforms of the period of Charles XII. Our carriage drew up, footmen opened its doors, scattering flowers to the ground as they did so. On each step of the main stairway stood a grenadier, topped with a huge bearskin cap. The whole palace resounded to the drums and trumpets of a military band playing the national hymns of our two countries.

The Prince and I mounted to a landing where, attended, the King and Queen awaited me. Directly behind them, in the shadow of a door I saw—could I believe it?—yes, *Dmitri,* in his white uniform of the Guards. I stopped in my tracks and stared at him, so completely out of countenance that the attendants could not keep from laughing. The King had brought him to Sweden, secretly, to surprise me, and make me feel more at home during my first days in a strange country.

After the first greetings, and presentations to the court as a whole, we were conducted to the suite of rooms that was to be our home until our house was built. My faithful maid, Tania, was there, and my favourite fox-terrier, leaping to greet me in transports of delight. In a few minutes Dmitri and General Laiming came; so I found myself, at the beginning of my life in Stockholm, surrounded by old friends.

But in spite of the King's delicate consideration, and my joy at seeing Dmitri, I could not but feel that it would have been better if his visit had been made later. I had cultivated for my entry into Sweden a special attitude of mind—a determination for those few days, at least, not to think of myself as I had been in the past, but to give myself fully to my new duties, and find pleasure in my new rôle. The presence of Dmitri somewhat distracted me from this purpose, and forced my thoughts backward, to the old life, rather than forward, to face the new.

After some days of celebrations, dinners, and receptions, we went to the country, Dmitri still accompanying us. My husband, as Duke of Södermanland, used as a rural retreat a little château in that province, two hours by rail from Stockholm. We were received with ceremony; the whole province was there that day to salute their Duke and his new wife. And of all the receptions we had undergone, this was the one that was the most trying. For the crowd did not leave the gardens; they remained all that day and returned the next, peering through the windows of the ground floor all round the house. We ate in public, in a veritable show-case—a dining-room with three large windows, and a glassed-in porch.

After a few days Dmitri went back to Russia. My husband and I were now alone, except for Baroness Falkenberg and Captain Klercker, my husband's aide-de-camp.

A pleasant calm replaced the excitement of the wedding journey and our arrival in Sweden. Our attendants discreetly left us alone. It may be supposed that they passed their time agreeably, as they were married soon after.

The estate offered little amusement. I suffered intensely from homesickness. My young uncle, Prince Christopher, came that summer to spend a few days with us. Droll, of active imagination, he did me good; I hated to see him go. And in the autumn, as had been promised, Dmitri returned, and we went on a cruise in a sailing boat among the islands off the coast of Sweden. By day we sailed, at evening dropped anchor in some small harbour, or landed on some island, often uninhabited, to bathe in rocky bays, and cook our meals over a wood fire. These were pleasant weeks.

The next autumn Dmitri returned and we cruised again with my husband on that small yacht. I liked the life on board, with its simplicity, calm, and lack of formality. Sometimes I took the tiller myself, and the Prince gave me lessons in sailing. It was a happy fortnight. We had with us only a crew of three, and a steward who looked after our cabins and cooked our meals. I had to do without a maid, and I recall tragic difficulties with my hair, which I simply could not succeed in doing alone. Finally I hit upon a device which I thought would be a great help; I ordered myself a wig!

But the wig gave me much more trouble than my own hair would have done if I had taken the trouble to learn how to dress it myself. To begin with it had to be combed; and it is harder, I can assure you, to comb a wig than to disentangle hair firmly attached to a head. Even after I had done my best, it always looked like a windblown haystack. Morning after morning, tired of struggling with the thing in the confines of a tiny cabin, I would go up on deck, my hair blowing in the wind, my wig in my hand; there, sitting anywhere, oblivious to teasing, I went on with the battle. Combing done, I had to get the wig on so that it would cover my own hair—and that was no easy matter either; I never entirely succeeded. Always some wisps of hair would escape. My bewigged head was, moreover, now so huge that no hat would go on. And all that display of hair made my head much too hot. What troubles!

After ten days we returned to Stenhammer and Dmitri went back to Russia. In October we left the country and settled in the palace at Stockholm. The rooms which we occupied were large and sombre, with magnificent furniture that was not enough to fill them, and with walls hung in old tapestries.

ii

THAT autumn I found I was going to have a child, and although I did not suffer at all physically, I was low in spirit, crushed and melancholy. The Prince, his vacation over, took up again his duties with the general staff of the Navy, and I saw him only in the evenings. Idleness and isolation weighed heavily upon me. I worked at embroidery and tried to read, but my education had been so uninspired and incomplete that reading was not much of a resource for me. I was not used to serious books, or trained to the systematic study of a chosen subject. The reach of my mind was limited to my own powers of observation and adaptation, and I was deficient in intellectual curiosity. I had lived surrounded by the traditions and the souvenirs of great periods without realizing them or identifying myself with them. The history of Sweden, the palace, the museum and collections, offered a field of study with immense possibilities. I never even thought of them.

I thought of charity work. It had always been the main occupation of my aunt and of those about her. But here in Sweden, it seemed, no help was needed. Everything was admirably organized, and I was deprived of this last resource.

Although my health never gave the slightest cause for concern, we hardly ever went out, and I was surrounded by so much care and so many precautions, that I ended by believing in my own fragility.

The winter passed. I longed for the presence of some familiar person and for the first time in my life felt acute regret that I had no mother. Aunt Ella refused to come to me; her life as a nun had absorbed her completely; she could not, she wrote, be spared from her work.

The time arrived at last. The pains began in the evening, but I was still able to sleep that night. In the morning my sister-in-law, the Crown Princess (daughter of the Duke of Connaught; she died in 1922), came to be with me and did not leave me all day. We lived through those long hours of pain together; and when, the night following, I was at last delivered of a son, it was she who held to my face the mask soaked in chloroform.

According to the custom of the Swedish court, the newly born baby was ceremoniously presented by the King to the members of the government and to the high dignitaries of the court. I cannot with certainty remember whether this presentation was made the same night or on the morning after the birth, but I retain a distinct picture of my equerry and Baroness Falkenberg, both in full court-dress, waiting to take my child from my bed to carry it to the King.

As soon as I was about again my son was baptized in one of the rooms of the palace. The hope which I had cherished of having some member of my own family take part in the ceremony was not realized. Only my old governess, Mlle.

Hélène, came from Russia to be present. I took consolation in anticipation of June, when the Emperor and Empress of Russia were to pay an official visit to the Swedish court.

They came on their yacht, escorted by a fleet of warships. Stockholm was gay with the flags of both nations. We went out to their yacht to greet them and escort them ashore. Their coming had to me a special meaning; it was as if they brought to Sweden the Russia that I longed for, and lifted for a while my banishment from home. So it was with genuine fervour that I greeted my sovereigns; and the warmth of their response made me feel as though I were indeed—as they playfully used to call me—their "oldest daughter."

But so implacable is destiny that even upon that small part of Russia which my Emperor and Empress brought to me, violence and death intruded. The welcome ashore was enthusiastic; the celebrations that followed were gay and pleasant; but as the guests were leaving the palace, after a state dinner, someone hidden in shadow fired a revolver at a Swedish general. He fell mortally wounded and died soon after. No one could ever discover the motive of this crime, or whether the assassin had mistaken the Swede for a Russian dignitary. It was centuries since such a thing had happened in Sweden. Everyone was horrified, I perhaps most of all, and I trembled for the safety of our guests until they left.

Soon after, my husband was ordered to sea for two months. This separation was followed by many others. I had to learn how to accustom myself to his absence and organize my life independently. It became more and more rare for us to be alone together.

I tried hard to make friends. Human beings, from whom I had been in the past so far removed, attracted me now with all the fascination of the unknown. I felt that by getting closer to them I would learn about life and how to protect myself from it. I was very young and very confident in my own method; it was not until much later that I came to realize how inexorable are the limitations of a princely education, heredity, and custom.

"Hens cannot be taught to fly or eagles to talk like parrots." Princes of reigning families are a race apart—a race that has been for centuries shut off in palaces, protected, restricted, compelled to live among its own dreams and illusions. Meantime the world and its needs pass us by. That is why we are destined to be destroyed or forgotten.

In Sweden, the attitude of the people towards their royal family seemed to me, coming as I did from Russia, somewhat curious. They appeared to regard us fondly, but rather as if we were big children—favoured children, whose life, interests, and possessions constituted a world apart, gorgeous, exciting, and necessary to the beauty and dignity of the world as a whole. The curiosity that was aroused by our least action in Sweden was definitely a part of this crowd psychology. The whole nation enjoyed the show. Our least characteristic, good or bad, was commented upon from every possible angle, always without ill feeling, always with a smile, as grown-up people discuss the escapades of their children.

In Russia it was different. There, the Emperor held, unchecked and undisputed, absolute power over his country and subjects. He was to some extent a god; and his family shared in this deification. Yet one never felt in Russia so bound by etiquette, so constantly on display, so circumscribed against natural inclination for an easy intimacy with other people, as one did in Sweden.

In Russia it was a much simpler matter to form a friendship. Public life hardly existed. Ceremonies were magnificent, but rare, and etiquette was only for purely official occasions. Our palaces offered shelter for the kind of life we wanted to live, and protected the intimacy of our homes. True we were of the family of the immortals, and no merely human flaw, discovered, was ever forgiven us; but the Russian talks familiarly to his God, and approaches Him trustfully. Such was the attitude of the Russian people towards us—an attitude uncomplicated by snobbery, a fault in which my compatriots are altogether lacking.

The situation can be described in a very few words: in Sweden life was complicated but people were simple, in Russia the contrary was true; life was simple, but people were difficult to understand. Those Russians who were admitted to our homes made friends with us easily, but—principally because of an intense pride almost morbid on their part—often took offence at nothing, and abandoned the friendship. And those not admitted felt themselves neglected, and vented their bitterness in criticisms which spread to the people at large, and were eagerly listened to and absorbed. So little by little Olympus was depopulated.

I have said that my husband's first absence was an ordeal for me, but at the same time it was useful because it made me see the necessity of making a life of my own. I had always numerous public duties to perform, and now took a certain pleasure in doing them. Dmitri came to visit me and we made calls, visiting together the estates and castles in the neighbourhood. Dances were given in my honour and I met the society of the province. I entertained people at my home, sometimes informally and in unusual ways. One young Prince of Prussia, a nephew of the Queen of Sweden, I contrived, for instance, to take out driving in an open dog-cart at a time when, knowing the weather of the locality, I was quite sure there would be a thunder shower. There was, indeed, a torrential one; and it amused me vastly to see the Prince exposed to the rains of heaven in all the glory of a frock coat and a grey top hat! He stood the test well and came again to Stockholm a few months later. I still remember as a bright spot in that summer his camaraderie and frank gaiety.

That same summer I went to Russia for the first time since

my marriage, and took with me my son, still only a few months old, to show him to my family and friends. I stayed first at Peterhof where I had been invited by the Emperor and Empress, and then went to Moscow to see my aunt.

This last visit was very painful to me. I went to the Nicholas Palace; my aunt no longer lived there, and had kept only certain rooms for her own use. The retinue had been much reduced and many of the old servants discharged. My own rooms were no longer available. Everywhere I looked I saw sadness, neglect, disorder, where once life had been planned for and regulated to the last detail.

My aunt herself lived at the convent she was planning, the more conveniently to direct the building of a great chapel, a hospital, and other new buildings for her Order. It was her aim to found a new order of nuns which in its aims would resemble the Deaconesses of early Christendom. Instead of living solely in cloistered contemplation, my aunt planned for her Order active good works—nursing, charity. This idea was so foreign to the Russian temperament that it aroused amusement among the people and stubborn opposition on the part of the higher clergy. She had designed for herself and her nuns a costume of great simplicity, austerity, and beauty. This provoked remark; everyone, it seemed, was laughing at her. But nothing could discourage her. She had somehow found within herself the courage to break the frame that held her in the rigid "position" assigned to her by birth and training. I noticed that, emancipated, my aunt was better able to understand people and to bring her life into relation with the world of reality. Coming nearer to the miseries and frailties of humanity, she accepted them; penetrating to the hidden motives and passions by which the world is moved, she understood all, forgave all, and was exalted.

But she remained true to her old habit of silence, never confiding in me her plans and difficulties. I had to seek information elsewhere, or employ intuition, for I was not in the habit of asking questions. And in Moscow, to which I had come eagerly as to a home, changes that had taken place made it seem to me, somehow, a city I did not know at all. I never recaptured my old feeling for it, and returned to Sweden with a sense of irreparable loss.

CHAPTER XII

OAKHILL

WE spent that winter also at the palace in the morose apartment, hung with Gobelin tapestries. The construction of our house was progressing and we had to think about furnishing it. I called the Court Chamberlain and asked him how much of my money would be available for that purpose. He calmly informed me that estimates had long ago been exceeded, and that the sum advanced by my aunt would only just suffice to finish the building itself. Since, under the terms of my marriage contract, I had to bear all the expenses of our household myself, I did not want to break into my capital, but I was forced to do so, and also to draw in a measure upon the generosity of my father, who made me a handsome Christmas present.

The material side of the alliance had been badly arranged at the very start by my aunt and the Russian court. Through misunderstandings and oversights, due in part to the negligence of certain persons at court, I was deprived of important privileges long established by custom, and involved in many vexations concerning my uncle's estate, of which my aunt enjoyed only the interest, the inheritance reverting to me. It was too late now to amend all that; nothing could be done; my aunt, with her customary disregard for things material, had dispersed many valuables that she had really no right to dispose of without my consent. The marriage contract had been drawn up and signed by the ministers of both countries and was sealed with the seals of state. I had no redress.

My money was in Russia. The interest was at first paid to me through one of the attachés at the Russian legation, who acted as my private secretary in Russian affairs and looked after my correspondence in that language. Later, as attachés at the legation changed often, it was thought better to pay the money direct to the Court Chamberlain, who controlled the accounts of my household. We were obliged to keep up a considerable establishment and all my money went into that, so that I had practically nothing left for my personal expenses. I could never, for example, when I went to Paris, buy clothes from the best houses. I bought dresses ready-made from the Galeries Lafayette and wore ready-made shoes.

This did not seem to me strange. I had very simple tastes, too simple when I come to think about it; and as to the value of money I was totally ignorant. So it never occurred to me to feel sorry for myself, or to object.

I did sometimes wish, though, for more and better horses. My means seemed never sufficient to keep more than three or four at the same time, and those I had left much to be desired.

Socially, our winter was gay. Entertainments, receptions, and parties followed so rapidly one upon another as to make the King wag his head in disapproval. He commented sharply upon our conduct to my husband, but never scolded me. To me, he was always most kind. I had in him a real friend—and still have despite all that has since occurred.

My high spirits, which no amount of etiquette could long suppress, amused him; I felt always at ease with him. We enjoyed each other's confidence completely. Sometimes he would take me on elk hunts where I was the only woman. During railway trips in his private carriage I played bridge with grey-bearded old gentlemen and rejoiced when I won a few crowns. In winter I was one of a group who played tennis every day with him on the excellent indoor courts of Stockholm.

In short, my father-in-law spoilt me, and we were such good friends that I could not resist playing tricks on him, which sometimes got into the newspapers and in an exaggerated form, but which were always accepted by him in good part.

OFFICIAL ENTRY INTO STOCKHOLM, 1908

The famous boa is in evidence

OAKHILL, STOCKHOLM

One winter, for example, as we travelled for some skiing to Dalecarlia in a special train with several carriages, I conceived the idea of dressing myself up as an old lady and presenting flowers to the King, who was playing bridge in the carriage ahead. My plan was applauded by the other occupants of our carriage, and I set out to contrive a make-up. We had no paint and very little powder. I made wrinkles with a burnt cork and rubbed slices of beet root on my cheeks. I hid my eyes with dark spectacles, and covered my head with a big woollen shawl. Then I borrowed from one of the maids a cloak lined with fur and put that on inside out. All was ready. The conductor had the train stopped at the first station, and I got off, carrying three fading tulips wrapped in a piece of newspaper. One of the aides-de-camp, in on the hoax, informed the King of the desire of an aged woman to pay homage to him. I was taken into his presence. As I entered the carriage, he rose and took a few steps towards me. I gave him the flowers, mumbling a few words in a shaking voice.

But then, seeing my absurd bouquet in the King's hands, his seriousness in accepting it, and the ceremonial aspect of the suite, I could contain myself no longer. I collapsed to the floor, trying to stifle my laughter, hoping it would be taken for tears. The King, thinking that the old dame had been seized with a fit of nerves, turned to his Chamberlain and said in French, not without emotion, "*Enlevez-la, elle est folle!*"

Two aides took hold of me. I had visions of myself being put off on the platform, and the train going on without me.

"It is I, Papa," I cried, through the laughter that shook me. The aides let go of me, their eyes very round. The King bent close to me, recognized me—laughed. It was a trick that really came off splendidly.

Another time, in spring, I took him driving in my dog-cart, behind my little American trotter, very fast and hard to hold, especially in traffic. On the main street of the town my horse took the bit in his teeth, and the general public had the opportunity of admiring their King, his bowler askew, and myself, equally devoid of dignity, with each of us tugging frantically at a rein in our efforts to stop that horse.

Such small escapades soon gained for me a certain reputation in Sweden. I was said to be a regular dare-devil, and this did not altogether displease me. All sorts of anecdotes were told about me and I was credited with exploits of which I had never dreamed.

It seems almost too bad, even now, to spoil such entertaining stories; but the fact is that I kept always within limits and always knew how far I could go without hurting anyone. But malice, however gay, may leave a scar.

Before settling in the country again, at the end of that winter, I went to visit my father at Boulogne. I loved these visits; the simplicity and peace of my father's household did me good after all the publicity with which I was so constantly surrounded in Stockholm. We went about, and sometimes attended the theatres, but more often stayed home in the evenings, my father reading aloud while my stepmother and I embroidered. Between my father and myself the ties of affection had strengthened with the years. When, therefore, during this visit, he felt it necessary to question me severely as to my escapades in Sweden, of which exaggerated accounts had somehow reached him, I was cut to the quick. From him I learned for the first time, with amazement, the cruel interpretation that was being put upon my childish foolishness; from him, heard the "reputation" I was getting. It was my first direct experience with the malevolence of humanity, and I was profoundly depressed. Long after my father had forgotten this conversation, I thought of it often, and always with a tightening of the heart.

I felt thereafter less at home in Sweden. My homesickness increased. In Sweden I found much to admire—her great civilization, her spirit of order, her immense capacity for organization. But I remained a spectator of all this perfection, and instead of finding the spectacle attractive, as doubtless I should have, I found that it only drove my thoughts back to my own vast country. This civilization, developed to the point where individual effort no longer counted, where there was no longer room for the exercise of imagination, weighed upon me. The more I saw of Sweden, the more I dreamed of Russia, so near on the map, really so far removed from modern life; and I felt, almost with a sense of guilt, that I was a Swedish Princess by title only.

In those days, however, my attachment to Russia had mostly a romantic and sentimental quality. I knew nothing of her needs, political, economic, or otherwise, and if at times I had felt a vague uneasiness about the situation at home, it was an unreasoned, intuitive feeling, a feeling which I could not put into words. Besides, in the years I had lived abroad, Russia had enjoyed a spell of comparative peace. The Duma, after a few unsuccessful attempts at acquiring independence of action, was forced into silence for the sake of its self-preservation. The government from 1906 to 1911 had been headed by Stolypin, a man of insight, integrity, and energy, the only political figure at that time approaching to the stature of a statesman. The only dark spot in the seemingly clear surface was the presence at court since 1907 of a certain mysterious figure called Rasputin. Other shadowy figures had preceded him, but their reign had been brief; his, for some unknown reason, was lasting, but his influence so far escaped definition.

Each visit I made to Russia persuaded me more fully that there, amid the increasing chaos, lay my true field of action. It was not that these visits were especially pleasant. I came as a foreign princess and was received accordingly. Nevertheless, I felt that here in Russia lay my life, my work, that here, not in Sweden, I would find an outlet for my energies.

Dmitri was no longer in Moscow. He had gone at the time of my marriage to live in St. Petersburg and had entered the cavalry school where he had worked so hard, and suffered so from loneliness, that his health, never good, became seriously affected. General Laiming, of course, was with him, and the Emperor and Empress, who were very fond of him, saw him often; but the counsel of human beings as far removed from all reality as were the dwellers of Tsarskoie-Selo at that period could not help him much; he was deprived of all real family life at a time when it would have been a precious and necessary support to him. And now in the Horse Guards he led a life, military and social, that was even more exhausting for one of his age and fragile constitution. His loneliness, his ill health, were constantly on my mind. I was always worrying about him, without being able to do anything about it; and this, too, had a part in drawing my thoughts still more towards Russia.

ii

To combat this tendency, I arose early and all day long kept myself busy. By the autumn of 1910 we were established at Oakhill, our new house.

My dear Cecilia Falkenberg, the lady-in-waiting who had come to Russia to escort me to Sweden, had married and left me. I sorely missed her, for she had surrounded me always with gaiety and an almost maternal tenderness, and she was, moreover, a person of great intelligence and tact. But in the choice of my two new maids of honour I was most fortunate, and Lieutenant Rudebeck consented to give up his military service to become our chamberlain and the permanent director of our household. We all four lived together at Oakhill, and I often gave thanks for such devoted and agreeable companions.

Oakhill was situated a little outside Stockholm, on a hill overlooking the sound. It was surrounded by the green fields of a public park, a mile or so around, and terraced with a garden that sloped down towards the water. Magnificent oaks gave the place its name.

The house was light and spacious, modern and comfortable; all in all, the most agreeable I ever lived in. I had, at the time, no taste; and the decorations must have showed it, but the general effect was pleasing and unpretentious; and I was delighted to be out of that sombre palace, in a home of my own.

As soon as everything was more or less in order, I gave a ball to celebrate my twentieth birthday. I remember it was a pretty occasion. I had flowers sent from Nice; the house was full of them; the guests took armfuls with them when they left.

My days were crowded. Disturbed at the aimlessness of my existence, I was determined now really to do something; my painting had been long neglected, so that winter I entered an art school.

The school I chose was the best in Stockholm. Prince Eugene, the King's younger brother, a painter of great talent, was the only one of the family who encouraged my desire to study; although from the rest of them my resolution met with no opposition—only astonishment.

Every morning at 8:30 I was seated, with a class of twenty-five, at a wooden table in a big room with grey walls. The first days were hard for me. My fellow-students were timid and distrustful. But as soon as they saw I worked hard and wanted only to be one of them, they became friendly and ended by heaping me with favours and marks of affection. It was chiefly due to their help and criticism that I made considerable progress in a very short time.

Often I stayed at the school during the eleven o'clock recess, eating a sandwich lunch that I brought with me. Sometimes my companions treated me to a repast of milk and gingerbread, which I liked particularly. Promptly at noon we turned again to our models and worked till three, when twilight, early at that time of year, obliged us to dry our brushes and close our sketch-books.

When I got home I changed quickly and went to the riding-school where I was learning to ride astride. I put in an hour or two of fairly violent exercise, riding without stirrups to improve my seat, even jumping without them. Then after a bath and tea I took a singing lesson, or practised on the piano so that I could accompany myself. In the evening I frequently prepared work for the test in composition which was held once a month at the school. I liked this; the competitions were wholly anonymous and gave me a chance to judge how I was really getting on.

It was through attending these classes that I made the acquaintance of a really remarkable man. He was a tram conductor on the line from Stockholm to my house at Djurgården. I sometimes travelled that way when I did not want to use my car. The trip took fifteen minutes, and as I usually saw the same people I fell into the habit of chatting with them. Thus I met this conductor—an old man with a white beard who had been with the company many years. I found out that he supported out of his earnings a little home for illegitimate children, abandoned by their fathers and mothers. I was so impressed by this evidence of actual, living Christianity that I asked him to my house one day for a cup of coffee, and heard more about his work. I can see him now, coming into my sitting-room with his hat and gloves in his hand and seating himself with the utmost dignity and calm.

The grey mornings of the Swedish winter always found me on my way to school. The time passed fast and happily. Satisfaction in accomplishment and a healthy fatigue quieted the black thoughts that occasionally would stray into my head despite all my efforts to keep them away; and the society of friends of my own age, together with the simplicity and lack of ceremony at the school, did me a great deal of good.

I asked the King to give a costume ball for me, and to add to the gaiety of the occasion I organized a quadrille of young women and men. Eight pairs of us danced a minuet and a gavotte; then with my husband I danced a mazurka, a quick dance, demanding great abandon and vitality. We wore beautiful Polish costumes. The spurs on my little green boots flashed and jingled to the gay music and we pirouetted so madly that I scattered the emeralds sewn to my dress.

The important court functions were held in January, commencing with the formal opening of Parliament. For that occasion we all had to be dressed by ten in the morning—the Princesses in court dress of black velvet, with long trains and slashed sleeves bordered with ermine; the maids of honour also in black but without ermine; the King, the Princes, and ministers in dress uniform. The men were grouped about the King on a platform in the hall; the Princesses, with their ladies behind them, occupied a balcony. The ceremony was not so trying; after a few speeches, rather long, we went home. In the evening we had to attend a supper given at the palace in honour of the deputies, after which we had to make conversation with them, for what seemed a terribly long time.

But the grand ball was a much longer and much more tiring function. All the Princes and Princesses assembled in one of the rooms of the palace, and memoranda were handed them, giving the names of their partners for supper and for the dancing. Then doors were thrown open, and we filed through rooms leading to the ballroom. In each room were grouped different ranks and degrees of people with whom we had to talk. In the big salon next to the ballroom were the debutantes of the season, lined up with their mothers. The Mistress of the Robes, list in hand, presented mothers, then daughters, to the princesses, who followed closely after one another down the line, saying something suitable to each. It was a fearful ordeal.

The ball began. We danced the quadrilles, of which there were three, with members of the government and the ministers of foreign countries. The King and the Princes danced with their wives. For the other dances we were more or less free to choose, but the partner had to be informed beforehand, and a chamberlain sent to tell him of the honour that was to be his.

In the spring of 1911 the King decided to send my husband and me on a journey, the prospect of which excited us both.

The King of Siam was to be crowned the following winter; invitations had been sent to European courts. We were to represent the family at the event.

I do not know whether the King had divined the distinct coolness in the relations between me and his son, and proposed this journey in the hope of remedying matters, or whether the interests of Swedish trade in Siam really required the Prince's presence for their furtherance. It was the latter reason, of course, that was given to us and to the public.

CHAPTER XIII

THE EAST

OUR trip was to last six months. We spent most of the summer in preparations, and at the end of October set forth, travelling by way of Paris and Nice to Genoa. There we embarked on a German liner of 8000 tons, bound for Singapore.

In addition to our regular suite, which consisted of my maid of honour Miss Hamilton, our chamberlain Rudebeck, and the aide-de-camp Heidenstam, we were accompanied by ten others —Swedish diplomats, professors, the Siamese consul to Stockholm, and others.

The voyage to Singapore took three weeks, broken by brief stops at Port Said, Aden, Colombo, and Penang. Wherever we went we were officially received; the English governors and residents came to meet us dressed in white uniforms and gave us lunch in the cool rooms of spacious palaces that seemed like paradise to us after the stuffy little cabins on our boat.

It would be only for a few short hours that we could be ashore, and the days aboard dragged on interminably. The heat, the inaction, the lack of comfort, became nerve-racking, and the passengers, mostly German colonials, were far from amusing.

At Singapore, where we were transferred to the King of Siam's yacht, we met other guests who had come from afar to the coronation.

Our reception at Bangkok was altogether splendid. My husband and I and the other Swedish guests were lodged in a palace, and most admirably served. A lady of the Siamese court and two chamberlains were attached to my personal suite, and several Siamese aides-de-camp to that of the Prince. We had numbers of pages to wait on us, all boys of good family, as royal personages could only be approached by the nobility; and brand-new cars, carriages, and saddle horses were constantly at our disposal.

Celebrations that began as soon as we arrived were so splendid and varied, so amazingly lavish, and of such fantastic beauty that they seemed dreamlike, unreal. Never in my life, I think, have I had such a gorgeous time as I did during my stay in Siam.

After the coronation festival all the other guests departed, but we stayed on to see the country and to take part in hunts organized in my husband's honour. We went up the rivers in sampans arranged as comfortable houseboats, and attended by a fleet of other boats bearing provisions and servants.

At each halt a repast was awaiting us, spread under a shelter made of bamboo covered with palm leaves; native musicians played softly in the reeds while we ate, and a motley crowd greeted us smilingly on the bank.

Gifts rained down; now it was a parrot, now a monkey, the plumes of rare birds, fruit, or pieces of silk.

Travelling thus we reached the sea, where had been prepared for us a camp of roomy tents, with every comfort imaginable.

We spent several days there, bathing, enjoying the comparative coolness. Every day the men hunted. I shall never forget the wonder of the sunset over the sea, or the splendour of the tropical night. We visited famous temples, where huge ancient Buddhas, in stone or gilded wood, watched in the gloom. We stopped at different estates belonging to the King, where we were received with the same pomp and lived in unheard-of luxury. We saw the festival of the rice harvest, we went to hunts, to races of oxen, and to cock fights.

After an enchanted visit of more than a month we left Siam for Indo-China, where my husband hoped to have good shooting. I, for my part, wished to visit the ruins of Angkor.

There was no road then between Saigon and Angkor, and we could go only part way by river. The expedition was planned accordingly. My husband came with us as far as Pnom-Penh, the capital of Cambodia. We visited King Sisowath and spent an evening admiring his ballet; then my husband returned to Saigon to hunt with the Duke of Montpensier.

I embarked upon a little river steamboat, with Anna Hamilton, two or three Swedes, the Resident of Cambodia, and several others. The next day we left the steamer and were crowded into big sampans. These took us as far up the river as the already low water would permit. There we transferred to ox-carts that lurched and bumped us to our destination, across streams and ravines and rough country.

Only part of the immense ruins had been excavated. The rest was covered with a thick tangle of vines. The whole gave an impression of impenetrable mystery. We walked for hours along dim galleries in a silence broken only by the cry of a monkey, or towards evening the flutter of bats. We saw the statues of the leprous King and his wife lying in the grass, and reflected on the glories of the Khmer civilization here, like themselves, entombed. We climbed to the tops of pagodas, up stairs wellnigh impassable, and looked out over an ocean of treetops as far as the eye could see. At night the natives kindled bonfires, by order of the Resident; and lit up by this coloured fire the ruins seemed more terrifying than ever—mutinous at human intrusion, menacing in their strange aloofness.

In two days we saw all there was to see and returned to Saigon. The Duke of Montpensier organized a hunt and took us for ten glorious days into completely wild country. We lived in bamboo huts set on piles, as a protection against the beasts of the jungle, and spent whole days in the saddle, hunting wild buffalo.

We sailed on to Singapore, from there to Burma, then on to Calcutta. In India the Prince again went hunting and left me to do some of the trip alone. I started with Benares, where

I visited the temples and viewed the troubled waters of the Ganges, with its marble steps and its bathers with glistening skins. I saw, on the bank, human bodies hung above wood fires, slowly burning, while the families of the deceased unconcernedly waited for the time when they should throw the ashes into the river. The Maharajah invited me to visit him and showed me Hindu dances and animal fights.

It took us a month to cross India. A month of temples, mosques, and monuments, heat and dust eternally, visits and receptions, faces white and dark. Towards the end I was so tired I hardly knew what was going on.

From Bombay we went back to Colombo, where we stayed several days, this time at Kandy, refreshingly cool and green. At the end of March we set out for Europe.

Despite my extreme fatigue I felt myself to be more alive. The voyage had been to me in some ways a revelation of my own personality; it had broadened my knowledge of people and given me a chance to develop independence of judgment. I had more self-assurance now and was not so shy.

I hated to go back. To surrender my new-found independence, to settle again into the dull routine of tradition and custom—it seemed to me more than I could stand.

ii

It was still cold when we got back to Oakhill at the end of April. My son had grown and seemed much changed during the months of our separation. My heart was heavy. Sadly I looked out at the trees in the garden, hardly in bud yet, and I could not feel that I was home.

The journey had not changed the relations between my husband and myself; my feeling towards him had become, in fact, almost hostile. It was without joy that, at the age of twenty-two, I looked forward to the future. Although I had tried hard and sincerely, I had not been able to make this family

WINTER SPORTS IN NORTHERN SWEDEN, 1910

my own, or to feel at home in Sweden. The setting remained foreign to me. My courage failed me at the thought of the years ahead. What should I do? Everything seemed to forbid my taking a decisive step—the principles of my childhood and my education, still strong in me, my idea of duty, reasons of state, above all, the lack of support and interest from my own family.

I was racked by remorse. Had I really done everything, tried everything? Could I not quell this restlessness and discontent, this curiosity which tormented my mind? Did I really want to? These were problems too big for me to solve alone; and yet I was alone, irrevocably alone, in my trouble and doubt.

The humdrum of everyday life claimed me again, smothered me. I submitted, but my nerves rebelled.

That spring the Olympic games were held in Stockholm, and Dmitri, who was to take part in the mounted events, came with his horses and grooms to stay with me at Oakhill. When the games began we passed whole days in the Stadium, a splendid structure put up for the occasion. The Russian contingent, with the exception of the Finnish group, did not distinguish itself in anything, and the officers, although they were all good horsemen, won no prizes. However, nothing happened to my brother and only one of his companions had a bad fall.

During the two months that the games lasted, there were many informal fêtes and parties; and, with Dmitri there, Stockholm seemed to me a different place. That made it all the emptier when the games ended.

Dmitri returned to Russia. All our guests and their followings scattered to the four corners of the earth. The Prince went off on a cruiser. I remained at Oakhill, with occasional short visits to Stenhammer or to see my parents-in-law at their estate.

Late in the autumn I took my son with me to Paris to see my father, whose position now had changed in several respects. The Emperor had not only called him back to Russia to be present when Dmitri took the oath of allegiance and joined a regiment, but had upon the same occasion lifted my father's banishment. I found him and his wife delightedly making plans to build a house on an estate at Tsarskoie-Selo, the imperial residence. Their son, my half-brother, had already been sent to St. Petersburg, and entered in the École des Pages, a military school.

I decided to open my heart to my father and tell him all my difficulties. He listened patiently but was firmly opposed to the idea of a divorce. In his opinion, apart from all moral and political aspects of the case, I was much too young to be alone in the world; and my stepmother strongly supported him in this opinion.

CHAPTER XIV

ANNULMENT

I WAS to have returned to Sweden for Christmas, but there came suddenly a telegram from the King, telling me to go to Italy and join the Queen, on the Island of Capri.

The Queen had for some time led the life of an invalid and, as she could not stand cold weather, always passed the winter months there. Now she was suffering more than usual and needed companionship.

I entrusted my son to the care of the Crown Princess who was passing through Paris, and set off for Italy with the two Rudebecks (who, by the way, were in no way related). A few days later, we crossed the Bay of Naples and landed at Capri. The Queen had a villa on the higher part of the island; it was here that I joined her.

Besides her maid of honour and her chamberlain, who lived in the villa, she had her doctor with her.

This Dr. M., whom I had not before seen, was a much-talked-of man in Sweden. Although Swedish by birth, he rarely went there. He owned two villas at Capri, in one of which he lived. He led a retired life, coming to visit the Queen once each day. He came to tea on the day after my arrival, and fell into the habit of returning each afternoon for an hour or so of music. The Queen was an accomplished pianist; she accompanied the doctor and me when we sang. Dr. M. was a middle-aged man. He wore a small beard, which like his hair was almost white, and always hid his eyes behind blue spectacles. He said that he was practically blind, but as I came to know him better I observed that not even the strong lenses of his spectacles could conceal the intensity of his regard; it had the sharpness of a blade, and perfect clarity.

He made obvious efforts to gain my confidence, no hard thing for him to do. He took me on walks and showed me the beautiful scenes of the island, which he loved. A man of great intelligence, he had a profound understanding of human nature. I had never yet met anyone who talked to me as he did. The solitary life which he had led for years had taught him a great deal, and he made plain to me the meaning of much that I had read in history, or observed in nature, and in human nature, yet had never really understood. I visited him in his villa, a former tower built in the days of the Saracens. He lived as a hermit, deep in reflection and contemplation of the solitudes about him.

The few rooms in his tower were simply furnished but each object was rare and precious. In the evening as it darkened, Roman oil lamps of chased silver were lighted. There was not one inharmonious note in all this strange house; all belonged there, from the silver lamps to fruit cakes made by an old peasant woman, and the curious cooking utensils that she employed in the kitchen.

Cleverly, gently, Dr. M. questioned me about my life. I gave him my confidence completely. I told him of my childhood, my education, and my marriage, and of the griefs and disappointments that life thus far had brought me, of my loneliness, of my most intimate troubles. I talked with him also about my difficulties in finding an aim for my life, and about my doubtful state of health—the result, I thought, of my worries, self-reproach, and general unhappiness. He listened patiently to it all, but it was my health that seemed really to interest him. He questioned me a great deal as to childish ailments, and about my heredity. I do not know to this day what conclusions he formed. What he told me, suddenly, almost abruptly, was this: that I showed symptoms of kidney trouble; and that to live in a cold climate might be bad for me.

He suggested getting the Queen to write to her husband that a longer stay at Capri would be advisable for my health and that, although I would, as planned, return to Sweden for New Year's, I should be sent back to Capri thereafter. The Queen did so; and I went back to Stockholm feeling that I had found a friend in Dr. M.,—perhaps a new and powerful ally.

In Sweden, winter sports absorbed, almost intoxicated me, and my ailments, real or imaginary, were for the while forgotten. My sister-in-law organized hockey teams for women and we played on the ice nearly every day.

In February the King went as usual for his holiday to Capri and took me with him. It was arranged that I was to have no attendants. The King stayed at Capri only a very few days; then went on to Nice. I stayed on alone at the Queen's villa, still unattended.

I had never before lived in such profound solitude; no sound of the outer world, not a soul penetrated to our retreat; the rest of the world did not exist for us. We fell back into the old habits, the doctor and I singing, accompanied by the Queen. We began again our walks and endless discussions.

But there was now a change in the doctor's attitude towards me; his gentleness had vanished; he was exceedingly severe. He accused me of levity and frivolity, and reproached me for the futility of my life.

I listened without resentment or protest. I was young and inexperienced; it seemed natural enough that he should speak to me as he did; and I honestly tried to find in what he said some help, some guidance for the future. But he so played on my lack of balance and other shortcomings that in the end I despaired, and doubted myself all the more. All my old diffidence, all my old self-mistrust returned; they were, in fact, increased; and I felt myself gradually losing such little independence and freedom of action as in the past few years I had managed to gain.

In March the doctor decided that a change would be good

for the Queen as well as for me, and we all went together to Sorrento and then to Amalfi. On the way back the Queen caught cold and became seriously ill. Her condition gave no cause for alarm, but called for complete quiet, and my presence in the house seemed to bother her.

Dr. M. had to telegraph to Stockholm for my attendants to join me in Capri, and to arrange to put us all in the big villa, then unoccupied. This did not please him in the least. He had hoped to isolate me from all influences save his own.

The arrival of the two Rudebecks seemed somewhat to restore my health and energy. We lived pleasantly and happily in that white villa, overlooking the Bay of Naples. Time passed quickly; soon it was spring, a lovely soft spring, scented with rosemary and sea breezes. The time had come for us to leave the island.

Again the doctor expressed grave concern as to my kidneys. He was sure now that they were seriously affected. I must, he said, come with him and the Queen to Germany and see a specialist; and under no circumstances must I fail to return for the next winter, there to Capri.

As soon as the Queen was well enough we left Capri and went from Naples to Rome where we spent several days at the Grand Hotel. Then on to Karlsruhe, then to Munich to see this specialist. After examining me the two doctors conferred, and the specialist confirmed Dr. M.'s opinion.

The winter climate of Sweden, they decreed, was dangerous for me. My fate was sealed. Hereafter, every winter, Capri! I realized, not without anxiety, that the whole aspect of my life would be changed. In the future I would have to leave my family and my house and spend more than six months of every year in a foreign country, surrounded by an atmosphere of invalidism. The decree was absolute, for the consent of the King and Queen had already been given.

But Dr. M. wished now to have also the approval of a member of my own family. It happened that my aunt Ella

DR. M.'S VILLA IN CAPRI

was abroad; for the first time since her widowhood she had decided to go to England to visit her sister, Princess Victoria of Battenberg, who had just undergone an operation. At the doctor's suggestion, I wrote her and asked her to come to Sweden.

Much to my astonishment, she came. It was at Stenhammer that I received her, dressed in her nun's habit, and I was genuinely glad to see her again. She brought to me in my confusion a breath of ordered activity and normal life. I so envied her serenity and the satisfaction she took in her work that her convent seemed, for the moment, a refuge where I also might find work, usefulness, and peace. I begged her to take me with her, to initiate me into her Order. She smiled sadly at my outbursts and gave me no other answer.

Dr. M. came to Stenhammer and they talked privately for several hours. It was easy for him to influence her in the way he hoped. She left, thinking that I was in good hands. Dr. M. now had all the authority that he needed to become the absolute dictator of the course of my life.

ii

THIS was in 1913, the year of the tercentenary of the rule of the Romanovs. Celebrations were held in Moscow that summer, and I attended them.

The Emperor and Empress and the imperial family had just returned from Kostroma, the cradle of the Romanov family, and were living at the Kremlin. Dmitri expected me at the Nicholas Palace. He had grown taller and very handsome. He served now with the Horse Guards in St. Petersburg, and led a quite independent life. I was astonished to see him so matured, so full of assurance, in this same Nicholas Palace where so few years ago he had been running around in his blue flannel blouse. Now he was a dashing young officer, roaring through the winding streets of Moscow in a hundred horse-power motor car.

The Emperor and Empress were, as always, charming. The fatigue of the fêtes and receptions was telling on the Empress, who was often indisposed; she had to spend days in bed, arising only to don state robes, with long trains and heavy jewellery, showing to the multitude for a few hours a face full of sadness.

Almost every afternoon Dmitri and I went to the palace, to see the Emperor and his daughters. As the Empress was resting, I served the tea. The Emperor was lively on these occasions; Dmitri made him rock with laughter, and all the children besides, with his jokes and anecdotes.

There were a number of dinners and receptions; I especially remember the grand ball given at the halls of the Cercle de la Noblesse, because Dmitri and I danced together seven consecutive waltzes, after which the Emperor signalled smilingly to us and sent an aide to tell us to dance for a change with the other guests. However, we had created quite a sensation for we both waltzed, it must be admitted, very well!

Returning, with vast reluctance, to Sweden, I found plans for the winter finally made. Dr. M. had already rented a villa for me at Capri and engaged servants. I must leave, he said, by the middle of October; he would precede me by ten days. My son was to remain in Sweden with his father and his father's people.

It was further arranged that on this particular journey to Capri I was to go, not through Paris, but by way of Berlin, where the Prince was to represent his father at the centenary of the battle of Leipzig. From Berlin I was to go straight to Italy, the Prince returning to Sweden.

In other words, Dr. M. feared the effects that a visit to Paris might have upon me; he wished for no influence hostile to his own, and had therefore arranged matters in such a way that it would be impossible for me to go and see my father.

I hardly knew what to think or where to turn. The whole plan filled me with apprehension. I was afraid of all that it involved; and the more I considered it the less I liked it. I felt trapped.

It is not surprising that, when I first met Dr. M., I wanted to believe that I had found in him the person who could unravel all my problems and give a new direction to my life. Our first talks had seemed to give good reason for this hope, but something very different happened. Of that very vitality, that need of constant activity, that intense curiosity about life—to which I had hoped this doctor might give bent and direction—he merely disapproved. It was something, he said, likely to lead me into rash actions. He set himself to curb it in me, to ride it down, to eradicate it. I was impressionable and easily influenced, and he had succeeded.

And in return for what he had taken from me, what had he given me? Nothing. No new horizons were opened for me, no new direction given my energies. He had done nothing to help me develop the possibilities which, despite everything, there really were in me.

Before I met him, it is true, the conditions of my life, the deceptions I had to practise, and my loneliness, worry, and unhappiness had reduced me to a nervous condition, a condition, however, not serious. He had persuaded me—as I saw it now—quite as much as he had persuaded others, of the gravity of my "symptoms." He had filled me with negative ideas only, which depressed my spirits and my physical condition equally. After ten months of this relationship with him I found myself in a worse state of perplexity than before. Nothing had been settled, no problem solved. I began to doubt the disinterestedness of the doctor, and to regret my own credulity. His fine words when we had first met seemed to me now as much a trap as his later projects.

If, while remaining married, I was condemned to spend half of every year away from my home, a supposed invalid, not seeing my son, and under a supervision which robbed me of the little freedom which I enjoyed at home—then what use to prolong a situation not only painful but ridiculous? Instead of striving to keep alive vain hopes, instead of continuing a struggle for which I had no heart—why not break such feeble ties as still held me, and embark on an entirely new life, a life in which I might perhaps find happiness?

My thoughts and intentions began to take definite form. I emerged from the mental fog in which I had for so long been living. And as my mind cleared, I recovered my energy and will power. I shook off the influence which had dominated me; I reattained to independence of judgment, and at the same time my physical condition improved. I was no longer in doubt as to the action to be taken:

I must leave. The scruples which had held me before no longer entered my mind. I had tried in every way to adapt myself to an impossible situation; I had failed. Now I must take my fate into my own hands.

A circumstance of apparently little importance fortified my resolve. One day Dr. M. set off on a journey without telling me where he was going; when next I heard from him he was in Moscow and had seen my aunt. This news gave me a disagreeable shock. Apparently his first meeting had not wholly satisfied him; he was determined to win her, it seemed, so completely to his plans that whatever he might decide as to my future would go absolutely unquestioned. My father, whom I was prevented from seeing, lived still in France; my aunt was really my only support in Russia. If Dr. M. succeeded in influencing her in the direction of his conversations with me, I was indeed lost.

I decided to act promptly. It was to my father, naturally, that I turned for help and refuge; but before approaching him I consulted the Minister from Russia, a friend of the family. We both wrote letters. I had already mapped out my plan of action. To make my leaving easier and to avoid useless scenes, I had decided to go with the Prince to Berlin, as had been arranged, and not until I had arrived there make known my intentions. Then instead of going to Italy I would go to my father in France.

My father soon answered my letter. He said he would wait for me at Boulogne and that Dmitri, then on leave in Paris, would come to Berlin to meet me there.

I made my farewells, accordingly, to the royal family and my friends, and took a last look around at all that I was leaving, all that had made the background of my life for more than five years. The thought of leaving my son was almost more than I could bear, but I hoped to have him again soon; I could not foresee that circumstances would prevent this for many years.

Towards the middle of October we started. Thinking it safer to confide in no one, I did not tell even the Prince of my intentions till we were out of Sweden.

In Berlin I saw with relief Dmitri waiting for me on the station platform. We had a long talk, then in the evening attended a military dinner, at which, together with the Prince, I had to preside. The next day I left for Paris, accompanied by Dmitri and by Ida Rudebeck, who did not wish to leave me. My father and stepmother welcomed me affectionately, but anxiously; they saw better than I all the complications my step involved.

The months of uncertainty and the last weeks of emotion had broken my strength. I fell really ill this time, with bronchitis which developed into pneumonia. A most thorough examination by a French specialist disclosed, however, no such functional kidney disorders as had been reported so insistently by Dr. M.

My father tried to reason with me, without success. My stepmother, fearing that some of the blame would fall on her, talked to me also. But all was in vain, and, as soon as my father realized that my decision was irrevocable and that no influence could shake me, he ranged himself courageously on my side and gave me his wholehearted support. He charged himself with all the arrangements and correspondence.

The announcement to the Emperor was rendered somewhat easier by a coincidence; it chanced that two highly placed diplomats had in the course of their duties met Dr. M. and had formed of him a thoroughly unfavourable opinion. I was further fortunate in being able to communicate my history to the Emperor verbally by one of these gentlemen. No comment was afterwards made and I do not know what impression it created.

To this day I do not understand how a matter of such grave importance could have been arranged so quickly and easily. The annulment of my marriage was announced in Sweden no later than December, and in Russia a few months later. I call it an annulment as the usual divorce procedure was completely omitted. The Emperor issued two decrees on the subject, one to the Senate and another to the Synod representing respectively the highest judicial and clerical bodies.

Rather than be completely idle I went, when my health allowed, to paint in the studio of a pupil of Detaille. In January we all went together to St. Petersburg for a final inspection of my father's new house.

In St. Petersburg I saw Aunt Ella, who happened to be visiting her sister the Empress at Tsarskoie-Selo. It was a meeting that I rather dreaded, but there was no cause for fear. Dr. M.'s visit to Moscow had produced on my aunt the opposite effect from that which he intended. His proprietary way of speaking about me and my future had displeased her, she said, and had so aroused her suspicion that she was preparing to write me and warn me when she heard that I was on my way to Paris. My aunt was, in a word, both understanding and sympathetic; she reproached me with nothing and went so far as to deplore the haste she had shown to see me married. From this time forth, we were intimates and got on wonderfully together.

In March, some of my troubles with lungs and nerves continuing, I set out for Italy, accompanied only by a maid, and from Italy went on to my destination—Athens. Greece was my mother's country and I had never been there. It did me good. The memory of my mother was still surprisingly fresh in Greece, and I was welcomed with open arms by all classes of society. It was wonderful spring weather. I went to the island of Corfu where my mother was born, an island of dreams, with rich and abundant vegetation and inhabited by people of classic beauty.

In Athens I met the military painter Scott, and the portrait painter Laszlo. Scott had been with the Greek army during its last campaign, and had returned to Athens to finish his pictures and make studies of soldiers. I asked permission to join him, and every morning we worked together in the immense empty shed which served him as studio.

In April a yacht belonging to the Russian Black Sea squadron was sent to the Piræus to take us to the Crimea. My mother's sister, her husband, the Grand Duke George, since assassinated, and their children went with me to Constantinople, where we stayed two days. It seemed to me the most beautiful city I had ever seen; I remember it as almost fairylike.

In May I returned to Russia, and spent that summer at Tsarskoie-Selo with my aunt, the Grand Duchess Marie, widow of my father's brother Vladimir. My father and stepmother were near by, living in their new house, and completely happy —especially my father—to be at home in Russia once more. My aunt gave dinners and entertained a great deal; my stepmother was picking up the threads of old friendships and forming new ones. Fêtes were held at court to celebrate the visit of M. Poincaré, President of France.

I did not know what my life was to be in the future and was vaguely troubled; and to this personal uncertainty was added a general uneasiness hard to define, an uneasiness which weighed upon me as it had weighed upon me in the old days at Ilinskoie at the approach of a summer storm. I remember solitary walks in the park at Tsarskoie-Selo when this feeling became so strong that it drove all other thoughts from my mind.

It was radiant weather; the sun shone always in a clear blue sky, but this very sky seemed to me full of threat, and my heart was troubled by a strange anguish, all the more painful because of the calm which surrounded me. I seemed, without understanding why, to be awaiting catastrophe.

It came. We were carried away by a storm which raged throughout Europe, and by the same storm dropped to earth, crushed, destroyed.

CHAPTER XV

TO WAR

THE report of the assassination at Serajevo reached us when we were in Krasnoie-Selo, awaiting the arrival of the French President, Poincaré.

It was the day of the Officers' Races and the Emperor and his family were present. Report of the murder spread rapidly among a dense crowd that recognized at once the importance of the news. The very air seemed suddenly chilled; the throng, well dressed and animated, was hushed and began whispering among itself.

My aunt, the Grand Duchess Marie, and I returned to Tsarskoie-Selo, disquieted. Her house, until then always filled with guests, had suddenly emptied. Now Aunt Miechen and I seemed often alone, interminably discussing the turn of political events, anxiously awaiting the outcome.

The weather remained extremely warm. In the daytime I wandered lonely through the park of Tsarskoie-Selo, dusty and lifeless, or went across the road to my father's house. There too I felt the same peculiar mood of unrest.

The inevitability of war became evident. I dreaded it, and dreaded above all another separation from Dmitri. As soon as the order for the mobilization was issued I moved to St. Petersburg to be near him. It was unspeakably hard for me to see him engaged in preparations for a possible campaign. I watched his boyish figure and his youthful face with almost maternal tenderness.

In spite of the exultation which he shared with every Russian, he regarded with great seriousness the task before him. There was no bravado in his attitude. I had, in fact, never seen him so grave at heart. We lived through these few crucial days in close contact, trying to comfort one another, and our relations became again quite simple and childlike. Our talk passed haphazardly from the gloomiest observations to the silliest jokes.

On August 2, Dmitri and I drove in an open victoria to the Winter Palace where a state of war was to be declared by the Emperor. Dmitri was a brave sight in the summer full-dress uniform of his regiment, and I was dressed in a gay, light gown; our brilliant appearance attracted the attention of the people in the streets. I hoped that they could not see my eyes, clouded with tears.

The square in front of the Winter Palace was so thronged that we had difficulty in passing and drove at a foot pace, continually stopping. In spite of its size, the crowd was quiet, with faces grave and rapt. Flags blew overhead, church banners glittered in the sun. It seemed that for the first time the people consciously faced the significance of events.

We entered the palace and proceeded with all of the imperial family, headed by the Emperor and the two Empresses, to the Nicholas Hall for the chanting of a Te Deum.

During the Te Deum I surveyed the assembly. Here also, in spite of the light-coloured dresses and festive array of the gathering, the faces were strained and grave. Hands in long white gloves nervously crumpled handkerchiefs, and under the large hats fashionable at that time many eyes were red with crying. The men frowned thoughtfully, shifting from foot to foot, readjusting their swords, or running their fingers over the brilliant decorations pinned on their chests.

After the service and the reading of the manifesto, the Emperor and the Empresses went out on the balcony. The people on the square knelt as one, and there arose from a thousand throats, impressive and harmonious, the surging measures of the Russian national hymn.

It was long afterward before the crowd could be quieted.

Each time that the sovereigns left the balcony the people clamoured for their reappearance with loud hurrahs and sang *God Save the Tsar*. As Dmitri and I drove back home, our carriage threading its way through the throngs, kind eyes looked now with sympathy upon tear-swollen eyes which I attempted no longer to conceal, and tender smiles met us everywhere.

Russia, already bidding farewell to her first regiments, was animated throughout by an almost sublime patriotism, the reality of which none could doubt. The feeling of national consecration, of national unity, was sincere. It was felt everywhere. The disorders in the factories which broke out early in July had subsided as soon as mobilization was announced; political workers of almost all parties enrolled in various military and auxiliary organizations. It was the only time that I ever remember when Russians, leaving arguments and differences aside, set themselves to their tasks with precision and zest. That vagueness of purpose which is one of our national characteristics had, for the moment, disappeared.

On the eve of the Horse Guards' departure for the front, a Te Deum was celebrated on the square in front of the cathedral. The regiment stood in square formation around the pulpits. It gave one a feeling of dread and pain to see these orderly lines of men standing at prayer, elbow touching elbow, caps in hand, dressed in their new field uniforms, their faces so young, so buoyant! As usual, the finest men of the country were to be the first to go. Where, in those orderly ranks, would the first gaps be torn? And how much reduced would those ranks be when the regiment returned from the war?

Yet, in spite of all my nervousness and sorrow, I remember how it hurt me to kneel on those cobblestones during the benediction.

On August 4, the day of departure, a mass was held, according to our wish, early in the morning in the private chapel of our old palace on the Neva, and Dmitri and I both took communion. The chapel had no windows; it was lighted by oil lamps burning before ikons and by candles in tall candlesticks. After the service we took breakfast with the Laimings in Uncle Serge's old study which served me now as a drawing-room. We were silent. Dmitri sat on the couch, his arm round the neck of his brown Eskimo dog, Palach.

When it was time to go, Dmitri and I took our seats side by side in the carriage. All the members of the household crowded to the door to see us off. Tears rolled down the cheeks of the coachman, who had known us since childhood and had taught us how to drive.

We drove to the barracks of the Horse Guards. The barrack yard, behind an iron fence, was a picture of resolute confusion. Men tramped about, officers shouted orders, pack horses neighed and chafed.

Dmitri joined his squadron. At his request I remained waiting in the carriage. "You can drive beside the regiment as we cross the city to the station," he said.

The wait was long, but finally out of confusion came order, and the regiment marched from the barrack yard. I followed, driving at a foot pace, the coachman keeping his dappled greys as closely as possible beside Dmitri's squadron.

At the railway station the men were packed into trucks. The train stood on a side track by a goods platform. A few of the officers' wives and myself formed a small group to one side apart from the hubbub. There was nothing for us to do except to stand there, endlessly smiling, and watch men climb, one after another, into the wagons. Dmitri and the other officers came up to us continually but, in spite of everybody's desire to be cheerful, the conversation lagged. There were awkward silences, lingering glances, hands inconspicuously pressed. The women kept their tears back. The men's eyes shone with a tenderness which they did not try to hide. I kept thinking: "This may be the last time I shall ever see him."

Leaping to the platform the trumpeter blew the call of

departure. There was a last quick exchange of embraces, kisses, blessings. The officers ran to their carriage and, climbing in, thrust their heads from the windows. The trumpeter blew another signal, then throwing his trumpet upon his back, jumped on the train, already moving. The squadron had started on its way to war.

I returned for a few days to Tsarskoie-Selo. Here, for the first time since my return to Russia, I began to consider my own situation, and for the first time completely realized the loneliness and the difficulty of my position.

I had been happy to return to Russia. But, because of my youth and inexperience, I had not realized the talk and noise that my divorce would arouse, or the difficulties which, as a young divorced woman, I would encounter. Moreover, everything connected with my childhood seemed now to have ceased to exist; nothing remained of those years, neither home, family life, nor former friends—nothing but painful memories.

Aunt Ella was absorbed heart and soul in the Convent of Martha and Mary of which she was Abbess. In St. Petersburg I knew hardly anyone. At Tsarskoie my father and his wife were so busy organizing their new life in Russia that they had no time for me; and Dmitri was at war.

I decided to go to war too, as a nurse.

To do so, I had first to receive the permission of the Empress. There was no time to lose. I went to Peterhof. Somewhat to my surprise, the Empress granted my request. I immediately moved to St. Petersburg to begin my training.

As special training courses for nurses had not yet been opened by the various Red Cross societies, it was arranged that I should take my practical work at one of the city hospitals. I went there every morning, and in the evening attended the lectures of several physicians. As the hospital's only pupil I received individual attention, and learned fast.

Princess Helen, sister of the Serbian King Alexander, began plans for a field hospital, the upkeep of which she and the family of her husband intended to take upon themselves. She offered me the chance to go to the front with this unit and I accepted. Helen's husband was, like Dmitri, an officer of the Horse Guards. We were to be attached to the sector of the front to which this regiment was assigned. That delighted me.

The first few days after Dmitri's departure I had not been so anxious about him; he communicated with me almost daily and his regiment had not yet reached the line. But when it became known that the Guards cavalry had arrived in East Prussia and had gone immediately into action, I was frantic. Even my work at the hospital could not distract me. The ringing of the telephone, the sight of a telegram, frightened me terribly. A telegram was brought to me one morning as I returned from the hospital. With trembling hands I ripped it open and looked first at the signature. It was from Dmitri. That calmed me; but after reading its contents I was horrified.

It told of the battle at Kaushin in which were killed more than half of the officers of the Horse Guards. Dmitri said only that he was well and safe but that the losses were tremendous. Later that day I received another telegram from him, naming some of his comrades who had been killed or wounded. The two brothers Katkov were among the slain; they had been among the few children who were permitted to play with us in Moscow.

A few days later when the first wounded officers of the Guards reached St. Petersburg, I went with hundreds of others to the hospital; I wanted to see Dmitri's comrades and to talk with them about him.

The departure of our unit was set for August 29. I took my final examinations as a nurse. The doctors who interrogated me had known me since childhood; and in spite of my nervousness and the short period of my studies, I was passed. Mlle. Hélène was never, I think, so proud of me as at that moment when she handed me the certificate authorizing me

THE GRAND DUCHESS MARIE AND PRINCE WILLIAM

Dressed for a ball in Polish costume, 1911

to wear the Red Cross on the bib of my apron; I also was happy; I felt that I had attained to something real.

Aunt Ella, to whom I had written of my decision to go to war, had approved it and indicated her intention of coming to St. Petersburg to bid me good-bye. All those who knew me were now so moved to kindness towards me that I felt almost ashamed of all this attention. It seemed to me that the work I had undertaken was nothing out of the ordinary; even if I chanced to lose my life that would certainly be no unusual sacrifice those days. And as to existing values, it seemed to me that I was sacrificing nothing—no home, no dependents, no social life and pleasures of any consequence. I felt, in fact, that I was gaining, at last, an opportunity to apply myself usefully, to find work for which I was really fitted and which I needed, to direct all my energies to one central purpose. Life beckoned to me and I could not pity myself.

My luggage was not complicated—a few grey uniforms, white kerchiefs which we wore as head-dress, aprons, white hospital smocks, cotton underwear and cotton stockings—all packed in one suit-case. An army cot, a rubber tub, and a few small rubber wash basins completed my field kit.

Aunt Ella came, as she had promised, on the day of my departure. That morning for the first time I had put on my uniform and I remember how embarrassed I was to go out on the street.

After lunch my aunt took me to the chapel in the little house of Peter the Great; it had a much venerated ikon of the Saviour. While we were there, our footman must have told the people who we were, for when we came out we were surrounded. They were mostly common people, greatly moved. Many of the women were crying; those who stood nearest began, to my great confusion, to touch my dress and to catch my hands and kiss them.

"Oh! our dear one, you too are going to war. God bless

you!" said an old crone, sobbing. Others joined in and showered us with tears and good wishes.

"Thank you! . . . You are going to take care of our soldiers. . . . God help you! . . . God save and guard you. . . . May God give us strength to overcome the enemy! . . ." And one poor old woman kept asking my aunt please, please, to find out something about her son.

Finally we freed ourselves and entered the carriage. I had never experienced anything like this before, and was stirred to the depths of my heart; so likewise was my aunt.

Aunt Ella, the Grand Duchess Marie, and Volodia Paley, my stepbrother, came that evening to the station to see me off. Our unit consisted of eight nurses, two doctors, a superintendent, a representative of the Red Cross, and twenty orderlies. Besides the Princess Helen and myself we had with us Mme. Sergeieva, recently appointed as my lady-in-waiting, without whom the Empress would not consent to let me go.

Our train carried not only hospital material but also a variety of equipment essential to field operations—an ambulance and other wagons, field kitchens, cauldrons, horses, and tents. Helen was also taking her automobile. Tremulously I kissed all who came to see me off. Tears stood in Aunt Ella's eyes as, placing her slim fingers on my forehead, she fervently blessed me with a wide sign of the cross. Word was given to entrain. We clambered into our compartment. The train began to move; last wishes and admonitions were shouted. There on the platform we could see many people crying. But my heart was easy, even joyful.

ii

THAT night for the first time in my life, I, myself, took out my nightgown and a pillow from a modest small travelling bag. I had seldom yet travelled overnight without a maid. As I hung my black apron and the grey cotton dress on the wall of the compartment that Helen and I shared, I reflected how easily and simply my life had changed, and how much easier and simpler I felt, myself. So musing, I fell asleep and dreamed of heroic deeds.

Our destination was indefinite. We only knew that we were to go to the frontier town of Eydtkuhnen, there to unload our equipment and await instructions. Arriving at Eydtkuhnen next day we found that town in great disorder. When we finally located the headquarters of General Rennenkampf's command in that sector, there were no orders whatsoever concerning us. His army, which included Dmitri's cavalry regiment, the Horse Guards, had advanced far into East Prussia, but no one could say whether Insterburg was occupied by our troops or not.

The small town of Gumbinnen, half way between Eydtkuhnen and Insterburg, was, however, in our hands, and we were advised to proceed there.

While the men unloaded equipment we nurses wandered about town. Quite obviously, this town was near the front. Everywhere were soldiers in field-stained uniforms; carts stood heaped together; smoke rose here and there from field kitchens; the air was full of mingled scents—the aromatic smell of hay and of horses, the warm smell of fresh-baked bread, the smell of trampled grass, the smell of smoke. Some families had apparently decided to leave town. Their belongings were piled on wagons in front of their yards or lay scattered on the street amid hay and straw. And here and there upon the street were articles dropped or forgotten; these the soldiers examined carefully and as a rule immediately appropriated, regardless of bulk or uselessness. I myself picked up a brand-new coffee pot which I proudly showed to my companions as my share of the common plunder. I tucked it under my arm and used it for a long time, always telling its history.

When the unloading was finished, Helen, Mme. Sergeieva, and I drove in the car to Gumbinnen while the unit was to follow in marching order.

Upon all this activity the inhabitants of the town looked

disconsolately. I would have much preferred to remain with the personnel and ride with them on the wagons but Helen thought that we should drive on ahead to Gumbinnen and if possible locate a place for the hospital.

It was not easy to reach Gumbinnen. That town had been quite recently a battlefield, and the roads had greatly suffered. With eager curiosity I looked at the trampled fields on both sides of the road, at the holes so recently dug by shells, at the broken trees. In some places there remained signs of encampments, in others, of open warfare—abandoned packs, broken rifles, empty ration tins, bits of clothing. I looked for the dead, dreading to see them; all human corpses had, however, by that time been removed, but the bodies of horses, with legs sticking upward and swollen bellies, were still there.

Neither trenches nor barbed wire were anywhere to be seen. The advance of General Rennenkampf into East Prussia—an advance undertaken in order to draw the German armies away from the Western front, at a time when they had already flooded Belgium and were ready to march on Paris—had to this extent been altogether successful; it had taken the enemy by surprise. They had not expected the Russian mobilization to go through with such speed and in such order. Our hurried advance had allowed, however, no time for fortifications and had left our rear defenceless.

Chaos reigned in Gumbinnen. As nearly as we could determine, the headquarters of Rennenkampf had been moved up ahead to Insterburg. Helen decided nevertheless to inspect some of the houses. We made a tour of Gumbinnen, accompanied by several of the town officials.

Never shall I forget that town. Outwardly, few buildings had suffered; at first glance, the neat German brick houses seemed clean and untouched. But inside, all was different. There was not an apartment which had not been ransacked. Doors were sagging open, locks had been forced, cupboards stood gaping, clothing was scattered all over the floor, crockery and mirrors lay smashed, furniture had been overturned and pierced with bayonets.

The inhabitants, not expecting the arrival of the Russians, had fled, leaving all their property behind. The alarm must have come around dinner-time, for in almost all the houses tables were set. Dry pieces of meat in thick cold gravy were lying on the plates, napkins thrown beside them, chairs pushed back. Were it not for the terrible disorder and destruction, one would have thought that the family had just risen from the table and gone into another room.

Yet, still more terrible was the deathlike silence hovering over it all. We did not decide upon any of the houses.

Dmitri and John, Helen's husband, having somehow learned of our presence in Gumbinnen, came to us in an automobile and found us making our inspection. I had not hoped to see Dmitri so soon and was transported with joy. But I noticed at once that he did not fully share my sentiments. He had seen terrible things; he looked sad and worn, and did not approve of my presence so near the actual fighting. The situation, he said, was very uncertain; headquarters were, for the moment, in Insterburg.

To Insterburg, accordingly, we moved our unit, and were billeted in a school. It was the largest building in town, but completely unadapted for living quarters and extremely gloomy. As soon as our wagon train arrived we quickly unloaded and very soon that school began to look like a real hospital. The nurses and I laboured in gay co-operation. We cleaned the whole building from top to bottom, scrubbing every floor, window, and staircase. The classrooms of the two upper floors we turned into wards, and transformed other space on those floors into bandaging- and operating-rooms. On the first floor, where the rooms were smaller, we lived, with packing boxes for chairs. The room assigned to Mme. Sergeieva and myself, like all the others, had a stone floor and grey, shiny walls. Our cots and suitcases and some boxes were our only furniture. We washed in the school lavatory in the basement.

The nearer one draws to a front the less, as a rule, one knows of what actually is happening there; and this was true of us. We had no real idea of the instability of our situation. The army of Rennenkampf was scattered, its positions were not fortified, its rear was undefended. Some of our troops were already before Königsberg, and the Germans, occupied on other fronts, seemed unprepared to make a firm stand or to counter-attack.

Our first days at Insterburg passed in comparative quiet. From time to time we heard sounds of cannonading, generally distant and dull, but sometimes closer, more distinct. Regiments of infantry, their boots caked with dust, passed singing through the town; squadrons of cavalry, automobiles, wagon trains, passed continually towards the guns.

Dmitri was stationed in Insterburg, serving as liaison officer at the headquarters of Rennenkampf's army. He came often to the hospital, accompanied by a Great Dane who somewhere along the line of march had become attached to him. Occasionally, Helen and I were invited to lunch at headquarters. Everyone there seemed still in that same uplifted state of mind in which, a few weeks ago, they had taken the field; and all expressed an unshakable certainty in the swift and brilliant termination of the war. With few exceptions, everything had gone well, and promised well. The army was as yet well stocked with provisions, and had more than enough equipment and munitions. Everybody was content; and our mutual relations were marked with that special cordiality which results from the realization of one's strength, and of comparatively light sacrifices in the name of duty. It was, if I may so express it, the honeymoon of the war.

Everywhere I was received with the warmest cordiality, although almost no one knew me. The nurse's uniform brought me close to those who wore khaki; we all lived the same life and had the same interests.

Once, towards the very beginning of our sojourn in Insterburg, Helen, Mme. Sergeieva, and I went out into the town to do some shopping. The few stores were situated around the town's square, not far from our hospital. Around this square centred the life of Insterburg. This day it was crowded, as usual, with people. Wagons were parked here and there, officers walked about, mounted orderlies rode by. As we were crossing the square an infantry officer rode towards us. He was mounted; his horse was lathered from hard riding. He showed us a hand in a dirty bandage partly unwound, and asked:

"Little nurses, haven't you by chance a dressing to rebandage my hand?"

In my pocket I discovered a piece of clean bandage that I had slipped there that morning in the bandaging-room.

"I have one," I said. "Get down, give your reins to some soldier and come into the shade."

He dismounted and throwing his reins to a private standing by, followed me. Choosing a spot away from the crowd I placed my patient in front of me and turned my back to the square. Hardly had I begun unwinding the dirty upper layer of the dressing than I heard an unknown voice behind me.

"Your Imperial Highness, may I take your picture?"

I turned around in confusion and recognized one of the officers attached to headquarters. He held a large camera in his hands.

"No, for heaven's sake, don't!" I replied, blushing painfully.

The hand that I was bandaging shook slightly. A searching glance stopped for an instant upon my face, then was lowered again, but not a word was said. Confusedly I hurried my work, in silence winding the fresh bandage. When I had finished the officer raised his eyes; they were brimming with tears.

"Let me ask you who you are," he said.

There was no longer any reason for concealing my name and I told him.

"Then you are the first cousin of the Emperor?"

"Yes."

Once again in silence he scrutinized my face; then suddenly kneeling there on the pavement in front of everybody, he lifted the bottom of my cotton dress to his lips and kissed it.

I was completely taken aback. Without looking at him, without saying a word of farewell, I shied away from him and rushed across the street into the store. There I found my companions, who were very much surprised at my agitation. On the way back to the hospital, I was so confused that I dared not lift my eyes for fear I might see some witnesses of the recent spectacle.

Another time, when I was walking on the street a farm cart passed me with several officers. By their shoulder straps I saw that they belonged to the Kiev Grenadier regiment, stationed in Moscow, of which at one time Uncle Serge was honorary Colonel. They recognized me at once, stopped their carriage, and rushed to me with expressions of enthusiasm.

"Is it really true that you are at the front, Your Highness? How wonderful this is. Now we shall fight with greater joy, knowing that you have come to take care of us."

I felt that they were sincere; for them the realization that the dangers, hardships, and changing luck of war were shared by a member of the imperial family had real significance. We were suddenly equals in the face of the trials which had befallen our fatherland.

Still another time, one of the nurses and I went in a cart to a village for some apples. It never entered our heads that it might be dangerous for two women to go out of town alone, into enemy territory, inhabited most likely by a hostile civilian population. It was the beginning of autumn, the sun was setting over harvested fields, the leaves on the trees that bordered the deserted road were still green. We drove to a small, neat farm, behind whose fences we could see apple trees heavily laden. An empty carriage stood by the gate.

The nurse stayed with the horse while I went in search of the farmers. I found them in the orchard, talking with three Russian soldiers whose business was apparently the same as ours. One of the soldiers offered to watch our horse for us while two others, together with the nurse and myself, began to shake the trees and fill our bag with ripe apples.

One of the soldiers, a fine, upstanding young sergeant, kept looking at me with a particularly searching glance; it was as if there were something he wished to say to me, but dared not. Finally gathering his courage and looking at me sidewise, he exclaimed:

"I know you! You are our Grand Duchess Marie from Moscow. I recognized you at once, only I did not trust myself because you are dressed as a nurse."

We conversed with animation, as people do when, coming from the same town, they meet. I found that he had served in one of the regiments of the Moscow garrison.

"It isn't right for you to drive alone with a nurse here in the country," he said. "The enemy is not far enough from here to make that sort of thing safe; besides, you can't trust the inhabitants. Whether you want it or not, I am going to escort you back to town myself." And in spite of my protests he rode in with us, joyfully grinning, all the way to Insterburg.

A few months before, this same sergeant would have stood at attention before me, rigidly saluting. Now in his manner towards me there was something good-natured and patronizing; there was even a touch of familiarity, though no trace of impudence, and I was vaguely surprised.

I was glad, however, that my uniform broke down barriers and smoothed out differences in rank. Whether this was good or bad, I do not take upon myself to judge; but my white headdress inspired trust in the common people, drew me, thus attired, nearer to them, made me more understandable to them.

iii

Helen, older and more experienced than I, became naturally the head of our unit. I worked as an ordinary nurse, well knowing that I had still a great deal to learn. I quickly grew accustomed to my duties, shirked no work, however disagreeable, and became adapted quite easily to hospital routine. Already it seemed only natural to me to make my bed in the morning, to shine my shoes, to brush my clothing, to clean my room.

The Russian advance had been halted and the Germans were stirring. Enemy aeroplanes began to fly over Insterburg, first at long intervals, then more and more often. Our anti-aircraft guns were still few and the planes flew so low as to frighten both soldiers and horses, who were not used to them. So great was the confusion brought upon our town at the first air attack that even officers took out their revolvers and attempted to fire at the planes. The casualties were many; these wounded became our first patients.

I clearly remember the very first case. Our hospital was empty. I was on duty that afternoon, reading a book. An orderly rushed in:

"Nurse, quick, come into the reception room. Two patients are there on stretchers. One is hurt very badly, the soldiers say."

In the reception room were two stretchers side by side. The four soldiers who had brought them stood shifting from foot to foot and crumpling their caps in their hands.

"What has happened?" I asked them, bending over the stretchers. One of the men was unconscious. His face was of a horrible yellowish hue. The other man was conscious; he moaned.

"We serve on a supply train, nurse. A plane came flying over us and the horses bolted. This one fell from the wagon and the wheels passed over his chest," one of the soldiers replied.

I felt the pulse of the man who was unconscious. It was very weak. I was frightened.

"Run for the doctor," I said to the orderly, "and also tell them to bring me some camphor and a needle from the bandaging-room."

The wounded man began to choke and blood appeared on his lips. I did not know what to do. Unbuttoning his collar I slipped my arm under his shoulders and lifted him a little. He stopped choking, his head dropped heavily over my hand, and his eyes opened slightly. When the doctor arrived he was already dead. I freed my hand, and with great difficulty got to my feet; my knees shook violently.

"Go, drink something," advised the doctor, smiling at me. Scarcely able to move my feet, I walked out of the room. I was shaking all over. It was the first time that I had ever looked upon death face to face.

My next patient was altogether different. The soldiers' wards were filled to capacity, but those for the officers still stood empty. Our first officer was a very young sub-lieutenant; he had an inflammation of the periosteum from contusion.

I had not yet seen the patient when, the morning following his arrival, I entered the room where he was lying. He had been forbidden to get up, and I was to attend to his morning toilet. I still felt somewhat constrained in the presence of the patients and to hide this I bade him good-morning with unwonted buoyancy and cheerfulness. His reply was somewhat sullen. I brought the wash basin, placed it upon the bed, poured water into it and, holding soap and towel in my hand, suggested that he wash himself. He had been silently watching my movements with what seemed to me more than a hint of animosity.

"I don't want to wash myself," he announced petulantly. "It is your business, and you have to do it."

Rather surprised, I attended to my duties without saying a word. Silence soon bored him, and he tried to start a conversation. Not knowing exactly how to act, I decided to make my answers very short. Noting this, he attempted to hinder my work by awkward movements, watching at the same time the expression of my face. When he saw that this would not arouse my temper, he started asking questions:

"Nurse, what are you going to do afterwards?"

"Bring you tea or coffee, according to your preference, and then go to the bandaging-room."

"Don't you want to stay with me? It's so dull to be alone."

"No, I cannot stay with you," I replied.

"Why not? I am also a patient."

"Because I am very busy and also because you don't know how to behave yourself," I told him, trying hard not to burst out laughing. "Which do you want, tea or coffee?"

I was standing by the door at the other end of the room. Suddenly he threw at me the towel and the soap which I had forgotten on the bed. His youthful face, with hardly a vestige of a beard, was distorted by a funny childish rage.

"If you need anything, call the orderly who sits by the door in the hall," I said coldly, picking up soap and towel and leaving the room with what seemed to me a showing of dignity.

Throughout that day he sent the orderly to fetch me under a number of pretexts, but I did not go. Towards evening a party of wounded officers of the Guards were brought in. Some of them knew me. After dressing their wounds and changing them into hospital clothes, I placed them in the ward and went to supper.

We were still at table when an orderly from the upper floor came to report that my sub-lieutenant had hysterics. I understood at once what had happened. The officers must have told him who I was.

I went to the ward and stopped by his side. He was lying

MOTHER AND SON

The Grand Duchess Marie with Prince Lennart, 1910

flat on his stomach, his face buried in the pillow and was sobbing desperately. I placed my hand on his head and said gaily:

"Well, well, stop it now; everything is all right; I am not angry with you."

The officers were laughing. But he continued sobbing, lying in the same position, and my pleading was of no avail. After that, whenever I entered the room he invariably turned his face to the wall. Only on the day of his departure did he gather enough courage to apologize; and this he did in a very low voice, with bent head, his hand nervously fingering the edge of his topcoat.

Our work was hard and all-absorbing. To that ward, the four walls of which seemed to encompass a world unrelated to any other, death came often; and there was always suffering. The attitude of the soldiers towards us was deeply touching. It was as if we personified to them all that was dear and close to their hearts. We somehow represented, in our white head-dresses, that highest feminine being in whom were united all the qualities of motherhood and wifehood with the additional conception of a saintly nun, a conception especially dear to the Russian people. Here, in this world of hospital beds, white smocks, and long, monotonous hours, the doctor and the nurse occupied the places next to Divinity. The doctor, for some reasons incomprehensible and mysterious, often caused pain, yet the soldiers never asked an explanation; they did not question God when He sent them trials. The nurse was more human and nearer to them because she tried to alleviate their suffering, to comfort them, to show them kindness.

We felt all this with greater force during those first months of the war, when we were all still fired by the same impulse, responded alike, and served, all of us, an ideal comprehensible to all.

The soldiers bore their suffering with extraordinary patience and resignation, and their attitude towards the hospital personnel was invariably tactful and considerate. They appreciated what we did for them and knew how to show it. But as to the officers, the matter was somewhat more complicated. That simplicity in relations which existed between the nurses and the soldiers was here absent, especially towards me when they knew who I was. And to none of us did the officers evidence that boundless, almost mystic trustfulness that was shown to us by the ranks. The officers were, quite naturally, more exacting; it was more difficult to satisfy them; yet they too unflinchingly endured pain that was at times almost unbearable.

The soldiers brought to our hospital in Insterburg were all cavalrymen, strong, good-looking young boys. I spent all my days in the wards working with an enthusiasm that was untiring, and insensible to fatigue. My happiness was so great that I was at times remorseful at experiencing such ecstasy in the midst of all this pain. The wounded, however, with the perspicacity inherent to common people seemed intuitively to feel the warmth of my inner fire, and were drawn by my cheerfulness.

"Do you know that the patients call you the 'cheerful nurse'?" I was asked by the other nurses with whom from the very beginning I was on the best of terms. When I made the round of the wards I knew that the patients not only were looking forward to the sound of my laughter and were thinking of answers to my jokes, but I had an almost mystic feeling that, looking into my eyes, they would see and rejoice in my spiritual unity with them. Those were wonderful days.

The crowning point of my happiness occurred when General Rennenkampf—his whiskers well combed and his waist tightly belted—descended one day upon the hospital, accompanied by Dmitri and by the staff. It was at supper-time. All the personnel rose hurriedly from the table at the unexpected arrival of their commanding general.

The General was visibly nervous. Taking a small box from the hands of one of his officers, he turned to Dmitri and, with a brief greeting, presented my brother with the Cross of St.

George, pinning it on his chest with a hospital safety-pin. The decoration was given to Dmitri for bravery shown in the battle of Kaushin. The General thought that it would please me to witness the presentation, and he was right. I was happy and proud beyond words.

It was only then that I learned that my brother, besides taking part in a cavalry attack in which an entire battery was captured, had saved the life of a wounded corporal. He had dismounted, loaded the man on his back, carried him to safety, and then jumping into the saddle again rejoined his squadron.

Our stay in Insterburg was fated to be cut short. The Germans were beginning, little by little, to drive our men from occupied positions too quickly taken. Troops and supply trains began again to pass through the town, this time in the opposite direction. Suddenly came an order to transfer all our seriously wounded to sanitary trains and to prepare for retreat. Planes now flew over the town every day, singly and in formation, dropping bombs, trying, as usual, especially to damage the railway station. The bark and rumble of artillery drew nearer each day.

Helen was away on the day we received final orders to move. She and her husband had gone to the rear of the army on business. It took us all that day to transfer our wounded to the station. They had to be driven very slowly in uncomfortable, springless wagons, the nurses walking beside them on the hard pebbles. I made several such trips. The station had been almost completely destroyed by the bombs and we had to place the stretchers on the pavement in front of it. Aeroplanes kept flying over us and on all sides we heard the explosions of bombs. I shivered with apprehension, expecting every minute to see a bombing plane appear above the station, and our helpless wounded. Incidentally, it was for this day's work that I received the St. George's medal.

Towards evening, having finished the loading of the wounded in sanitary trains, we began to pack the hospital equipment. The unit was to leave in the night; then I, by order of General Rennenkampf, was to follow the next morning with his staff. He would not hear of my going with the unit in marching order. As the evening wore on I felt completely exhausted. At midnight I stretched myself on the bed without undressing. It seemed that I had hardly time to close my eyes when I felt a hand on my shoulder shaking me. Dazed by sleep I could at first distinguish only a sort of buzzing noise, seemingly far away.

"Wake up! Come into the yard. There is a Zeppelin flying over us. Wake up, *please* wake up!" It was the voice of Mme. Sergeieva, my lady-in-waiting.

Still so much in the grip of sleep that I could hardly understand what was wrong, I forced myself to my feet.

"A Zeppelin. It is flying over the city. Throwing bombs," repeated Mme. Sergeieva. As if to confirm her words, there came immediately a loud explosion. Restored to my senses, I hurried into the yard.

The night was clear and starry but the air was filled with that same curious buzzing noise. Suddenly in the sky above me I saw an immense object radiating silver rays that seemed to plunge from space directly down into our yard. A terrible explosion followed, then another. I understood at that moment the meaning of mortal fear. I felt sorry for myself, sorry for everything. I remembered the sun . . . blood was throbbing in my temples. . . . Those bombs had not fallen into the yard but very close to it.

In a few seconds all was over. The silvery object disappeared with a dull rumbling that grew fainter and fainter. The relief I experienced cannot be described; it was just as oppressing as the fear. I wanted to laugh, to cry, to feel that every fibre in my body was alive. The rumbling noise had again turned into a buzz that slowly dissolved now in the darkness of the sky. From the distance came the sound of one final explosion; then all was quiet.

The stillness seemed now especially beautiful, the night especially peaceful. Looking around I noticed for the first time that almost all the personnel of our unit was assembled in the yard. In silence we exchanged glances. After a while, having satisfied ourselves that the danger was over, we went inside. An excited officer from headquarters came running to inquire if everything was all right. Headquarters was situated almost next door to our hospital; a bomb, the officer told us, had exploded between our two buildings.

We resumed our packing. When everything was almost ready, the horses had to be harnessed, but the supply train orderlies were nowhere to be found. We searched throughout the building and finally a nurse and I bethought ourselves of the cellar. There we found the orderlies lying side by side on the stone floor, sleeping the sleep of the dead, surrounded by a great many empty beer bottles. At the sight of this spectacle, we burst out laughing; but there was no time to lose and we tried to awaken them. This proving impossible, we had to fetch the superintendent. Together with him we dragged the orderlies to a water-tap which we happened to discover and gave each one in turn a cold spray of water straight into the face. That worked. The unit moved before dawn, leaving Mme. Sergeieva and myself alone in the empty building.

Early in the morning one of Rennenkampf's officers called for us in a car and we joined the automobile train in front of headquarters. Rennenkampf, wearing a general's coat of grey and the tall fur cap of the Siberian Cossacks, appeared on the steps. He came to shake hands with me, took his seat in his car and the procession started, our automobile the second in line. The abandoned town seemed to hold its breath as though fearful or unwilling to show its elation. Somewhere quite near the artillery roared and the machine guns rattled. It was a clear and cool morning. Our destination was Gumbinnen.

Outside the town the cars stopped. Rennenkampf alighted and came towards us.

"Your Highness," he said, "there was stationed here a park of artillery and picket line into which the Zeppelin threw a bomb last night. Would you care to look about?"

Reluctant to refuse, I jumped out of the car. We climbed over a ditch and walked along the field. The sight that met my eyes was horrible beyond the wildest imagination; I remember it, to this day, down to the slightest detail, but I cannot write about it.

Our progress was slow. Supply trains moved along the road several abreast. I had been guarded from a full knowledge of the situation, and did not know how closely we were followed by the enemy, but I was nevertheless conscious of a sense of alarm that seemed to hover in the air. I noticed it especially by Rennenkampf's agitation when we caught up with supply trains driving in disorder or at a trot. Our cars would then stop and officers of the staff, under the direction of the general, would seek to straighten out the line. All this, I learned later, indicated the beginning of a rout and a panic.

We arrived in Gumbinnen in the evening. The town was dark, quiet, and gloomy. Mme. Sergeieva and I were given quite decent lodgings, facing the street, and a sentinel from headquarters was placed at the door to guard us. Somewhat later, the hospital doctor sought us out to report that all had arrived safely and had found lodgings.

Exhausted, we were undressing with joyful anticipation of deep sleep in real beds, when there was an insistent knocking at our door. It was one of Rennenkampf's officers with whom we had travelled that day.

"The General begs you to get ready to leave Gumbinnen without delay," he said. "You are to be taken to Eydtkuhnen, and I have been assigned to accompany you."

There was no use arguing; we dressed. An automobile was found and we drove in haste out of that dark town. The Germans had begun an outflanking movement. Headquarters did not know whether we were cut off from Eydtkuhnen or not. This time the officer did not try to conceal the seriousness of the situation. We were threatened by all kinds of danger, the least of which was being taken prisoners of war.

It was impossible to drive fast at any stretch; headlights were too dangerous; we had to feel our way along in complete darkness. No one spoke. It may have been because I was so exhausted, but I did not feel the slightest fear.

We reached Eydtkuhnen without hindrance, but once there we did not know where to go. It was quite impossible to stay at the station over which remained only part of the roof. In the waiting-room, amidst broken and twisted furniture, were soldiers, so tired that they had dropped to sleep where they stood, without taking off their caps or their ammunition. Some of them were sick with dysentery. It was a sad spectacle and we could be of no assistance.

The officer went in search of the station commander to whom he explained the absolute necessity of getting a carriage and an engine ready to take me immediately to the next flag station. This was done by what means I cannot imagine. Later we spent two days stationed in a field getting our food from the field kitchens of the passing squadrons. It was from officers of our acquaintance in these squadrons that we learned that the personnel of our hospital had been able to escape in time but that our equipment had been left behind, while the French unit, headed by Dr. Kresson, had been taken prisoners.

Thus ended the first phase of my war experience. I was sorry to part with the personnel to whom I had grown accustomed and sorry that my work at the front had ended so soon. Without being unfeeling, I can say that I look back to it today as one of the happiest times of my life, a time of real service and of that allurement which is linked with danger.

CHAPTER XVI

COMMAND

I RETURNED to St. Petersburg in the middle of September and arranged immediately to begin work at the nursing home of the St. Eugenia chapter of the Red Cross, from which I had graduated. My former unit would now have to renew its equipment. This would disable it for a long while and I did not wish to wait. Besides I had been forced to the conclusion that, however inspiring might be my work at the front, my place was not there. My presence on the line might have caused a great deal of trouble to the authorities and distracted them at crucial times from more important duties. I hated to give up the idea of being near Dmitri, but I saw that I must.

My Red Cross chapter was organizing a large hospital for work at the rear of the army and I was appointed head nurse.

I spent three weeks at the St. Petersburg headquarters of the Society, working in the morning in the bandaging-room and in the afternoon in the dispensary for the city population. Sometimes I was assigned to nurse a dangerously ill patient or an officer just off the operating-table. Whenever I could find time I attended lectures. The harder I worked, the more I was pleased.

By the middle of October our hospital was ready for departure. It was a large unit—twenty-five nurses, five doctors, a superintendent, and eighty orderlies, and it could accommodate two hundred and fifty wounded, a capacity that later was increased to six hundred. To assist me in my duties as head nurse, I was given an old experienced nurse, a veteran from the days of the Turkish War.

The wounded officers who had been in my charge there at St. Petersburg had grown accustomed to me and regretted to see me go. They gave me a dinner on the eve of my departure, and presented me with a bouquet of white flowers tied with a large white ribbon. On the ribbon was written in gold letters: "To our beloved nurse, from her wounded officers." They called me that because in the beginning no one knew who I was, and I succeeded in preserving my incognito for a long time—an incognito which I guarded most zealously and which was disclosed only at the very end, and then through a stupid mistake. By this time the habit of calling me "nurse" was so rooted in my patients that they never thought of giving me the other, more complicated name.

My new hospital was ordered to Pskov. It went there in marching order, personnel and equipment, and I followed two days later. We were assigned to the Ecclesiastical School for Girls, occupying the lower floor only, while the school, in crowded quarters, continued its activities and tried not to intermix them with ours. I was given a small but cheerful room in the apartment of the directress of the school. I was to spend two and a half years in that room.

The work was already in full swing when I arrived in Pskov. Wishing to show the personnel, whom I scarcely knew, that I was not afraid to work, I armed myself with a wet rag, tucked up my skirts, and washed and scrubbed floors and furniture together with the rest of them. In a few days everything was ready and the results were more than satisfactory; our hospital had the appearance of a real peace-time hospital.

We were quite a distance back from the front, situated in a small provincial town, the outward life of which was hardly ever disturbed by the war. Nothing ever seemed to happen unexpectedly, and our life drifted on with the life of the town, peacefully, steadily.

Here I realized that, amid these humdrum surroundings, my task of adapting myself to life, and discovering in myself new capacities, would be more difficult, much more complicated, than it had been at the front.

First of all I was now surrounded by a large personnel composed of a class of people whom in ordinary circumstances I would never have met. It was plain that, at the beginning, they avoided me, and I did not know how best to approach them; I vaguely felt that one awkward word would spoil everything. Yet I must, I knew, establish some sort of equilibrium in my relations with them.

I was head nurse. This meant that I had to assume command over twenty-five women, see that they performed their duties well, defend their interests, look after them in every way. And I had never in my life given an order.

On the contrary I had since childhood been taught submission and obedience. It was easy and perfectly natural for me to carry out orders; but I could not, did not know how to, give any. I had been brought up in the spirit of humility, always to believe that everybody knew better than I. By purpose and by the accidents of convention, my life had been enclosed in such narrow bounds, my personal initiative thus far so limited, that now, having acquired a certain amount of authority, I did not know how to use it.

At first I tried to establish working relations with the personnel and to perform my own duties, without any definite display of authority. The orders that I was supposed to give were issued by my elderly assistant, Nurse Zandina, who knew all the rules by heart. She possessed inborn tact and life-long practice, and throughout all her term of service under me, she never placed me in an awkward position. A type, rare even in those days, a simple peasant girl, very young and without any education, she had gone to the Turkish War animated by the same sentiments that induced Russian women to take the veil. At that time there was no special training for nurses and all she knew she had learned by experience. She had never mastered the science of writing, and read very painstakingly, only in ecclesiastical books. When I knew her she was about sixty years of age and had already retired from work, but at the declaration of war she immediately offered her services. She was absolutely untiring. From morning till night she rushed through the building, always attending to some important business, always arranging something or giving orders.

But her favourite occupation was the dressing of the dead. She performed this task with a peculiar enthusiasm, as though it were a special ritual, incomprehensible to others. She contended that a dead man lives a definite, though mysterious life in which he is helpless and above all lonely, and she took it upon herself to comfort him in this loneliness. She herself washed every dead man, dressed and placed him in the coffin, read the psalm book over him, and sobbed disconsolately. Having done all this, she would display not only pity but a certain pride. Walking back a few steps she would gaze with admiration on the results of her handiwork. Sometimes, while working, her lips moved and by the expression of her face one could surmise that she was chiding or tenderly reproaching the dead man. Her psychology interested me. I asked her several times how she could cry over every one.

"But how can I help it! Think only of the many trials the poor soul has to go through in the other world and all alone! So I am helping him with my tears," she replied reproachfully, throwing a tender glance at the coffin. Then all of a sudden her tone would change and she would ask for my praise: "Now, Your Highness, doesn't he look handsome?"

She treated me with respect in which there was a slightly patronizing touch. Every morning as I was having breakfast she came to my room to report. She never consented to sit down in my presence when we were alone although I never failed to offer her a chair.

"Please permit me to stand," she would answer. "I am more comfortable this way."

I can see her standing in front of me. She was rather short

and thickset, with a freckled, homely, but intelligent face. She wore the head-dress on her grey, thin hair set back far from her forehead. Her hands were always folded under the apron, pulling it forward and making her appear quite round in the waist.

Having reported some shocking news of hospital life and noticed that I was duly impressed, she would reply to my anxious questions with a judicious air.

"Don't you worry, Your Highness; you must not concern yourself with such affairs; I'll investigate and report to you. Then whatever you decide will be done."

"But listen, Theodosia Ivanovna," I would answer, feeling altogether helpless. "It can't be done that way. I must examine it myself."

The old woman would then pull her hands from under her apron, and resting her cheek on one of them, would look at me with an air of genuine commiseration.

"These are petticoat affairs; they are of no importance," she would say. "There is plenty of more useful work for you here."

I soon gave up trying to remonstrate with her and left the management of the feminine kingdom, so well known to her and to me so incomprehensible, in her hands entirely. Later, however, when I gained experience, I began making independent suggestions. These she always heeded and later carried out with great willingness. Only twice—and that happened much later—did I have to interfere and personally investigate a quarrel. The old woman was right. I had not yet seen the difference between unimportant details and circumstances worthy of attention.

All our doctors, with one exception, came from the same hospital in Moscow. They were men of thorough training, knew their business, worked in unity. The superintendent was, on the other hand, very young and quite inexperienced, with no idea whatsoever of the way to manage a large hospital.

The head doctor was invested with full powers and, although in his particular field extremely able, he did not know how to maintain discipline; his subordinates soon became slack, especially the orderlies.

As head nurse I had no duties in the wards and as this left me not enough work to occupy me, I started helping in the operating- and bandaging-rooms—work which from the first had fascinated me. After a while the doctors were giving me the most difficult and important dressings to do, and no operation was ever performed without me. If something unexpected occurred in the night, I would be called from my warm bed and, throwing a smock over my nightgown, I would run shivering into the operating-room. Later when we had so many patients that the five doctors could not attend to all the work, I had of necessity to perform some slight operations such as extracting a bullet or amputating a finger. At first the responsibility frightened me tremendously, but I soon grew accustomed to it. Sometimes it happened that I had to administer the anæsthetic and, if we had many operations, I would become myself somewhat chloroformed and would leave the operating-room walking unsteadily, as if drunk.

We had hard days. When in 1915 the front drew nearer and we were obliged to increase the number of our beds, we sometimes received very large parties of wounded. Then we would work unceasingly, day and night. The wounded arrived from the front in such a condition that two or three baths were needed to take off all the grime accumulated during their long months in the trenches. Hair was to be shaved, clothing burned. The front was only about one hundred and fifty miles from Pskov but the wounded men we received had generally spent several days travelling that distance, in goods trucks without any care. Their bandages were as stiff as if they had been made of wood, saturated with clotted blood, soiled with pus and vermin. To remove such bandages was almost as painful to the nurse as to the patient. I ought to say here that there were a considerable number of well-equipped hospital trains running between the front and the rear, but somehow never enough of them. We saw them very seldom, for they went directly, most of them, by special schedules, to St. Petersburg or to Tsarskoie-Selo, and stopped at Pskov only if patients stood in immediate need of an operation. The sort of trucks we received, loaded with dirt, suffering, neglect, and misery, were seldom shown in the capital and were usually sent to provincial towns.

At the beginning of the war the military department had prepared over twenty thousand beds at Pskov for the wounded, and the entire town now had the appearance of a vast hospital. All the school buildings had been requisitioned in whole or in part, a circumstance which aroused countless misunderstandings and quarrels with the school authorities. There was also a feud, long standing, between the military department and the Red Cross.

The Red Cross was an independent organization. It had large sums at its disposal and was able to equip its nursing homes in a manner that aroused the envy of those in the hospitals of the military department, institutions run on very small subsidies, inadequately equipped, and of a personnel not only insufficient, but often inexperienced.

Having received reports of scandalous neglect and mismanagement in these military hospitals, I decided soon after my arrival in Pskov to investigate. This I could do only superficially, as I had no official power; but I started without announcement to visit the military hospitals, seeking always to arrive at an unexpected hour. By the fright displayed by officials and attendants during those unexpected visits of mine, I could see that many consciences were uneasy. I remember especially clearly one such visit that I paid to the barracks where there were several hundred sick and wounded prisoners of war. Our first difficulty was in finding the doctor on duty. Finally he came running, his face sleepy and swollen. The linen in the wards as well as the patients themselves were dirty; and apparently they were badly fed for they all looked exhausted and weak. The bandaging-room was far from clean. Everything was in such a state of disorder that I found it necessary on this occasion to overcome my timidity; I sent for the head doctor and scolded him soundly. It was the first time in my life that I ever scolded anyone. The head doctor, a gynæcologist, was so frightened that he could hardly answer me for stammering.

Several such inspections convinced me that the military hospitals needed help, if only with linen and bandaging supplies. I wrote a letter to the Empress, asking her if she could do something for them. It would have been for her an easy matter; she had organized a workshop in the Winter Palace and had there created a storeroom of linen and hospital supplies; but her reply to my suggestion was in no sense encouraging. She hinted that I was meddling in what did not concern me, that I would do better to concentrate on my own duties. She had, however, her letter ended, been planning to come to Pskov anyway, and she then could verify the correctness of my account. So my first attempt to show initiative was not much of a success.

The Empress did come to Pskov, but this did not improve the situation in the military hospitals. Late one evening in, I think, November, the Governor of Pskov arrived at the hospital, bearing a telegram. He told me that the Empress Alexandra was coming to Pskov next morning but had asked that I be not informed; it was all to be a surprise. We nevertheless discussed the details of the reception and made a schedule for the day, well knowing that such a visit could not be permitted to proceed unplanned. For one thing, she had, because of her bad heart, always to be carried upstairs; and men and chairs had to be provided beforehand.

I went to the station to meet the train. The Empress was astonished to see me there, and disappointed that she had failed to surprise me. She seemed not to realize that such an event as a visit of the Empress of Russia to the city of Pskov could not pass casually or unnoticed. Directly from the station she drove with me to my hospital and was met by the personnel and the pupils of the Ecclesiastical School, headed by their directress. The Empress was accompanied by two of her daughters and by Mme. Vyrubova. They were all dressed in nurses' uniforms. The wounded, who had been told beforehand of the Empress's visit, were plainly disconcerted by the sight of these four nurses all dressed exactly alike. Their faces throughout the wards expressed surprise and even some disappointment; it was as if they could not imagine that one of these women could be their Tsaritsa.

The Empress, who spoke Russian very well, made the round of the wards and talked at length with every patient. I was walking behind her and did not so much listen to words, always the same, as watch faces. No matter how sincerely the Empress sympathized with the men's suffering, no matter how she tried to express it, there was something in her, eluding definition, that prevented her from communicating her own genuine feelings and from comforting the person she addressed. Although she spoke Russian quite correctly and almost without any foreign accent, the men did not appear to understand her; her words remained to them distant and inscrutable. They watched her move about the ward with eyes that were anxious and frightened, and their expressions did not change after she had approached and spoken.

I have many times been present when the Emperor visited hospitals. That was quite different. The Emperor possessed real simplicity and exceptional charm. His entrance seemed immediately to create a special atmosphere, grave yet uplifted. In spite of his small stature he always seemed taller than anyone else in the room, and he moved from bed to bed with an extraordinary dignity. After he had talked with the patients a few minutes, the expression of anxious expectation in their eyes would be replaced by one of rapt contentment. His own eyes were grey and luminous. They radiated life and warmth and established in the person addressed an almost mystic sense of contact. I have often seen patients, after the Emperor had walked away from a bed, close their eyes as if to retain his image in complete and blissful beatitude.

From my hospital the Empress made the round of several military hospitals. I accompanied her. She invited me to lunch in her train, and after visiting the local chapter of the Red Cross, left Pskov. It surprised me that a person of her precarious health could endure such a long and fatiguing day; I was so tired myself that, returning to the hospital, I was obliged to lie down for a while.

Trifling but entirely characteristic was an incident just before her departure. Pskov had a large Military School of Cadets. I knew its director. The older class of cadets, boys of eighteen or twenty years of age, was graduating and leaving, to go soon after to the front. The director asked me if the cadets might have the joy of seeing the Empress before they went to war; and I of course promised to arrange it when I met her at the station that morning.

To my great surprise the Empress absolutely refused to acquiesce to the request and none of my arguments were of the least avail. She said that she had come to visit the hospitals, not the School of Cadets. Placed in an awkward position, I telephoned the director that the Empress was tired and could not come but that, as the school building was on our way to the station, he might draw up his boys in front of the building as we passed.

He followed my suggestion. The sound of the cadet band reached us when we were still at some distance from the school, and as we drew nearer we could see the straight ranks of the boys, standing at attention. I suggested that we stop just for a second, but she refused even that. Fortunately, however, the coachman held the horses back, and we drove slowly past the cadets. Her face a spotty red from confusion, the Empress bowed stiffly. She did not, however, guess that I was responsible for this annoyance, so I escaped a chiding.

Such conduct—which was, as I have said, representative of the Empress, rather than otherwise, at that period of her life—grew, I think, out of an almost fanatical absorption in home affairs that left her no affection or consideration to expend elsewhere. For years before the war she had shut herself within her family circle; and, since the birth of the heir to the throne, had devoted herself wholly to his care. His health, from the first precarious, had not improved with the years; there were days when it seemed that all hope must be abandoned. Watching the course of the terrible disease in her son, this poor mother became more and more distracted, and lost in a measure, I think it may be said, her mental equilibrium. Only the most official ceremonies, those which it was impossible to avoid, now took place at the court; and these ceremonies were now the only connexion of the imperial couple with the outside world. They lived in such seclusion that word to them or from them had to be passed through people often ignorant and sometimes unworthy.

Upon the declaration of war the Empress, like the rest of us, felt the need of participating in the common cause. Her maternal instinct led her to choose as her war work the same which, for other reasons, I myself had chosen. She undertook the care of the wounded, or thought she did, forgetting that Russia had thousands of women perfectly able to do this work, while she alone, as Empress, could arouse emotions and inspire loyalties which no one else could. But she had already grown accustomed to looking upon herself only as a mother and a nurse and, having donned a nurse's uniform, she worked in a hospital at Tsarskoie-Selo, unconscious of the larger encouragement, that was daily becoming more necessary to Russia as a whole. She came to Pskov to visit hospitals as a nurse. She had no time to see healthy youths eager to give their

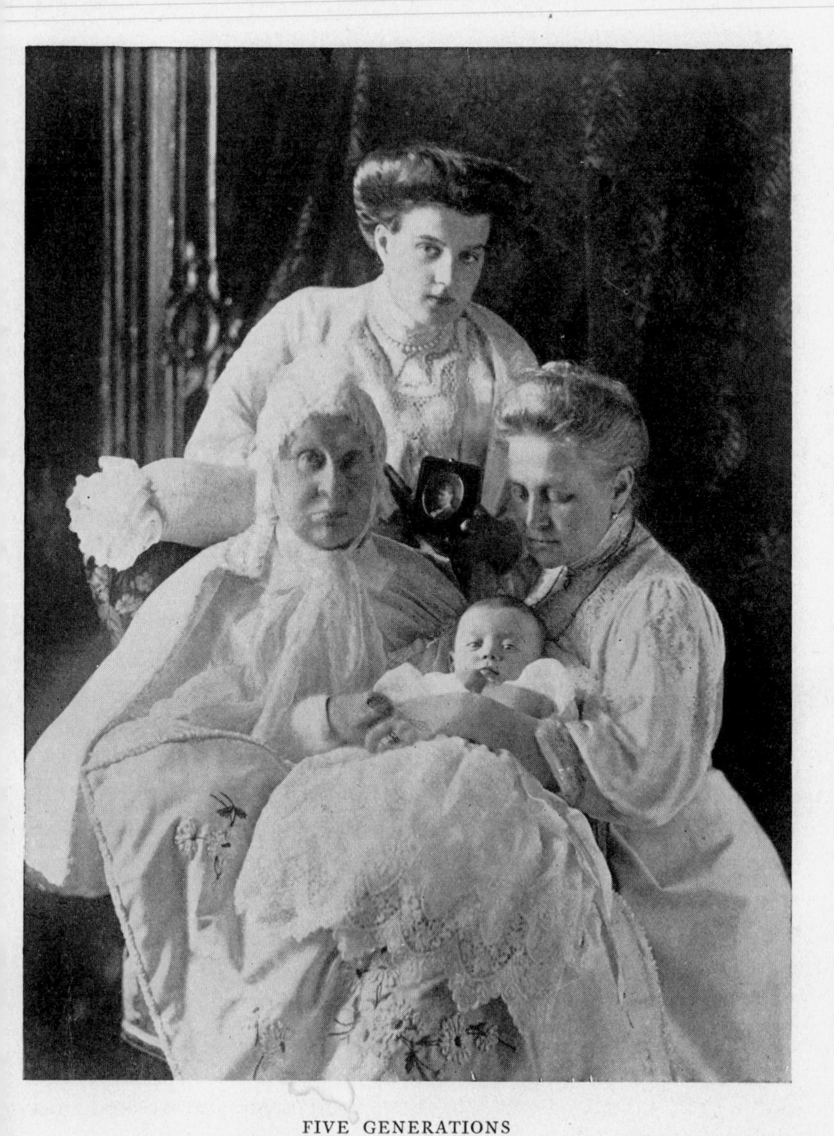

FIVE GENERATIONS

The Grand Duchess Marie, with a photograph of her mother, stands behind her great-grandmother, the Grand Duchess Alexandra, and her grandmother, Queen Olga of Greece, who are holding her son, Prince Lennart

lives, if need be, for the sake of their Fatherland and their Tsar, her husband.

I do not mean to speak unkindly, nor to dwell on these small, but ultimately tragic deficiencies of an unfortunate woman. I must own, however, that her attitude towards the other feminine members of the royal family who showed any initiative or independence bore a kind of unavowed jealousy. The restrictions that she placed upon us sometimes descended to rather absurd trivialities. Once, when paying her a visit in the Alexander Palace, I happened to speak of the diversion I found in going skiing on occasional Sunday afternoons with cadets from the Pskov Military School. The Empress disapproved and asked me in the future not to repeat such excursions. I was head nurse, she pointed out, at a hospital. Very well, then; let my interests and activities end there.

Such incidents, while trivial, express, I think, something of that increasing inner rigidity and that fading sense of proportion which in this unhappy mother, who chanced also to be Empress of all Russia, could not but sway the judgments of her husband, the Emperor; and through him send forth undercurrents of incalculable effect on history.

ii

Towards the close of 1915, early in December, I took two weeks off and visited my father at Tsarskoie-Selo and my aunt at Moscow.

My aunt had greatly changed during the last few years. In spite of the fact that she was living in a nunnery, she came now into contact with a greater number and variety of people. This had broadened her outlook, made her softer, more human. Not only did she come face to face with phases of life of which previously she had known nothing, but she had now to take into account opinions and viewpoints entirely at variance with her own. She remained, however, always a little puzzled, never quite able to attain a complete balance. Seeking in Orthodoxy to build her life and by Orthodoxy to establish a religious order firmly founded upon ancient Russian precepts and customs, she still remained a foreigner in her psychology, and her attempts seemed often naïve and unco-ordinated.

But the atmosphere that she had created around herself revealed so clearly and so charmingly her inner self, that in spite of all my love for life, I was attracted.

In contrast to her sister, the Empress, my aunt clearly understood that she had no right to bury herself entirely in her own affairs and preoccupations. She never ceased to participate in charities quite apart from those of her nunnery, and during the war enlarged her outside work tremendously. Yet deep within her heart she harboured the dream of retiring completely from the world, even from the management of her beloved nunnery. She wanted to go to a hermitage, and secretly hoped that I would replace her at her post. She never tried directly to influence me in this direction, but she watched attentively my spiritual growth and the direction it was taking. As in Sweden, at a certain time of my life, so now during the war, although for entirely different reasons, I was not averse to this thought and, strange as it may seem, were it not for the Revolution, perhaps today I would have been Abbess of the Martha-Mary Convent of the Sisters of Pity.

During my trip to St. Petersburg and Moscow I heard many things which did not reach Pskov, where we were reading only newspapers censored strictly to official data. The war apparently was going to last a long time. There would be no easy victory; the struggle promised to be fierce. A wave of superficial nationalism had engulfed the capitals and was expressed, among other things, in the accusation of pro-Germanism against both the Empress Alexandra and my aunt the Grand Duchess Elizabeth. The rumours spread in this connexion were absurd in their stupidity and pettiness.

I learned moreover that Russian rule was being enforced in

occupied Galicia in spite of the promises to the contrary, and that uniatism was being uprooted. Poland, uplifted by the manifesto of the Grand Duke Nicholas, granting various liberties, was now losing confidence in the sincerity of Russia's expressed intentions.

And at home, that enthusiasm which had swept us all off our feet in the beginning of the war, even in spite of certain losses, had definitely begun to subside.

CHAPTER XVII

FRIENDS

RETURNING just before Christmas to my hospital in Pskov, I found there, as a patient newly arrived, the Archimandrite Michael. Paralyzed, he had been taken seriously ill at his monastery near Pskov, and had been received at my hospital at the special request of Aunt Ella. Both he and his former teacher, Father Gabriel, were old friends of hers. They had retired from actual work and lived together in their poor monastery. Father Gabriel was my aunt's confessor.

Father Michael, when still a very young man, had been nominated the dean of a seminary in a large provincial town. During the disorders of 1905, one of the pupils shot him in the back, injuring his spine, and ever since then his body had been paralysed from the waist down. He spent his time in bed or, when he felt strong enough, in a wheel-chair.

At the time when I met him he was not yet forty and had already been for nine years an invalid. Thoroughly capable, well educated and intelligent, he had been robbed by his assailant of a brilliant career; but he bore his infirmity with great patience and simplicity and preserved an astonishing buoyancy of spirit. This even-tempered, gentle, and gay man turned in his suffering to spiritual interests entirely, yet refrained from forcing these interests on other people. He was one of the few persons I have ever known in whom a genuine spiritual loftiness did not seem, at times, rather oppressive.

He had erysipelas when he came to our hospital, and to receive him was against all rules; but my aunt's influence prevailed. I had him isolated from the rest of the patients in a large room, adjoining the apartment of the directress, in which I lived.

For some days he lay at the point of death, then slowly recovered. I went to see him quite often, for Aunt's sake, but when he was convalescing, we both felt constrained and my visits were short. From my early youth, ever since the time Uncle Serge had appointed the red-haired priest to teach us religion, I had retained for all the clergy an instinctive dislike. To me they did not seem to be men, but some kind of vague creatures always uttering the same words, and thinking always the same identical and servile thoughts. One had to speak a different language with them and to conduct oneself differently, with a pretence of almost inhuman virtue. A clergyman, it seemed to me, was supposed constantly to maintain authority without probing its essence, for all power came from God. This sounded to me false, and falsity I despised.

But Father Michael's simplicity quickly disarmed me. He never uttered the stilted phrases proper to various occasions, as I had expected him to; and I came to see him not as a priest but as a man, and a very unusual one. His embarrassment, mainly produced by the feeling that a woman had somehow penetrated into his monastic way of thinking, disappeared little by little, and he began to show interest in me as in a human being.

Thus began our friendship. My short visits were lengthened, our conversations became more and more interesting. We discussed everything, from newspaper reports to the most trifling details of everyday life. This contact filled a certain void in my life. Having worked all day long among people, I used previously to spend my evenings alone in my room reading or writing, but now after supper I went to see Father Michael.

Dr. V. I. Tishin, who was in charge of Father Michael's case, often joined us. Of all our large personnel only two people possessed definite personality and character—the old nurse Zandina and Dr. Tishin. He was born in Moscow and came from a family of Old Believers, of modest means but strong principles. In spite of the surroundings in which he grew, he had succeeded in entering the Medical Faculty of the University of Moscow. After graduating he had gone to Switzerland to continue his education.

His unusual intellect made Tishin, while still comparatively young, an outstanding figure among his colleagues at the hospital. He loved his vocation and worked with enthusiasm, seeking continually to increase his knowledge and his command of it. Having studied Röntgenology before the war, he fitted out in our hospital a splendid X-ray cabinet, that served also for the other hospitals of Pskov.

My desire to go to the core of things drew me continually towards Dr. Tishin, and he always gave me clear and detailed explanations. I worked under his guidance not only in the laboratory but also in the X-ray cabinet. I took notes on much that he told me, and added greatly to my knowledge and to the scope of my interests.

It would be difficult to imagine people more different at first glance than Father Michael, Dr. Tishin, and myself. One was a monk, the son of a provincial priest, a man of high spiritual standards and culture, who had suffered great moral affliction and withdrawn from life. The second, an intellectual, born of a poor family and brought up on pennies, who had won his way solely because of his own capability and energy, a man honest and sincere, but an unbeliever, indifferent to ideas which did not correspond to his own. Finally, I, brought up in all the traditions, all the prejudices of my milieu, which still constituted my outlook, inexperienced and naïve, with unformed opinions, but avid of every escape into other worlds. There grew up between the three of us, in spite of all these differences, a friendship which remained unmarred during the two and a half years that we were together. This friendship left a deep impression on me and affected all my future life. When by the turn of events we were forced in different directions, with little probability of ever meeting again, I felt that I was parting with people very dear and close to me. They gave me what no one else had ever given me—they gave me a chance to grow—and prepared me, each in his way, for what was to happen later. Without them, I do not know what means I should now have to live.

Father Michael gave an inner meaning and beauty to spiritual beliefs and teachings which formerly were but empty sounds to me. From childhood I had seen in the religion of those surrounding me either superficial sentimentality, or official pompousness, or disciplinary measures for the safe conduct of both private and social life. The insincerity of such a religion had always irked me. But the talks that I had with Father Michael showed me clearly that Orthodoxy was a part of the Russian soul, that it was closely connected with the psychology of the people, that it was broad in its viewpoint and full of a poetry both simple and profound. Under his guidance I began a new study of Orthodoxy from this point of view, and imbibed its true spirit. We read together the works of the fathers of the church and studied the regulations of church services and the Bible. Religion became alive to me. Father Michael accompanied these readings with explanations and stories of his own experiences; he described to me life in the monasteries and told me of the touching and curious customs of the Russian clergy.

Tishin, on the other hand, personified for me points of view and opinions entirely contrary to those in which I had been brought up. I had only suspected their existence and had never known exactly what they were. While not a revolutionary nor an "uprooter of foundations," as they called radicals in Russia, Tishin was radically inclined, although himself unallied to any party. In his youth he had never taken part in students' riots, so frequent in those days. Owing to his upbringing as an Old Believer, he had conserved a certain respect for religious as well as social principles in which he personally was unable to believe.

I represented to him a principle in which he did not believe but which he respected; and his attitude towards me was one of thoughtful consideration. He carefully sought to broaden my outlook and tried little by little to destroy in me all preconceived opinions.

He argued so well, and was so logical, that at times, not knowing what to say and how to answer, the only thing that remained to me was to get angry. I had no political or social training and so was unable to enter into such a discussion; Father Michael and Dr. Tishin were therefore the chief speakers, while I sat silent, listening attentively, trying to form a definite opinion. But in the beginning I was unable to do even that, so far did I stand from the public in general and from the questions that were agitating all of Russia.

Father Michael and Dr. Tishin often disagreed, but it was precisely these differences of opinion which were of service to me. There was however one question on which they invariably agreed and that question was myself. Neither of them could understand my painful modesty, my desire to efface myself, and the complete absence in me of any assertion of authority. Father Michael, who welcomed meekness in church life, found it out of place in worldly duties and especially in my case, for my position demanded the shouldering of certain obligations and the assumption of a certain amount of power.

Tishin knew only too well the laxness of discipline in our hospital, a laxness arising from a want of firmness on the part of the head doctor. He had heard also of the neglect and the disorderly organization in the military hospitals of the town. He felt—and Father Michael supported him—that I should assert myself and take the hospital and sanitary organizations in my hands. I was unable to explain to them at that time that every manifestation of will had been from my earliest childhood systematically uprooted, and that even now any display of initiative on my part would meet with disapproval in the circles upon which I depended.

My teachers insisted that my moral helplessness was no defence, especially in these days of mediocrity and narrow-mindedness which had engulfed Russia. They saw it as, first of all, a source of danger to myself, to rest thus unprepared for struggle and unable to uphold my own, except desperately, when driven to extremity.

The process of my re-education was painful and slow. It was, I remember, just about at this time that the nurses became involved in a scandal of such dimensions that it fell outside the jurisdiction of Zandina, and I had to look into the thing myself. I had to conduct an investigation and question each nurse separately. I kept on putting it off until one day Tishin came to see me and made me cry, shaming me for my pusillanimity. I took up the matter and having concluded it, I do not know how, I cried again, this time as a relaxation from the nervous strain.

Another time I was forced, willy-nilly, to intervene in a quarrel between two nurses which took place in the bandaging-room in my presence. Under Tishin's stern glance I led the nurses to my room, but there, before I was able to say a word, I burst into tears. It happened in this case, that my tears produced a better effect than any scolding. The nurses rushed to me, kissed my hands, and made up immediately!

ii

GRADUALLY, however, I became stronger and began to assume power.

The head doctor had spoiled his subordinates outrageously. I was struck during the Easter festivities of 1915 by the extreme luxury of our table—a luxury little in keeping with the conditions of the time. I sent for the superintendent and learned that there existed only a vague accounting of running expenses. This accounting he did not himself keep, but sent requisitions to the Red Cross whenever necessary. He was in all probability within his rights; the Red Cross did not seem to verify the accounts, made no inquiries as to expenditures, and always sent the money demanded. But I gasped to hear the sum spent each month for the upkeep of our hospital.

In Sweden—although there, as elsewhere, I had never touched money nor managed my own affairs—I had learned of the practice, there general, of living according to a certain budget prepared beforehand. And in spite of my inexperience in household and business matters, I determined, with great confidence, that I would myself straighten out this practical problem in hospital management.

I took all the account books and with the help of Father Michael began to verify them. We spent several weeks over these books, using the abacus, adding small bills into immense sums, looking over the vouchers and requisitions. Whenever I met the head doctor, he pulled nervously at his moustache, not daring to ask about the progress of my work; and the superintendent looked at me with round, frightened eyes. But I paid no attention to their embarrassment and was not concerned whether they knew or not that I suspected them. The accounts were in a state of disorder and neglect that bordered on dishonesty, if it did not indeed shield actual graft.

There had been no system whatsoever. Provisions were bought at any price, used without supervision, and the items never checked. Crossing out old sins, I established new rules and in a short time obtained excellent results. From the start I encountered nothing but opposition; it took a great effort to uproot the careless habits which were everywhere deeply rooted, and this effort made more work for me. I had to learn the prices from the weekly bulletins issued by the local commissariat and in accordance with these prices plan the menus. I had also to be present in the kitchen at the delivery of the provisions. But our expenditure was noticeably lower and, although we no longer ate game and fowl, we still had a very good table.

But I remained unsatisfied with these results. The abuses in management that I had uncovered in my own hospital led me to think that similar mismanagement would probably be found also in other war organizations under the auspices of the Red Cross. I wrote to Mlle. Hélène, my old governess, who occupied an important position at Red Cross Headquarters and, never doubting that she would appreciate my zeal, asked for information on this point. I described in detail the state of our book-keeping, my efforts to bring it into order, and the results I had attained. I pointed out that it would be easy to avoid similar disorders provided that certain rather simple measures, which I indicated, were taken and a firm control instituted.

I was inexperienced, and did not know that I was fighting windmills. Mlle. Hélène saw in my words something quite supererogatory and, frightened by the new direction my work was taking, she came to Pskov. As I told her with pride of all my achievements, she listened distrustfully and without interest. She herself, I noticed with some surprise, understood very little of the questions of practical organization. Neither did she understand my plans for a more strict control and the periodical examination of accounts. She said that this, if it were done at all, was done by some department of which she knew nothing, and which was certainly not her own.

She paid, on the other hand, great attention to the length of our nurses' dresses, demanded that their hair be not curled, that they wear thick stockings, and that their head-dresses be made according to the standard Red Cross pattern. These standards, she said, had now been legalized, in a sense, by time and usage, as had also the set of procedures for provisioning and accounting; and to seek faults or suggest changes was in rather bad taste.

Our conversation revealed to me clearly how far I had outdistanced myself and showed me the deep abyss that had opened between my present mental attitude and that of my milieu.

My former governess's indifference to my practical suggestions considerably cheered both the head doctor and the superintendent. She was the chairman of the Executive Committee of the hospital school from which all the nurses and myself had graduated and therefore our immediate superior. The personnel, which had quivered at her visit, soon saw that they had nothing to fear; her inspection of all phases of our hospital life was equally superficial. Her visit disappointed and depressed me. Besides, it sapped the authority which I had been at such pains to attain. I did not completely give up the idea of control and examination of accounts. I tried to carry it into effect in spite of her; but in the end I became convinced of the uselessness of reforms which no one really wanted, and gave them up. Since this seemed to leave me no really important work to do, I busied myself with tasks less significant.

iii

From time to time, I came into contact with the pupils of the Ecclesiastical School in whose building our hospital was quartered. I came also into contact with the bearded priests of the school's board of directors, and with the directress, who embodied all of the traditions of this school for the daughters of the clergy. With the elders, my relations were anything but pleasant—especially when we were obliged to requisition the entire building for our use.

But the girls were a delight. To them our hospital was a source of continual interest and rare entertainment. Between classes the entire school would gather on the landing of the second floor in front of the church, and the girls' heads hung like grapes over the balusters, as they watched our every movement. The slightest mark of attention on my part they received with rapture. Noting this, and wishing to know them better, I sometimes joined them during their play-time in the yard.

They were of a class of curious traditions and standards.

Since ancient times, the Russian clergy had formed a separate and distinct caste with its own peculiar customs.

Persons of clerical extraction could be recognized by their names. The daughters of the clergy were educated in ecclesiastical schools for girls. The sons were sent to seminaries from which some proceeded to ecclesiastical academies. Graduating from the academies, they sometimes became monks and found a career among the black clergy; or they devoted themselves to pedagogy. Most often, however, the pupils of seminaries and academies were ordained as priests and, before ordination, had to be married. Parishes, particularly those in villages, passed as a matter of course from father to son; and in families with no sons, the priest chose his own successor, marrying him to one of his daughters.

The graduating seminarist, when the time came to wed, married a pupil of an ecclesiastical school, coming there purposely to choose his future wife; this was deemed simpler and easier than travelling throughout the province in search of a mate. There was probably, moreover, a sounder reason: for the difference in interests, the fundamental dissimilarity in the curricula of lay and clerical schools, created in these youths an altogether peculiar psychology; they thought and acted quite differently from lay children.

Some years before the war, under the influence of progressive ideas, innovations began to penetrate even into this clerical class of Russian society. Children of clergymen had begun to choose other professions; but still very few laymen became priests.

So far as I was able to observe, the education given those girls in the ecclesiastical school corresponded in no way to the conditions of life from which they came, and into which they would return. It was a boarding school and the parents were in most cases so poor that their daughters could not be brought home during the winter vacations, but only in the summer, spending thus nine months of the year in school.

Discipline was strict, even monastic; the pupils spent many hours in church and observed all the fasts. The chief subjects of the curriculum were religious. No attention was paid to practical subjects. The girls knew how to embroider, to play the piano, to sing in the choir, and that was all. Sport was of course taboo. They wore dresses of thick material, tight in the waist. Almost without exception they were pale, undernourished, sickly-looking. Returning to their villages to families for the most part poverty-stricken, they did not return with either that health which might have regenerated this sickly ecclesiastical class, nor the useful knowledge which might have transformed village and country life.

At first shy in my presence, the girls grew quickly accustomed to me and readily answered all my questions. I became especially friendly with the class that graduated in the spring of 1915, assisting, at the request of the pupils, at their commencement exercises and afterwards attending a gala dinner. In the interval between the exercises and the dinner, I went with the girls into the garden; and one of them, sitting astride on the wall, entertained us by singing factory songs, accompanying herself on the balalaika. That comical figure on the wall in the brown uniform and white cape, the balalaika, and especially the words of the factory song made such a contrast with the bishop, the stiff and stern directress, and the solemn and sanctimonious atmosphere of the commencement, that the girls and I laughed to the point of tears.

Next day we said good-bye almost tearfully and many of the pupils kept writing me long afterwards from their remote villages throughout the province.

iv

OCCASIONALLY, as time permitted, I made short visits to my father at Tsarskoie-Selo. Our troops were experiencing in that winter of 1915-1916 another series of reverses, due, it was said, to a shortage of ammunition. Our work multiplied; I was pretty well tired out, and needed a rest.

The house in Tsarskoie-Selo which my father and his wife were building with such love, and in which they expected to spend the rest of their lives, was now to all appearances completed. There were still some details to attend to, but these were to be done after the end of the war. The collections brought from Paris were in their places, the glass cases were filled with valuable porcelains, Chinese stone knick-knacks, antique silver, beautiful cut glass. Pictures and portraits hung on the walls, the rooms were furnished with magnificent antique pieces. All these things had been selected by my father and his wife with special care and each represented to them some pleasant memory.

Father had changed very little during all these years. At the age of fifty-five he had the figure of a youth and could still make me laugh to tears over stories and anecdotes which he told incomparably. He had transferred to Tsarskoie-Selo all the habits so well known to me and so beloved; his dressing-room was permeated by the scent of the perfume he always used, and his clothes were laid out in the same way upon the spare bed.

Exactly as of old, we went for a walk at eleven in the morning; exactly as of old, he took his nap between lunch and tea-time; while after dinner, as in days gone by, we gathered in his study while he read aloud. In spite of the fact that now my life was filled with entirely new and different interests, that I myself was imperceptibly changing, I always returned with joy to this well-known home atmosphere. It seemed at that time that outside of the stress and self-forgetful atmosphere of my hospital I could find pleasure and peacefulness only in my father's society and in his house.

CHAPTER XVIII

DEATH

EARLY in the winter of 1916, our sector of the front became active and our hospital filled with wounded. The railway station of Pskov, as in many other provincial Russian cities, was some distance from the town; it was more than two miles from our hospital and that made the transportation of our wounded a real problem. I made known to St. Petersburg our lack of transportation facilities, and as a temporary expedient mobilized the older pupils of all the schools of Pskov who were strong enough to carry stretchers.

Followed by a crowd of young stretcher-bearers, I used to go out to the goods station in an open field outside the town and direct the unloading. Men lightly wounded I sent to town afoot accompanied by nurses. The others we carried out of the trucks and placed on the stretchers. The file of stretcher-bearers often extended over the whole length of the highway, moving slowly, often stumbling in deep snow. Some days we had to make two trips; and one such day, when it was unusually cold, I got my feet badly frostbitten. In spite of this, I continued at this work until ambulances were finally provided.

My frostbitten feet gave me some trouble, but I could not often afford to think about them. We were all of us constantly busy—on our feet all day long in the rank air of bandaging- or operating-rooms, or in the wards. Cries and groans, bodies motionless under the spell of anæsthetics, surgical instruments, blood-stained bandages—these all became in time part of our familiar surroundings. Our feet swelled in our shoes, our hands grew red and raw from constant washing and disinfect-

THE GRAND DUCHESS MARIE

A camera portrait in 1911

ing; yet, in spite of all, we worked on tirelessly, with concentration and enthusiasm.

Once Dmitri, passing through the town on his way to the front, came to see me at the hospital without letting me know beforehand. I was in the operating-room when they told me of his arrival. I washed my hands but did not glance into the mirror and ran out into the hall where he was waiting. His attitude in regard to my capabilities as a nurse had always been tinged with mistrust, but this time he looked at me with a shade of awe.

"What have you been doing?" he asked without further greeting. "Murdering someone?"

My face and the front of my smock were covered with blood. From that time on, Dmitri was convinced that I was at the apex of my calling.

The endless suffering constantly surrounding us at first depressed me terribly and tired me more than the actual work. I was especially impressed if I had to pass through the wards at night. These immense rooms were dimly lighted by a single lamp on the desk of the nurse on duty, and this lamp was usually shaded so that its light fell upon the book in front of the nurse. There was quiet except for the heavy breathing of certain of the patients, and then suddenly there would come from out the darkness a choked, moaning cry. Some of the patients snored and once in a while one talked in his sleep or sighed heavily. It seemed to me always that with the coming of darkness suffering took on shape and lived its own peculiar life, awaiting only the opportune moment in which to creep upon its victim, and bear him down when he was least prepared for struggle. I felt at times a hysterical impulse to confront these phantoms, or to call to the patients and warn them of their danger.

Most deaths came between three and five in the morning, and though I lived, so to say, side by side with the dark angel, I was never able to grow accustomed to his triumphs. The simplicity with which our soldiers met their end did not comfort, it frightened me. Their spiritual resignation was too complete; they accepted death meekly enough; but in their bodies still resided the will to live, and fought to the very end.

So many of our patients were still young, strong, and sturdy in appearance; they had not been sick long enough to lose an appearance of life and health; and their last struggles were especially painful to see.

As life struggled with death I would watch with dread and terror, waiting for the last sigh, gazing fearfully upon the body suddenly grown rigid and lifeless.

Some, as they felt their end approaching, insisted on talking with me, expressing last wishes, sending messages to relatives. I dreaded these conversations, yet could never take it upon myself to avoid them.

Two of our deaths I remember particularly. One day a soldier was brought to us with several severe wounds and a fractured skull. He had lost the use of his tongue, and it was not possible to determine exactly whether this was because of the fractured skull or from some other reason. He had no identification papers, and he did not know how to write, so that no one was able to tell who he was nor where he came from. With no chance whatsoever of recovery, he lived on for several days. Most of the time he was unconscious, and during those rare moments when consciousness returned to him, his dark, deep-set eyes wandered silently over his surroundings. He neither mumbled nor moaned, and his lips did not move; he only looked at us, and all that he wanted and could not say was concentrated in his eyes.

I came often to his bed and every morning I dressed his terrible wounds. It seemed that he recognized me. A few minutes before his death I stood above him, looking down on his small, tanned, pitiful face. Slowly he lifted his eyelids and turned his head towards me. It was plain that he was now fully conscious and that he knew me. He looked at me attentively for a long time, then his face lighted with a barely noticeable, wavering, tender smile. I bent over him. Two tears appeared in the eyes still fixed upon me and slowly rolled down his cheeks. Then, with a scarcely audible sigh, he died.

The other death that I shall always remember was that of a child. She was the daughter of the young priest who performed in our hospital the services for the dead. This priest had been recently widowed; and since the white clergy of Russia were required to marry before ordination, and forbidden for ever after to remarry, he had lost with his wife all possibility of family life.

His only consolation in his grief was his little daughter. She was about four or five years old. He was very poor and had no one to help him, yet the little girl was always tidy and clean. Sometimes he brought her to the hospital at my request and I gave her apples or occasionally a new dress.

Suddenly the child fell ill. Dr. Tishin went to see her and found that she had meningitis. When a few days passed and the child showed no improvement, I had her brought to the hospital and placed in a private room.

She had long spells of unconsciousness, could hardly breathe; only by the reflex movements of her hands and the shaking of her little fingers could one tell from seeing her, at times, that she was still alive. The father came to see her very often, and stood for hours in silence by her bed. It seemed that even when she was unconscious his presence gave her peace.

Two weeks passed. I was sitting, towards evening, with Father Michael and Dr. Tishin. Old Zandina came to fetch Tishin.

"Our Taniusha is going, Victor Ivanovitch. I have sent an orderly for her father."

Tishin and I went to the child's room. She lay, tensely writhing, with her head thrown back; her breath hissed and gurgled in her throat. We could do nothing. By the time her father came running she was dead.

Entering the room, he glanced at us with frightened, questioning eyes and by our silence understood what had happened. He approached the bed, knelt beside it and, putting his head upon the small white hand, remained motionless. It was simple, even ordinary; yet I have never seen such desolate yearning, such terrible suffering, as was expressed in that silent figure on the floor by the bed.

The body was placed in a coffin. Two days later her father performed the funeral service. One could clearly see that in burying her he was burying all that bound him to life. In a few weeks he left Pskov, and we learned that he had entered a monastery.

ii

WINTER passed and Easter was approaching, the greatest, the most joyous holiday of the Russian year. I tried to lend to its celebration all due solemnity, and to make of it a break in the monotony of our hospital routine. A week ahead we started preparations. Batter was mixed; suckling pigs were roasted; eggs were coloured. Under the supervision of Zandina all the wards were scoured, and every window made to shine.

Meanwhile in the church we held Holy Week services, solemn and sad, fraught with poetical and with soul-stirring meanings.

Father Michael in his wheel-chair spent almost his entire day in the chapel now, directing services, overseeing the singing; and on the eve of Easter it was he who supervised the placing of the decorations. The pupils of the Ecclesiastical School, whom otherwise we seldom saw, sang in the choir and helped us with the decorations of the church. We nurses snatched time between our work in the wards and operating-room to peep both into the church and kitchen. Animation was in the air.

The Greek Orthodox Church begins its Easter worship by a short service at midnight of Holy Sunday, followed by a mass. I invited to this service the Commander of the Armies of the Northern Front, whose headquarters were now in Pskov, the Governor of the city, and other high officials.

Long before the appointed time our wounded, dressed in new clothes, their hair thickly greased, were lined up in orderly rows. Nurses in starched, rustling aprons and head-dresses ran aimlessly up and down the stairs. Doctors, thoroughly uncomfortable in their tight uniforms and high collars, paced the landing, stumbled over their swords. Behind the ikonastasis, priests whispered, while the pupils of the school stood quietly ranked in the place assigned to the choir, exchanging sly merry glances with the wounded.

A few minutes before midnight arrived the Commander of our front accompanied by a large staff of officers and the city officials. They came into the church with a jingle of spurs, and took their places.

Now the priests came out from the altar and formed a procession. Lighted candles appeared in everybody's hands. The service began. After the first words of prayer proclaimed by the priest, the clergy intoned the verses of a hymn; and the sonorous words were taken up by the fresh young voices of the choir. Louder and louder rose the triumphant tones of the Easter psalms, more and more joyfully sounded the hymn to eternal hope and eternal life.

After the service I made the round of the wards, followed by Zandina and several orderlies who bore baskets filled with porcelain, chocolate, and soap eggs for all the wounded. The last ward I had to enter was the one where we had several patients suffering from tetanus. Three of the men, whose cases were especially serious, had boards on both sides of their beds to prevent them from falling when they had convulsions. Several strong orderlies were continually in attendance. Yet all the three smiled joyously when I came to them and placed into the hand of each a porcelain egg with a red ribbon.

This done, I rejoined the personnel, for whom also I had

prepared small gifts. And together, in high spirits, we broke our fast, separating only towards morning.

Making her report next morning, Easter Sunday, Zandina told me that the three men so ill with tetanus had died, all of them, that night. Next day three open coffins stood side by side in the church. And each of the dead men held in one hand a porcelain egg with a red ribbon.

The pupils, free on account of the holiday, offered to sing the funeral service. And again their young voices rose in joyful tones, proclaiming in the words of hymns the victory over death.

I went to the cemetery. The wooden, unpainted coffins were placed on three wagons. A priest with a cross in his hand and the choir of pupils led the procession. Then came the wagons, and behind the wagons walked Zandina and I. It was the beginning of spring and the weather was fine. The sun was becoming noticeably warmer; it was turning the snow underfoot into a deep grey mash. The rooks were rowdy; sparrows, chirping provocatively, rose in flocks from under our very feet, and the doves, cooing loudly, strutted along the walks.

All along our way, too, we heard before us the exulting chant, "Christ is Risen!", a chant drowning, fading before, again arising above a disorderly, or a harmonious, but an always triumphant peal of Easter church-bells. And at the cemetery, as we lowered the coffins into the still frozen earth to the accompaniment of those soft spring sounds, eternally young, eternally joyous, I thought that it was at this time of the year I would like to die.

And then, tired by our long walk in the deep wet snow, we returned to the hospital, riding in the same wagons which had carried the coffins.

CHAPTER XIX

DISSOLUTION

IT was only when I made brief excursions into the outer, civilian world that I became really depressed. There, everybody, without exception, complained, criticized, was horrified; yet it was all so ineffectual, so impotent. The unfortunate course of internal politics seemed not only a condition, but an excuse, a cause for doing nothing. I was always glad to get back to my hospital, or, if I were visiting at Tsarskoie, to my father's house.

He, at least, seemed to be sustained by courage, wisdom, and the power of abstract reasoning. The Crowd's moods left him untouched. He followed attentively, though not without agitation, the unfoldment of fanatical developments and the changed psychology at court. The Empress devoted herself completely to the care of the wounded; the Emperor continually visited the front. Their lack of popularity increased while Rasputin's influence was mounting, and the tides of gossip about him spread farther, day by day. All this talk contributed to the glorification of Rasputin, especially in the eyes of dishonest men who sought through him to obtain important posts.

On all hands, the Empress was criticized violently, and continually accused, quite unfairly, of desiring a separate peace.

My aunt Ella, the Empress's sister, was also under incessant attack. During the anti-German demonstrations in Moscow a crowd had gathered in front of her nunnery, shouting insults and threats.

This news, when I heard it, led me to ponder seriously for the first time, I think, on the peculiar instability of Russian public opinion. In Sweden, I reflected, the crowd mind moved always in some measure according to reason, unswayed by that instinctive distrust of the ruling class that here was evident. My aunt's life, works, and loyalties, were certainly writ large, as on an open book, to all of Moscow. She had lived many years in Moscow. She had done a great deal of good. Everybody knew her by sight. Her benefactions were innumerable, some of them of a public character; and she had been, almost to the moment of the crowd surge against her, the object of general veneration and enthusiasm.

But Russians, in their very nature, it seems, pass quickly from the highest enthusiasm to complete dejection and distrust. They yield to their moods quite sincerely and go the whole way, entirely forgetting all moods preceding and opposite. They do not see any contradiction in such behaviour; or if they do, they readily find excuses for it.

Incurable pessimists, they actually dislike to look forward with hope, and prefer to expect of the future nothing but misfortune. To rise, to fight, to ward off such misfortune, seems so hard as to make such effort futile; and, thus reduced by their own reasoning to inaction, they complainingly await the realization of all their forebodings.

Strenuous action, resistance to fate, would permit them, moreover, hardly time enough for their favourite pastime—talk, analysis, criticism—tearing situations, characters, movements, mercilessly to tatters.

During these few months of the war the public mood had changed completely. Enthusiasm had disappeared; there seemed no longer any urge to unite in a common cause. The high fires which at first had driven us forward now had died.

Our driving force—the tremendous rusted engine of Russian governmental life—had been set in motion at higher speeds without ever having been repaired, or even oiled. And now that it was cracking, no one seemed to know what to do. The oldest and most trusted of our leaders stood by, shaking their heads ominously. Younger men, ignorant and hopeful, hastily fitted new levers or tried to replace the old wheels with new ones. But it was no use; the engine was too old; it was falling to pieces.

Russian industry, headed by Moscow manufacturers, seeing the incapability of the old mechanism of the state to adjust itself to modern demands, had offered at the beginning of that summer to follow the example of the West and to mobilize itself for unified action. But in that too there seemed little hope. How could our embryonic manufactories, quickly banded together, catch up with the tremendous development of events?

Lacking machines, we had to replenish the fires of war by and with human material. We had to throw into the struggle such tremendous masses of men that the equilibrium of the whole country was disturbed and in time destroyed.

It appeared for a while that there was a ray of hope for a more discerning attitude at the head of the government. The post of the Procurator of the Synod was given to Samarin, a clever and cultured man, respected by everybody, and devoted moreover heart and soul to the throne. And at Samarin's insistence, this time listened to with patience, Rasputin was sent home to Siberia. Moreover, a new and more liberal Cabinet was formed and the Duma was again convoked.

But our military reverses continued, with staggering losses. Our soldiers went over the top without rifles, and our artillery had no ammunition.

When finally came report of the fall of Warsaw, the Duma openly discussed the military situation and accused those in command of tactical ignorance and general incompetence.

With Headquarters of the Front at Pskov, I had always exact information as to the extent of our military reverses; such rumours of internal dissension as reached our province seemed to me by comparison doubly depressing; they were so vague, so impossible to verify.

We heard again and again, for instance, of the Emperor's intention to take upon himself the supreme command of all his armies. Towards this step, it was said, he was being urged by the Empress and by Rasputin, who hated the Grand Duke Nicholas, then commanding, and suspected him of overweening ambitions.

Rasputin, back again at court, was for the first time being attacked, though covertly, in the press. Among those who prior to the time of Rasputin's virtual regency had been closest to the throne, the news of this, his latest counsel, aroused apprehensions especially acute. However valuable a gesture it might be for the Emperor now to take the field, it would be, in all probability, a gesture of but momentary effect and after that far too costly. In assuming direct command the Emperor would assume direct responsibility for every future defeat, and every new criticism would be translated into a direct blow at his prestige.

The behaviour of the court became at this juncture all but incomprehensible. Such a view as I have just expressed could not be very well volunteered. The rumours upon which it grew remained always vague; and to remonstrate with the sovereigns at that time was not only unwise; it was as vain as trying to argue with shadows.

All their thoughts and methods had become shadowy and indirect. The Empress, for instance, wished to know the opinion of Paléologue, the French ambassador, as to her project of sending her husband to the front. She knew that my father and his wife were on friendly terms with Paléologue; so she asked them to give a dinner for him, and sent to that dinner Madame Vyrubova, her bourgeoise counsellor, with instructions to find out Paléologue's attitude. Madame Vyrubova was, in her own way, sincerely and altogether disinterestedly devoted to the Empress, but because of her shallowness in general and her blind worship of Rasputin in particular she did not command respect. M. Paléologue was dumbfounded at the thought of so important a mission being entrusted to such a clod. He told her, diplomatically, that it seemed too late for an outside and contrary opinion to be of any avail. Stammering, she repeated, one by one, his polished phrases, and said she would try to repeat to the Empress all that he had said. This conversation took place on September 2, 1915.

On the same day, Dmitri had dashed by special train from General Headquarters; his mission, undertaken entirely upon his own impulse, and without the knowledge of the Grand Duke Nicholas, was to dissuade the Emperor from assuming the supreme command.

At that time, the Emperor still treated Dmitri as a son; he was always the most welcome guest at Tsarskoie-Selo and the Emperor liked to talk with him. This time, however, Dmitri upon reaching Petrograd was obliged to telephone repeatedly to Tsarskoie-Selo before the Emperor seemed ready to receive him. This had never happened before. The Emperor finally asked him to dinner and afterwards proposed a game of billiards. Then Dmitri, seizing his chance, proceeded to say what he had come to say. He was well aware of the responsibility that he thus took upon himself, but felt that it was his duty to tell the sovereign not only his own personal opinion, but that of the majority—at the front, as well as in the rear; he could not, he felt, afford to care how this frankness might affect him personally.

The conversation was difficult for both of them. The Emperor listened attentively and without a shadow of impatience to all of my brother's arguments. At first he made occasional answers; later, he was silent.

It seemed as though he clearly saw to what he was exposing himself if he assumed command; yet now hearing a definite confirmation of his fears, he appeared to waver. At the end of the conversation, Dmitri was certain that he had carried his point; the Emperor was dissuaded; all was well. And instead of incurring the displeasure of his sovereign, Dmitri received thanks for his devotion and frankness. Before returning to the Empress's boudoir, the two men, deeply affected by the conversation and moved almost to tears, silently embraced. Dmitri, in speaking of this moment afterwards, said that they had never seemed so close to each other as they were then. He left the Alexander Palace that evening with a feeling of joyous and profound relief.

Two days later the Emperor assumed supreme command over the armies; and Dmitri, still in Petrograd, learned about it from the newspapers.

Hard upon this report and the Emperor's departure for the new General Headquarters at Mogilev, came the dismissal of Prince Orlov, chief of the Emperor's field chancellery, and then of Dzhunkovsky. The first was deeply and sincerely devoted to the Emperor but did not hide his opinion about Rasputin, and for this the Empress could not forgive him. With his discharge there remained no one in the palace sufficiently independent and courageous to withstand the dominance of those mediocre and unscrupulous personalities now in the saddle. Dzhunkovsky was Assistant to the Minister of the Interior, and had supervision over the police. His discharge came by reason of an investigation the police had conducted some time before, with indiscreet minuteness into several Moscow debauches of Rasputin's.

In September also, despite all the risks the step involved, the Duma was declared dissolved. This was immediately followed by strikes at the Baltic and in the Putilov factories which were engaged exclusively in the manufacture of materials for national defence.

The strike spread to other factories in Petrograd and continued for only three days, quite peaceably. There was as yet no open thought of "Revolution," but this strike did give rise to a prophetic byword; it was called "The Dress Rehearsal."

Dmitri was summoned to Headquarters, there to assume the duties of aide-de-camp to the Emperor. About that time there was a convention in Moscow of the Zemstvo and Town Unions, organizations with many branches extending from the rear throughout the army. The convention passed a political resolution which, in terms sufficiently polite, pointed out the hardships and trials that Russia was experiencing, and the absence of close contact between the government and the people. It emphasized the necessity of expeditious measures, and first, the appointment of a cabinet which would enjoy public confidence, and the re-summoning of the Duma.

The Emperor sharply refused by telegram to receive the delegation bearing this report. This telegram the sovereign handed personally to Dmitri to forward. Dmitri, knowing its contents, took it to his rooms and did not send it. He felt that this unreasonable outburst on the part of the Emperor would bring about consequences too grave to contemplate.

This time, my brother's boldness was not so well received. He was transferred for a time from Headquarters, together with the aide-de-camp Drenteln, with whom he had conferred. The delegation of the Zemstvo was not received. From that time forth, a more or less open war was waged between the Tsar and the reasoning part of the population.

ii

The Emperor was more than ever a psychological enigma. Personally almost indifferent to power, unconscious of his possession of it, he nevertheless would abide no inroads upon his absolute sovereignty. He felt it a mystical and sacred duty to keep intact the heritage of autocracy handed down to him by his forbears. This conviction had been instilled in him by the example of his masterful predecessor, Alexander III, in internal politics, and had been strengthened with time, first by those charged with his education, then by his ordinary surroundings.

For generations Russia had been governed by Tsars whose will was administered through a caste completely isolated. To the minds of these guardians of the autocratic ideal—a cult in which we all, headed by our Emperor, had been reared—Russia was the bearer of some special ideals, the purity and loftiness of which the West could never understand, and certainly never attain. Russia thus was permitted, in our eyes, to be centuries behind the times in terms of progress, yet eternally superior.

It proved, however, quite impossible to prevent this Western culture from penetrating in some measure into our midst. Those at the helm of our government received it suspiciously or rejected it outright. They might have shaped these new influences to our national peculiarities; but this task they disdained. Consequently, these Western influences, instead of becoming diffused, swirled into close, intense circles of new thoughts and ideas, all centered in one class, the intelligentsia.

Given free and open play to all their Russian love of theory and discussion, the matter might have ended among that class, in a whirl of talk and suggestions. But all such talk, all such suggestions from without, were sternly repressed or scornfully rejected by the ruling caste. There had been, in their opinion, no change. They completely refused to take into account the establishment of a public opinion, and the general interest, continually growing, in national affairs. They hastened at every possible opportunity to place on an illegal footing Russia's slow striving towards self-consciousness.

Deprived, then, of their right to apply their mental force for the good of their country, prevented in all ways from participating in its government, and constantly suspected of wishing to undermine the foundations of the state, the intelligentsia was goaded into open and active opposition, and a difference basically irreconcilable was thus established between these only two classes that could have shared the responsibility of government. The Emperor believed in the divine origin of his authority. He considered himself responsible for the welfare of the country only to God—in no case to the country itself. An opinion expressed outside the milieu from which he chose his advisers was not to be taken into consideration; it was deemed irresponsible, irreverent, and above all, troublesome. Those deputies of the convention of the Zemstvo and Town Unions, headed by Prince Lvov, appeared to the Emperor as impostors, guilty of a revolutionary gesture, taking advantage of the hardships of war to interfere in what did not concern them in the least.

To prevent such incidents from ever happening again, he decided at once to discharge the liberal ministers whom he had himself chosen so recently, and to return completely to the former reactionary system. To this decision the Empress gave earnest encouragement and support.

iii

The retreat of the army, continuing all along the northern front, gradually shortened the distance between Pskov and the front. During that summer we were obliged to put the Ecclesiastical School altogether out of its building and augment the number of our beds to almost six hundred. We had, however, to content ourselves with the same number of doctors, and the Red Cross could let us have only five additional nurses. Consequently we had still more work to do, and were very tired.

It was also during that same winter, the winter of 1916, that I organized a dormitory and an intermediary station for nurses travelling to and from the front. This dormitory caused me a great deal of work and unpleasantness. At that time, nurses were taken from all walks of life; some of them were extraordinary personalities, especially some of the girls from provincial Red Cross chapters. Besides, quite often adventuresses donned the uniform of a nurse and made their way to the front, where no one, it seems, ever thought of verifying their documents. I had many such cases sent to me by Headquarters or by the Military Commander of the railway station.

I also undertook, again upon request of the local authorities, to give some measure of practical experience to a flood of prattling girls in training for the Red Cross. They were always fainting at the sight of blood; always making mistakes; always in the way. On the whole, they brought so much disorganization into our hospital that the doctors prevailed upon me to turn them out.

iv

In October, while standing in church I put forth my hand to pull up a chair and suddenly experienced such a pain under my left shoulder-blade that I remained with the outstretched hand, afraid to move. It turned out to be dry pleurisy with a slight temperature and Tishin begged me to go to bed, but I refused. That evening the Emperor was passing through Pskov, accompanied by my father and by Dmitri, who by now was more or less forgiven. I had been asked to dine on the imperial train and I did not intend to miss it. I went to the appointment covered with a thick coat of iodine and swathed in cotton.

After a very lively dinner—and while the Emperor was receiving the report of the Commander of the Northern Front—my father and Dmitri came with me to the hospital. We had all secretly hoped that the Emperor might pay us a visit and everybody was still awake. Noticing the general disappointment, my father went into the officers' ward and talked with them. I was very happy to be able to show him my hospital. But he, so deeply attached to beautiful surroundings, could not understand how I was able to endure it. With polite astonishment and a certain hidden squeamishness, he listened to my tales of the work. He kept exclaiming that I did not have even a comfortable chair to sit in. He and Dmitri seemed to fill my room with their height and broadness of shoulders, and everything that surrounded me appeared in their presence especially modest and wretched-looking.

At the time, my father was troubled by ill health that, to-

THE GRAND DUCHESS MARIE IN RED CROSS UNIFORM

gether with his advancing age, prevented his taking active part in the war. Later he recovered to such a degree that he assumed command of an army composed of the Guards regiments and spent several months at the front, but throughout that winter he was so ill that once his wife summoned me hastily to Tsarskoie-Selo.

I will never forget how struck I was by his sickly appearance when I arrived and how keenly I felt my love for him. After coming into his room and seeing him emaciated and weak, I rushed into my room and cried for a long time. The possibility of losing him seemed unbearable, he meant too much to me. Yet I have since been sorry many times that he did not die then.

My pleurisy continued. Throughout that winter I ran a temperature, and for two years was subject to occasional seizures of inflammation and pain. But I remained on duty. Since the beginning of the war I had not taken off my grey cotton uniform or white head-dress, not even when I was away from the hospital. For convenience, I bobbed my hair; this in 1916; it horrified my father when he saw it. My hands had become coarse from continual washing and rinsing in disinfectants. My face knew only the touch of cold water for I had long forgotten about powders and creams. Never very particular about my personal appearance, I now took no thought of it. My grey dresses faded from washing, my shoes were down at the heels. There were no social distractions and I did not miss them. I was completely satisfied with my existence, and asked no more of life.

As I look back now, indeed, I can say in full sincerity that the years I spent doing war work were the happiest of my life. Each day brought me wider contacts, fresh impressions, new opportunity to escape from the old restrictions, and growth. Little by little, I spread my wings and tested my strength; the walls which for so long had fenced me off from reality were now finally pierced.

CHAPTER XX

RESPITE

I CONTINUED to carry my new ideas to Father Michael and Dr. Tishin, and to talk with them at length. I felt that I had reached at last to within striking distance of that goal towards which I had striven since childhood. I was now aware, at least, of the reverse side of life, and heard opinions which no one of our circle ever heard.

But the wider my eyes were opened, the better I saw how little I actually knew; and I realized, at times ruefully, how much time and effort it would take for me to come to a real understanding of all these things.

A corner of the veil was scarcely lifted, but I began to have some idea of the entire picture. I saw that Russia was sick; this I could detect, so to say, from the beat of her pulse; but beyond that I was certain of nothing. The contradictions which I encountered at every turn, between the ideas to which I had been brought up and reality, bewildered me. I did not know where to turn next in my groping for the truth; and daily I had to face disappointments and the wrecking of old ideals.

But I felt that I had at least started on the road of discovery; at least a beginning was made, and I had all my life before me. That thought sustained, even exhilarated me. I was, in a word, after all these years, really beginning to get an education.

Russian literature, with which since childhood I had been, I began to realize, only casually acquainted, now acquired a new significance for me. It spoke of feelings and emotions which at last I could share. I asked Tishin to indicate authors not previously included in my reading. Tishin himself read very well; he had a good diction and a pleasant voice; besides, he was interested in plays. Father Michael and I spent many an evening listening to him; sometimes we read some classical play, distributing the rôles among us, or discussed an author whose very existence, as often as not, had been kept in the past a secret from me.

I also turned my attention to the history of my country. This was a subject that had attracted me since childhood; but history, like religion, was taught us by rote, always from the official point of view, never deviating from its principles and premises.

In Pskov, surrounded by relics of antiquity, the study of Russian history and of the Russian Orthodox religion became alive to me. It served me, too, as diversion, respite, from strain and suffering; and perhaps it may do the reader of my book a like service if at this juncture I set down some of the more fascinating of the things I learned.

ii

PSKOV was the product of shifting trade routes. At the close of the thirteenth century, when the importance of Kiev as political centre of the first period of Russian history had begun to decline, the population started to migrate; some trekked west in the direction of the Carpathian Mountains, some northward into the forest-covered regions.

Thus new principalities were formed on the outskirts of the Russia of those days. The largest of these was Great Novgorod. At the time of its zenith of power, in the thirteenth and fourteenth centuries, the lands subject to Great Novgorod spread from the Bay of Finland to the White Sea.

In the west and the south-west, as a protection against foreign invasions, Novgorod had several fortresses. Pskov was the most important.

Vast commercial interests were centred in Novgorod; raw

materials from the central districts of Russia were bartered in the west in exchange for dry goods, metal wares, and wines. The first foreigners who came to Novgorod were merchants from the town of Visby on the Island of Gotland.

Novgorod had a republican form of government—the *vieche*, a people's council, in which every householder of Novgorod or its districts had the right to participate. When in the fourteenth century Pskov became strong enough in trade and in arms to separate from Novgorod, it set up a like government by vote; and the Pskov *vieche* was even better organized and more stable than that of Novgorod.

It was in 1916 a beautiful city, little changed by time. It rose on and around a rocky promontory at the point where the river Pskov falls into a wide and deep river, the Velikaya. The imposing ruins of the wall of its ancient inner fortress, the *detinez*, are still to be seen. In ancient times the city was built around this fortress and was then surrounded by an outside wall, in several places still preserved. In the middle of the *detinez* rises the immense and somewhat awkward-looking Cathedral of the Holy Trinity, first built in the twelfth century but burnt many times since, and restored to its present state in the reign of Peter the Great.

I used to look particularly, in walking through that old city, for its ancient churches. They were of an architecture extremely peculiar—low, squat, with uneven walls and cut-off corners that became larger towards the foundation; it was as if they had forced their way clumsily out of the ground. They were always whitewashed, and usually had green cupolas and roofs.

Beside these churches but apart from them rose the bell towers, like flat square columns, and under the smaller green roofs of these towers, through oblong openings, you could see bells of all dimensions. The walls of these old churches were so thick that the interior was surprisingly small; and their vaults were supported by two or four pillars so massive as to leave, in the end, very little room for a congregation.

Pskov was especially attractive in winter. Then, for some reason, it seemed less provincial; probably because the snow hid its unsightliness and dirt. Behind the hospital on the high bank of the river Velikaya was situated an old orchard which must have belonged to some ancient estate. This orchard seemed to lean against the remnants of the city wall, over which there was a wonderful view of the wide channel of the river, of the glittering white expanses stretching for many miles on all the sides of the city, and of the town itself—crushed, it seemed, under the weight of the snow. Here and there, on both sides of the river, the sun played cheerfully upon the golden crosses of the churches; and opposite, in the very middle of the river upon a low island, stood a lonely, almost deserted monastery surrounded by a wall that was falling to ruins. Only a few grey-haired, age-bent monks lived there and led a beggarly life.

This view became so well known to me that I grew fond of it and it seemed to me one of the indispensable requirements of my life in Pskov.

In the ancient churches I so often visited, I found objects of art neglected for centuries. Once, in an isolated cemetery of a church a little distance from Pskov, I discovered a mural painting of the twelfth or thirteenth century, covered with whitewash. In some places the whitewash had peeled, revealing painting beautifully preserved. I was enraptured with my find; I remember to this day my pleasure, and the sharp silhouettes of those lean saints. I planned to undertake, after the war, the cleaning of that church.

I began visiting nunneries and monasteries where modes and customs of ancient days were faithfully preserved. Sometimes I rose early, so as to be able to assist at an early mass in the neighbouring nunnery before beginning work in the hospital. If this happened in winter the streets were still dark and the dimly lit church was almost empty.

The nuns glided noiselessly about the church, changing

candles in the large candlesticks in front of the ikons, and sang in the choir with childish, passionless voices. Their faces were framed in black wimples upon which were set black caps and their hands were lost in the wide sleeves of their dresses. The service was performed slowly and with decorum, for they had hardly any other occupations except prayer. At the end of the service a novice would approach, bringing me the invitation of the abbess to take tea. And then, accompanied by this novice, I would leave the church, and go across the yard to the apartment of the abbess. In her drawing-room the furniture was hidden by white slip-covers and small palms stood on the window-sills. The table was already set; a boiling samovar, surrounded by cups, was placed at the head of the table; further down were hot wafers and jam.

The abbess, holding the wide sleeve of her cassock, would ask me to be seated. Soft-footed novices, with eyes modestly lowered, brought and removed trays and whispered at the doors.

Sometimes the abbess would send for the Mother Treasurer, asking her to bring from the workshop some piece of embroidery just finished, of which she was especially proud.

And always before the tea was over, she would complain of the hard times, of the high price of flour and of the poverty of the nunnery. One felt that generations of abbesses before her had spoken exactly these same words and had thought exactly these same thoughts.

I collected ancient ikons and restored them—clambering into layers of dust and cobwebs, carefully and reverently carrying my finds back to the hospital. A specialist in the art taught me how to clean these boards, blackened with smoke and age. Slowly, very carefully, I would scrape off a thick layer of dirt and little by little there would come to life bright colours and gilding, and ornaments, and groups of saints.

Antique objects appeared to inspire in the clergy no sense of value or veneration. When they could serve no longer they were simply thrown out. The priests treated these precious symbols barbarously, often damaging them beyond recognition, breaking them completely, or losing them altogether.

Absence of any systematic research among the Pskov antiquities and the danger of their complete destruction led me to undertake a catalogue, illustrated whenever possible by photographs and by my own sketches. I obtained permission from the local bishop and set to work. The photographs of the ikons and of the mural paintings had to be taken on the spot, by a special process and with great care; I did both this and the developing of the plates myself. Embroideries and the smaller objects I took home and sketched in my room.

At the end of my sojourn in Pskov I had collected a great many data, but am unable today to make any use of them; they remain in Russia.

I was at the outset completely untrained as an archæologist, and had a difficult time at first, but Pskov had an Archæological Society and I could turn to it for aid. Before I finished, I was corresponding with Petrograd and had arranged periodical lectures on historical and archæological subjects at the local Archæological Society.

I felt now that I need not worry about my future; here at my hand was enough work, and engrossing work, to keep me happily occupied to the end of my days.

iii

One of the strange new worlds into which my expanding interests led me was that of the Old Believers. These particular members belonged to a priestless sect that controlled almost the entire wheat trade. Its adherents lived according to the ancient customs, sedate and secluded.

In Pskov, they constituted a large colony. Learning of my interest in ikons, the local warden, a rich wheat merchant, invited me to visit their public prayer-house and his private chapel.

The Old Believers referred their beliefs to a distant past. Before printing was established in Russia, church books were transcribed by hand, and this led to mistakes and inaccuracies. Besides, these books in the course of centuries, were repeatedly translated from the Greek, and the translations were never identical. In the middle of the seventeenth century the Moscow Patriarch, Nikon, entrusted Greek and Russian theologians with the verification of the translations and the correction of all mistakes in the books of the church.

This measure seemed to a portion of the people a downright sacrilege. They were fundamentalists, adhering to the letter and not to the meaning of the word. When the corrections, despite all protests, were finally accepted, many of the people remained faithful to the old versions. These separatists in the course of history divided in their turn into many smaller groups and sects, some of which refused to recognize ordained priesthood. All the various sects of the Old Believers, however, carefully preserve not only the ancient books of the church, but old ikons and church utensils, of which they are great connoisseurs.

In spite of the persecutions to which the Old Believers had been subjected ever since their separation from the State Church, they had always remained, as to politics, extremely conservative, and wholly devoted to the throne.

This Pskov wheat merchant, the warden, showed me first the public prayer-house. Here I was met with low bows by several respectable, bearded merchants. They were dressed in long coats gathered in at the waist, and their hair was cut to the nape of their necks in a round even line. Their women servants wore black sarafans, white sleeves, and black kerchiefs. The wall in front of the entrance was hung with ikons, their arrangement resembling an ikonostasis; but I did not find among these ikons anything particularly interesting.

At the private chapel in this Old Believer's house, it was an entirely different matter. There, one felt the breath of true antiquity. The whole house with its thick walls and grilled windows had the air of a retreat—a retreat, however, in which the people had for generations been accustomed to comfortable and prosperous, as well as contemplative, living.

The entire family gathered in the drawing-room to receive me. The women wore heavy silk dresses with narrow bodices buttoned all the way down, and wide skirts gathered at the waist. Their heads and shoulders were covered with old-fashioned silk shawls.

The chapel, a small vaulted room, was filled with the fragrance of incense, rising from antique censers. Some of the ikons were truly remarkable, painted earlier than the seventeenth century by the famous Moscow ikon painters. Old metal lamps, burning oil, hung from the ceiling on perforated chains. In front of the ikons burned candles in home-made candlesticks, ancient and low. Crosses and rosaries decorated the wall. Church utensils shone in the dim light here and there. On a high *prie-Dieu* reposed in honour a very ancient manuscript book in a dark leather binding with metal clasps.

With love and reverence my host showed me these relics. All, he said, had been in the family for many generations.

After the visit to the chapel tea was served during which my host spoke not without bitterness about politics and the attitude of the authorities to this community of Old Believers. In spite of all the persecutions they remained profoundly devoted to their Tsar, accusing the government officials of instigating these persecutions.

Some years before the war great military manœuvres took place in Pskov and the Emperor was expected to be present. According to the Russian custom the Old Believers wanted to greet their sovereign with bread and salt upon a magnificent silver platter. But the governor, having learned of their intention, prevented their delegation from being received. The platter had not served its purpose and the warden, showing it to me, begged me to accept it. I refused it, for myself, but promised to give it personally to the Emperor.

In the spring of 1916, instead of spending my vacation in Tsarskoie-Selo, I went to Novgorod, still following my trail towards the past. I stopped at a nunnery because the hotels were so filthy, and visited all the places of interest in the town.

The most remarkable was the Cathedral of St. Sophia, built in the tenth century by Yaroslav the Wise. This cathedral had been badly damaged by unskilled restoration, but had preserved nevertheless a memorable majesty of appearance both within and without. In the lower row of the ikonostasis were some very ancient ikons, painted, it was believed, in Byzantium. Along the walls, encased in silver shrines, reposed the relics of numerous saints—princes who in ancient days had defended the city from foes, bishops who had pacified the barbarous populace. As was the custom I made the round of all the shrines and kissed all the relics, noticing, not without a shiver, that almost all the bodies have been preserved intact.

I visited also the near-by village of Mikhailovskoie, where a century ago lived our famous poet Pushkin. The house in which Pushkin lived had been burned down long ago but another had been built in the same style and it contained the furniture and the things that had belonged to the poet. I spent a night in this house in an immense antique bed of solid mahogany with pillars and bronze medallions.

In the evening my companions and I sat on the veranda from which opened a view of the limitless fields. We watched the sunset reflected in a river overgrown with reeds. Everything breathed of peace and quiet; it seemed as though nothing had changed during a hundred years, and that nothing ever could. I have kept a wonderful memory of that trip.

iv

All such diversions and excursions were, it must be understood, of short duration, and were widely spaced throughout the greater part of two years. I did not neglect my work at the hospital; it was principally because I had so many other things to think about that I did not find the routine of our provincial life monotonous.

But to please my personnel, which was getting dissatisfied with inglorious drudgery, and very restless, I asked that our unit be transferred to the front and I organized, meanwhile, a mobile sub-unit which I sent to the front at Dvinsk, about seventy-five miles from Pskov.

The work of this smaller unit was chiefly in the trenches, but it was necessary that it should also have a place in town where the gravely wounded soldiers might stay until they could be sent to our Pskov hospital. The connexion between Dvinsk and the hospital was maintained by a sanitary train which bore my name and over which I had full command.

In the winter of 1916, I went to Dvinsk and found a building for our detachment. It was the first time I had been to the front since 1914, and I was amazed by the changes. Changes in everything, beginning with the soldiers' faces and ending with the complicated constructions demanded by trench warfare. It seemed as though these structures were fortresses, built for permanent occupation. The town was half in ruins from aeroplane attacks, and the filth of it was shocking. The soldiers were neither young nor brave-looking; they seemed on the contrary to have shrunk in stature, and looked thoroughly shabby and miserable. Neither song nor laughter was heard anywhere. Everything was grey, dull, and dismal.

The day when the unit began its work I went into the trenches with the nurses and worked with them the entire day. The impressions I received were terrible. It was pitiful to see those poor muzhiks sitting for weeks at a time in the mud and the cold, knowing neither the position they held, nor even what was expected of them. It was clear that they had had enough of the war, that they did not, and did not wish to, understand anything about it. They had become so completely indifferent that when German planes circled over them, not one of them so much as raised his head.

I made several such trips to the line and each one distressed me more.

Princess Lucien Murat, whom I had known in Paris, had somehow made her way to Russia, regardless of all the hardships, to acquaint herself with the conditions under which we were making war. She came to Pskov at my invitation; it was strange to hear her vivacious French speech in those provincial surroundings. She was interested in everything and much impressed by my new and graver attitude towards life. (Strange to say, this lively Parisienne, who had never known me well, was the only person to notice this change in me; my family did not.)

The day after her arrival I drove her to Dvinsk in an open car. It was very cold and the driving was difficult on account of the snow, but I brought her safely to our destination. We spent the night in a railway carriage; the local officials came to pay their respects to us there. We were at the most forward firing-line and my guest yearned for thrilling experiences, but neither that evening nor the day following, when we went into the trenches, was there a shot fired. And not a single enemy plane came over. The Princess seemed disappointed by such an inhospitable reception.

She had been for some time in Petrograd and told me all the rumours about town. Among other experiences, she had been moved by curiosity to seek an interview with Rasputin and had been amazed by the awe-inspiring power of his eyes.

That anyone should seek to meet Rasputin surprised me, I remember, very much. I had heard a great deal about him, yet my father, my brother, and I had never seen him. We simply despised him and I could not understand at the time how a cultured woman could suffer herself to be introduced to him, or to seek his presence. Up to his death he was surrounded always by a group of excited, hysterical women and exerted over them, it was said, an unaccountable power.

I had attached little importance to all this talk; it seemed to me, at times, fantastic. His influence over the Empress seemed to me to be entirely a personal matter, explained by her constant anxiety over the health of the Tsarevich and her belief that only Rasputin could help him.

But the words of Princess Murat seemed in my mind to gather up and give definite shape to all that until now had been separate pieces of rumour and gossip, of no import. Here was the Princess—clear-headed, for all her excess of restlessness, a foreigner, a rather dispassionate observer of Russian affairs from the outside—and she quite obviously believed seriously that Rasputin's influence over the Empress—and, through the Empress, on the course of national affairs—was a real influence, a crucial factor, in the way things were going. I was dumbfounded.

CHAPTER XXI

RETREAT

TOWARDS the close of the spring of 1916 I had become so tired out and weakened by the constant attacks of pleurisy that Dr. Tishin insisted upon my taking a rest. A long journey such as to the Crimea or the Caucasus was out of the question. It was arranged that I go with Father Michael to the monastery, some twenty miles from Pskov, that he and the others of his order had evacuated the summer previous under threat of the German advance. Father Michael himself was recovering but slowly from recurrent attacks of erysipelas; he needed the change as much as I did; and he longed to return to his retreat.

I chose for myself a small house within the walls of the monastery grounds.

Father Michael moved into a little house of his own—one with a private chapel, built by Aunt Ella especially for him and his friend Father Gabriel, now dead. Once a week a car came from Pskov to take me to the hospital and keep me in touch with things there.

I remember my few weeks in that small cottage with a feeling of deep contentment. It had two stories, each with only one room. I lived on the first floor, my maid above; my only constant companion was the dog that had been given me by Dmitri and that had been with me throughout the war.

The monastery dated from the thirteenth century. It stood in the midst of an old pine forest, and was surrounded by a thick, low wall on the corners of which stood round towers with green pointed roofs.

The monastery was poor and modest, lost in the woods, far

from any habitation. The monks were very few. Taciturn, glum, completely uncultured, they went about in worn-out cassocks, their long, unkempt hair hanging down their backs. They divided their time between endless church services and work in the fields.

All day long I wandered with my dog through the virgin forest under the immense pines. I would sit for hours on some stump and inhale the fragrance of that forest or, lying in the grass by the brook, idly follow the flight of clouds across the sky. Sometimes I brought a book along but seldom opened it.

In the depth of the forest was a calm, deep pond fed by springs. I used to go there to bathe. The stillness of the forest was such that there would be no other sound than that of my splashing. On the shore, guarding my clothes, sat my dog and watched with shining eyes my every movement.

Days went by and I did not feel the weight of my inactivity. It seemed to me that I had come for the first time close to the soil of my native country, and could feel for the first time running in my veins Russia's vastness, her potency, her strength.

In the evenings after a modest supper, Father Michael and I sat for a long time on the small veranda of his house and talked. We spoke of Russia, of life, of the future, and planned how in that future, I might be of use to my country. Sometimes I went into the church where the monks prayed patiently and where a somewhat inharmonious singing rose to the vaulted roof.

On holidays mass was served in the little chapel by a monk especially appointed by the abbot, while Father Michael and I read and sang. The church was very small but friendly. A light breeze would bear through the open window the sleepy chirping of birds. Sunshine lay bright on the floor in vibrant spots and a stray wasp beat rapidly at the pane, seeking to escape.

On Saturdays and especially on the eve of holidays the service held by the monks in the church lasted throughout the night and, returning home from Father Michael's, I could hear the hum of their voices and see through the windows the flickering, brilliant specks of the candles. My room was filled with nocturnal coolness and the smell of pines and of grass touched with dew. I went to bed without lighting the candle and before falling asleep watched through my window the far stars above the dark trees.

The peasants of the vicinity soon learned of my presence and came to have a look at me. When in the morning I went out of the house there often would be several women and children patiently waiting. I sat on my cottage steps and talked with them for hours. They told me all their family affairs and I learned a good deal at first hand about their life. They never complained, but, oh, what a joyless existence they led! Sometimes I went to the villages and visited their huts. In this part of Russia, at least, the peasants lived poorly and in filth. But as they had never seen anything else, their pitiful condition did not trouble them and, even if they were somehow to grow richer, I could see, they would continue for a long time to live in the same way.

Some of the women brought to me sick children and I had to send to Pskov for an almost complete assortment of medicines. Always grateful, the mothers brought me presents—a few fresh eggs tied up in a handkerchief, some mushrooms, or a basket of berries. Their husbands and fathers were most of them at the front, some were killed. This war seemed to them by now to have lasted so long that they did not even remember when it began, and could not imagine that it would ever come to an end. They knew that we were fighting the Germans, but if they had ever heard of the Allies, they had forgotten it.

A considerable crowd of old muzhiks and peasant women attended the mass on Sundays and holidays. They came on foot or drove in wagons drawn by scraggy little horses. The monastery grounds became filled with bright-coloured kerchiefs and, in spite of the heat, sheepskins. After the service they

THE HOSPITAL UNIT AT PSKOV, 1914

The Grand Duchess Marie in the centre

gathered in groups and talked, scratching their necks and eating sunflower seeds. Sometimes I joined them and listened to their discussions about the war. Occasionally I even tried to explain to them what was taking place at the front. They did not know anything about internal politics or the Duma and were not interested in them, but in mysterious ways they sometimes got hold of the most fantastic and legendary rumours about the Tsar. These were always personal tales and anecdotes, full of details and dialogues, and in all that I heard there was never a shadow of malice or criticism. The old saying, "The Tsar is gracious, but his dog-keeper is not," was a perfect illustration of their train of thought.

They told how the Tsar, while visiting the front, would forgive delinquent soldiers and would reward others according to their merits and would punish those in command for their unjust attitude towards their men. They liked these stories of theirs much better than my explanations as to the meaning of the war and the activities of our distant Allies. All that was incomprehensible to them, beyond their understanding, inaccessible to their imagination.

On the other hand they quite definitely were expecting the division of the land after the war. They found it only natural that the earth they tilled should be taken from the landowners and given to them.

Looking at them, hearing them talk, I often was conscious of something close to fear. Millions of peasants throughout Russia, I thought to myself, are reasoning exactly this same way. They bear us no ill-will; but neither we, the government, nor a public opinion headed by an intelligentsia has the slightest power to reach and sway this stubborn, instinctive judgment of the overwhelming majority of our population. We have failed to understand the peasant psychology, or to enlighten it; and it is now too late.

Somewhere far away parties joined issue, conventions assembled, members of the Duma made their speeches, ministers were discharged, groups pulled this rope and the other. Yet none of this reached the people, none of it was done in their behalf.

Those were my thoughts in that summer of 1916. And even now, even at the moment when I am writing this, the situation of the Russian peasant remains, I believe, unchanged.

It has always puzzled me how my relatives and the people surrounding me could have failed even to worry about the agrarian problems in Russia. During their travels abroad, they must have observed the comparative welfare of the Western agricultural class. In Sweden before the war, every hired hand had his own bicycle. The farmers lived in clean houses behind muslin curtains, and their children were college graduates. I was never able to get used to the thought that those healthy, cheerful people, always cleanly dressed, were peasants.

It is true that public education of the Russian peasantry was —and is—fraught with such difficulties as to make a complete conquest over ignorance all but impossible. Climatic conditions, transportation problems, the vastness of the land, the psychological inertness of the sons and grandsons of serfs—all this had to be taken into account.

It is also true, however, that such attempt as was made to educate the peasantry was badly organized, and on an entirely wrong basis. Those entrusted with this education (that is, the village priests and the village teachers) had themselves received an education which did not in the least prepare them for the task. Their knowledge was academic, superficial, purely theoretical; they did not know anything of any use to a peasant. They excelled, on the other hand, in vague abstractions and half-baked revolutionary dogma. Sent to remote villages they yearned for more expansive subjects and neglected teaching the children in preaching sedition to their gaping elders.

Such ideas, slow to take root in that class, fell nevertheless upon soil prepared. For the peasants, freed from servitude in 1861, did not own the land individually but as a community and this arrangement, imperfect in its essence, was the source of all their troubles. They longed to possess their own land and they waited, with rising impatience, for a general redistribution.

Certain landowners, realizing the danger of the situation, did what they could. They tried to introduce new methods of culture, better breeds of cattle, new agricultural machines, and to explain to the people the importance of personal hygiene. But such attempts did not get very far, and they were all too few.

I do not presume, from my few weeks' sojourn directly among the peasants, completely to understand their problem. It is true that I did not have enough time to study anything, but I did understand a great deal more than I had before; I now saw plainly that our former existence, as a ruling class, was founded on illusions alien to real life; that the basic fabric of our national life was pitiably flimsy and insecure.

CHAPTER XXII

DOUBTFUL RIDDANCE

WHEN I returned to Pskov and again received first-hand news of the fighting from General Ruzsky, Commander of the Armies of the Northern Front, I found these reports far from comforting. Behind our lines, too, dissolution continued. The sudden appointment of B. V. Stuermer as Prime Minister had raised a wide-spread muttering as to German influence. Moreover, Samarin, the Procurator of the Synod, had been discharged; and Vladimir, the Petrograd Metropolitan, had been transferred to Kiev. His post was given to Pitirim, a trusted partisan of Rasputin.

In July of 1916 Sazonov was discharged as Minister of Foreign Affairs, and with him went the only hope and support of the Allies; his post was temporarily entrusted to Stuermer, the suspected pro-German.

In September Protopopov was appointed Minister of the Interior. This choice amazed everybody. It was a Rasputin appointment. Protopopov was a curious and very much discussed figure in the political world.

It was about this time that I first heard people speaking of the Emperor and Empress with open animosity and contempt. The word "revolution" was uttered more openly and more often; soon it could be heard everywhere. The war seemed to recede to the background. All attention was riveted on interior events. Rasputin, Rasputin, Rasputin—it was like a refrain; his mistakes, his shocking personal conduct, his mysterious power. This power was tremendous; it was like dusk, enveloping all our world, eclipsing the sun. How could so pitiful a wretch throw so vast a shadow? It was inexplicable, maddening, baffling, almost incredible.

ii

The winter of 1916 was extremely severe. Frosts which began in November gained in intensity as days went by. Our hospital had expanded tremendously and we faced increasing difficulties in obtaining supplies. Materials at first plentiful were now scarce and of a lower quality; and some things could not be had at all. For instance, rubber gloves; even gangrene operations had to be performed with bare hands.

Our spirits lagged. Our work went forward by mere force of habit. Our patients were depressed and bore their sufferings with less patience. Their attitude towards the personnel had undergone a noticeable change, and they returned to the front with a feeling of unconcealed aversion.

Pskov, however, did not change. The days were cold and bright. On the river Velikaya ice was being sawn to fill the ice cellars. The buzz of the saw, the cries of the workers, floated far and wide through the clear air. Long files of peasant sledges—upon which the immense, blue squares of ice had been loaded with hooks—drove screeching up the high bank of the shore. In the fields a mellow, downy snow was waist deep. Dry wood burned hotly in the stoves, the furniture and the wooden frames of the windows cracked.

People avoided going out if there was no special need for it. The few pedestrians in the street went at a trot, their collars raised high, their hands thrust deep into their pockets.

I was not afraid of the cold. Every day I would go into the woods with my skis. These walks held a special charm for me. There was so much snow that treading my way amidst the branches it seemed to me that I was climbing upon the tops of the trees. The sun became towards dusk an immense fiery circle, glimpsed through the black trunks of the trees, and the purple shadows became sharp. On the way home I would watch the thickening of the blue winter evening, and the dawning of the stars.

It was when I returned from one of these excursions that I heard the first report of Rasputin's death. I do not remember who told it to me, but I clearly remember the unprecedented excitement at the hospital. Neither will I ever forget the vague and contradictory rumours which crept through the town that evening and clothed in mystery the disappearance of this ominous being who had been hated so violently and for so long, and who now was blamed for all the misfortunes which had befallen Russia. The news of his death was met everywhere with a joy bordering on hysteria; people in the streets embraced each other as they did at Easter, and women cried.

Rasputin's presence at the court since 1907, with only a few absences, was known to all Russia, but had become still more noticeable from the beginning of the war. Now in 1916, almost everyone considered Rasputin morally responsible for all our reverses at the front and all disorders in the interior. Minds corroded by criticism and discontent had made him the scapegoat of their indignation. People were tired of sacrifice and the efforts of war. Russian patriotism, possessing an altogether abstract character, could not stand the strain. For many people Rasputin served as an excuse for their own slackness.

Fundamentally, despite all the harmful gossip, the reason for his presence and power at the court was very simple. The Empress, who adored her son, well knew that the hæmophilia from which he had suffered since his birth was incurable, and certain to grow worse as years went by. Internal hæmorrhages had become more and more frequent; the lightest blow could cause death and each new attack caused the poor child unbearable suffering. This suffering, Rasputin alone seemed able to alleviate.

There was therefore nothing strange in the fact that the Empress regarded Rasputin as her only hope and saviour. The days passed full of gloom in the Alexander Palace. The nerves of the Empress, completely unstrung by constant anxiety, turned her into a sick woman. It was quite natural that Rasputin should acquire such a tremendous significance if we think of the abnormal conditions in which she lived, the solitude to which she had gradually doomed herself, the four walls of the nursery where on his little bed her only son moaned and tossed about.

Repeating continually that the Tsarevich would not live if it were not for him, Rasputin cunningly and adroitly took possession of the Empress's mind. But his domineering character could not be satisfied with the comparatively modest rôle of a household's miracle worker, he needed a vaster field of action.

Now that many of the documents concerning that period have become public property, it is possible to say that at times Rasputin's advice was not devoid of that common sense which seems inherent to the Russian peasant. Yet like any other peasant he had a deep and firm distrust of the nobles and a conviction that they not only oppressed the people but continually prevented them from communicating with the Tsar.

Having acquired influence, but possessing little discrimination, Rasputin began to test his power. He incited the Empress against everybody, first including all the people nearest to her whom he knew detested and distrusted him.

His calumnies fell upon fertile soil. The Empress, shy and secretive by nature, had been unable, during all the years since her arrival in Russia, to make the Russian psychology her own; it always remained alien to her. Even the Russian Orthodox religion, which she had embraced at the time of her marriage, and the Russian language which she had carefully studied and spoke better than many of the foreign Princesses, did not help her to understand the true character of the people over whom she reigned.

Moreover, it seemed that ill luck followed her every step. At first, each two years, instead of the son expected with such impatience, a daughter was born to her, and when at last the Tsarevich came, he was affected with a disease which she herself brought into her new family.

This was a blow from which she could never recover. It seemed to her that people constantly looked askance at her, especially those who belonged to the highest ranks of society; and she did not like them. Brought up very strictly at a small German court and strongly influenced by her domineering grandmother Queen Victoria, she learned narrow-mindedness from childhood and was intolerant of the weaknesses of others. The Russian aristocracy seemed to her to be dissolute and, if they treated her coldly, she returned the feeling with scorn. She firmly followed her own way, that of a good Christian, an exceptional mother, a devoted wife. As long as she limited herself to her family interests, everything went fairly well, but as an Empress she was not loved.

Rasputin, acting in his own interests, turned her attention from household to state affairs, giving them his own interpretation. The sly peasant used the influence he thus obtained to satisfy first of all his inherent dislike of the nobility. Now he could amuse himself to the full by maliciously inciting them against one another and by humiliating them at court.

All that befell Russia through Rasputin's direct or indirect influence can, it seems to me, be regarded as the vengeful expression of a dark, terrible, all-sweeping hatred, kindling for centuries in the heart of the Russian peasant for the higher classes who never learned to understand him or win him over. In his own way Rasputin was devoted to both the Empress and the Emperor. He was sorry for them, as one is sorry for children led into error by adults. His seeming sincerity and candour appealed to both of them. His talks—the like of which they had never heard before—pleased them by their novelty and their apparently simple logic. The Emperor himself longed for closer intercourse with his people.

But with no education whatsoever, and unaccustomed to such

surroundings, Rasputin very quickly grew conceited from the boundless confidence shown him by his high benefactors. Brazenly, he surrounded himself with a clique of rogues and adventurers who played on his lowest instincts and involved him in a net of intrigues which he was unable to understand. To those who were constantly with him, he began to boast of his importance at the court in terms that led to disgusting gossip which gradually spread throughout Russia. He was dissolute and, loving wine, drank and bragged.

Such was the being who perhaps more than anyone else governed Russia; for the unbalanced, sick Empress blindly acquiesced to the demands of the only person necessary for her peace, and the Emperor, deeply attached to his wife, and pitying her, unfortunately did not have the strength to contradict her. And the circle of intrigues in which Rasputin involved the imperial couple closed around them day by day tighter and tighter.

His death came too late to change the course of events. His dreadful name had become too thoroughly a symbol of disaster. The daring of those who killed him to save their country was miscalculated. All of the participants of the plot, with the exception of Prince Yusupov, later understood that in raising their hands to preserve the old regime they struck it, in reality, its fatal blow.

True, Rasputin had to be annihilated, but it should have been done earlier, and in such a way as to raise no hue and cry. Then the imperial couple would never have been submitted to the humiliating necessity of punishing their kinsman for a killing which had brought about general rejoicing.

iii

As I have said, several different versions of the murder circulated in Pskov. Among other things it was said that some girl of the people, seduced by Rasputin, had tracked him and killed him by several revolver shots. They even gave the name of the girl. The details of this story, invented from beginning to end, were so plausible that this version was accepted at once.

I awoke the next morning to the ringing of the telephone. It was Prince Shakhovskoy, the local representative of the Red Cross. He asked me to receive him at once. Fifteen minutes later he stood before me. His nervous bearing, his perturbed face, told me even before he spoke, that he bore tidings both serious and distressing.

"You know, of course, Your Highness, what has happened in Petrograd." He paused, fidgeting with his gloves. "The details that had reached us yesterday were incorrect. We know now what has really happened. Russia was freed from Rasputin by some heroes—heroes headed by Prince Yusupov. One of the participants in the plot was—your brother, the Grand Duke Dmitri."

I bent my head without saying a word. I never doubted for a moment that I was hearing the truth. All my thoughts rushed impetuously there, to my brother. Thousands of suppositions, like flashes of lightning, pierced my brain; memory reproduced words dropped inadvertently, sentences spoken casually, conversations heard at one time or another. Finally I raised my eyes to my visitor who was troubled by my silence.

"Are any details known?" I asked.

My parched tongue could hardly move in my mouth.

"Not yet, Your Highness. Rasputin's corpse has not yet been found. It was said that both the Grand Duke and Prince Yusupov have been arrested by order of the Empress. It is known that the Emperor was still at Headquarters yesterday. He received General Ruzsky."

I began to regain my self-control.

"Is this known in Pskov?"

"Yes. This is why I took the liberty of disturbing you so early, I was afraid that you might learn about it by accident. . . . Rest assured that the brave action of your brother arouses general admiration. The destruction of Rasputin is of the greatest benefit to Russia," added Shakhovskoy haltingly; and, seeing that I did not know how to respond, left me alone.

All my thoughts swarmed, rushing one upon the other, towards Dmitri, who appeared to me now in a new, unusual light. I was proud of him. But somewhere, deep within my heart, I was hurt because he had not found it necessary even to hint to me about his plans. For the first time in my life my brother appeared to me an individual being standing apart from me, and this feeling of unaccustomed estrangement made me shiver.

My first impulse was to go to him at once. But was this wise? Rasputin's corpse had not yet been found; an investigation was probably under way. I knew nothing of Dmitri's situation—his degree of participation in the plot; his accountability in the eyes of the law; my precipitate departure from Pskov, a sudden arrival in Petrograd, might compromise and endanger him.

But to remain in Pskov, in ignorance—that seemed to me unbearable. The details of the murder, to all appearances, would not be printed in the papers; news would reach me only as distorted gossip. To send a wire seemed unsafe, or even to write. Would he write to me—could he—now that he was deprived of his freedom? Torn by doubt, I paced the floor of my room. It seemed to me, and in this I was not mistaken, that from this moment everything was bound to change and never be the same again. What now had happened was too tremendous to fit into the pattern of the usual, or to allow events ever to reassume their old reassuring lines. At noon I went to the dining-room trying my best to appear natural, but as soon as I entered it I knew that everyone had heard the news. There was a sort of covert excitement and hidden admiration in the looks given me; it was as if they thought that I also was involved in this assassination. But no one said anything.

Repeatedly that day I sent orderlies to General Ruzsky, only to learn that he had not yet returned from Mogilev. But the next day towards evening, I was told he had arrived. I threw a coat upon my shoulders and walked to the wooden fence which divided our property from Headquarters. The sentinels at the gate recognized me and let me pass. I stood now in the old garden overlooking the river Velikaya. An alley of old linden trees led to an unsightly wooden house; there lived Ruzsky. Yellow lamplight came through low, uncurtained windows, while overhead the trees lifted high their mighty black branches. It was very quiet. Below could be seen the smooth, winter-bound surface of the river and the distant fields. The light of the moon was reflected in the snow as in a dull silver mirror.

I lingered in the garden for a strange, tense moment, almost at peace; then I approached the house and rang the bell. A Ural Cossack opened the door and the General's aide, waiting for me in the vestibule, led me to the study of the Commander-in-Chief.

Ruzsky was sitting behind a large desk, piled with papers. He rose as I entered; a short, lean old man with stooping shoulders, sunken cheeks, and thick grey hair cut in the German manner, so as to stand, in short bristles, all over his head. His deep-set and extremely bright eyes shone behind gold-rimmed glasses.

Without doubt he was one of our most talented generals, but he had been of late suspected of political intrigues, and was somewhat out of favour. As I came into the room I could see that he was very nervous. He offered me an arm-chair and returned to his desk.

"I would not hide from you, Your Highness, that in my opinion the event which has just taken place in Petrograd will have unexpected and distressing consequences," he said, directing upon me his lively, almost youthful glance. "I have come directly from Petrograd. I went there to get a clear idea of the mood of the capital. I regret to say that the situation is fai from cheerful. . . ."

I remained silent. He, too, sat in silence for a moment, as if to gather his thoughts, then he went on to speak of the general situation, military and political.

The generals commanding the principal armies had been assembled, he said, at the military council at Headquarters. He, Ruzsky, had made a report of the prevailing mood in the armies under his command, the slackness of discipline, the disappearance of all martial spirit. Propaganda had penetrated all ranks, and was taking insidious effect. There had even been outright insubordination, refusal to leave the trenches and attack. Severity, punishments, were no longer possible or safe. It was necessary to work out some new plan, to face an unprecedented situation, to organize a psychological counter-attack.

This report, Ruzsky continued, greatly displeased the Emperor. He had, apparently, other information from more intimate advisers, and preferred to believe that.

The conference, supposed to last several days, broke up at noon upon announcement that the Emperor was obliged to leave quite unexpectedly for Tsarskoie-Selo. At about this same time rumours of the murder of Rasputin reached Headquarters. The Emperor must have heard them earlier but he showed no sign of agitation or anxiety. He seemed, on the contrary, more animated than usual and more gay. It was as if Rasputin's final disappearance gave him a sense of relief.

My father, who also happened to be that day at Headquarters, later gave me exactly the same picture of the Emperor's reactions. (Neither Ruzsky nor my father knew at the time of my brother's participation in the plot.) My father heard of it only the next day, at Tsarskoie-Selo, from our stepmother.

The Emperor bade all at Headquarters good-bye, and the imperial train rushed to Tsarskoie-Selo.

Ruzsky followed, hoping for the opportunity to make a

further private report to the Emperor at Tsarskoie-Selo; but all his efforts to gain an interview had, he said, failed.

Petrograd, he continued, trembled with curiosity and agitation. He, Ruzsky, had visited factories and talked with the city authorities. The same revolutionary propaganda which was disrupting our front was cutting the ground from under us, and just as rapidly, in Petrograd.

The removal of Rasputin threw all internal movements and counter-movements entirely off balance. Everything now depended, said Ruzsky, upon the course that the court would take as to the murder of Rasputin and its reaction to this tremendous event. The fate of the dynasty as well as that of the country depended upon that; and all eyes were turned towards Tsarskoie-Selo.

The immediate reaction at Tsarskoie, alas, was altogether different. Without waiting for the Emperor's return the Empress gave orders for Dmitri's arrest. She sent General Maximovich, the chief of the Tsar's field chancellery, who took his sword and placed him under arrest in his own house. Prince Yusupov was transferred there also and both were guarded by sentinels.

Popular sympathy was wholly on the side of the prisoners. The vestibule of my brother's house was continually crowded with those who came to express their admiration and acclaim. All such enthusiasm aroused a new danger, a violent reaction in Tsarskoie-Selo, especially on the part of the Empress, whose grief at the death of Rasputin—Ruzsky concluded—was boundless.

I told him of my doubts and asked his advice. He advised me to write Dmitri a letter and send it to Petrograd by a trusted man. With a heavy heart I returned to the hospital; my anxiety had increased.

That evening I sat down to write to my brother, no easy task. I did not know into whose hands this letter might fall. Having written a number of rough drafts which did not satisfy me, I finally decided simply to say that I had been missing him and would like to see him. This letter I sent next morning to Petrograd by an orderly who before the mobilization had been a footman in our house. Then two days dragged by; each hour seemed endless. In those two days I heard that General Ruzsky had been relieved of his command in the Petrograd district. I heard also that the murder of Rasputin had taken place at Prince Yusupov's palace. The papers printed a sparse official communication without details. The court, satisfied for the moment with the arrest of the two young conspirators, now did nothing, and its intentions remained a mystery. The police were still looking for the corpse.

My courier returned from Petrograd twenty-four hours later, but brought me no reply. I was more anxious than ever. Finally came a laconic wire from Dmitri, asking that I come immediately to Petrograd.

I telephoned Ruzsky. He ordered a special train. In less than two hours I was on the way. Some of my personnel came to see me off and my departure made at the station something of a sensation—an excited morbid pushing and gaping, thoroughly disagreeable.

Never had the trip to Petrograd seemed so endless. General Laiming met me at the station. We exchanged glances and silently shook hands; there were now too many things to speak about. In the automobile we continued silent and I fought back tears. It seemed to me strange that the streets should be lighted as usual and full of people and animation.

Driving up to the palace on the Neva and entering, the first thing I saw were the sentinels and, just beyond, the welcoming servants who had been with us since our childhood.

We went upstairs to Laimings' apartment. Mme. Laiming was there awaiting me. The old butler brought me a supper and busied himself about the table. Not wishing to hurt him I dipped my spoon into the soup. But when I was alone with the Laimings I began to question them—seeking always, however, to avoid any mention of the murder.

Their answers indicated all too clearly that the same atmosphere reigned everywhere, in Petrograd as well as in the provinces. Tension had reached its limit. The slightest awkward step on the part of the government would be sufficient to bring on catastrophe. A terrible confusion reigned in the minds of the people.

Some few there were, better balanced, perhaps, than the others, who hoped that the general rejoicing at Rasputin's death would sober the Empress. But the majority rejoiced maliciously at each new sign of the poor woman's grief.

The chief danger, according to Laiming, lay in a lust for revenge now sweeping the partisans of Rasputin, who were not neglecting to fan in the heart of the Empress a similar sentiment. For the most part adventurers, or men with a blemished reputation, they had nothing to lose and were capable of anything. Laiming had been warned by the police to watch over Dmitri day and night. Outside, the palace was guarded by plain-clothes men; inside, the sentinels stood at each entrance. Suspicious-looking men had several times sought under different pretexts to get into the house. Protopopov, Minister of the Interior, whose career Rasputin had made, sent spies of the famous Okhrana to watch all that was happening in the house, but Laiming's vigilance kept them, perforce, at watch from without.

By this time the corpse of Rasputin had been found and buried in Tsarskoie-Selo. There was an inquest, and talk of extreme punishments, even of court martial, which it seemed the Empress demanded. The case was altogether exceptional, and it was still unknown how it would be examined. As one of royal blood Dmitri was presumably immune from civil prosecution. All Russia, moreover, knew that the Emperor treated Dmitri as his own son, and could put no other interpretation upon his act than that of loyalty to the throne. He and Prince

Yusupov had become the heroes of the day, especially among officers of all ranks, and somewhat among public workers. To prosecute them now would be not only dangerous but even fatal; it seemed likely to arouse an outburst of rage, the consequences of which could not be foretold.

The imperial couple had isolated themselves completely in the Alexander Palace, and would see almost no one. Such of the family who wished to warn them against too severe measures of punishment and insisted on being received were given non-committal answers and treated coldly and officially.

My father, returning from Headquarters, had come the previous day to see Dmitri. He was shaken to the heart by what had happened. The talk that he had with Dmitri was painful for them both.

As for myself, I did not know what to say or do. It seemed all a terrible dream, a madness which had taken possession of us all, a circle of fire with no way out.

CHAPTER XXIII

EXILE

LAIMING notified Dmitri of my arrival. Some of our relatives were with him at that moment. He sent word that he would come to me as soon as they had left.

Finally I heard his steps in the adjoining room. My heart stopped beating. He entered. Our eyes met. His forced smile, his assumed air of animation, were to me a perfectly transparent mask. For his face was drawn and he had black circles under the eyes; in spite of his extreme youth, he was old. My heart swelled with sorrow and pity and love for him.

He sat at the table where the tea things were still standing and asked me a few unimportant questions, but soon rose and began to pace the room. I said nothing. It was now long after midnight. Glancing at the clock he offered to take me to my rooms.

We said good-night to the Laimings, went down the stairs and passed through the endless corridors and drawing-rooms leading to my apartment. The old, immense house seemed that night gloomier than usual. Our steps echoed dully through the empty, high rooms. I did not seem to recognize this house, known since childhood; there was something alien, ominous in it now. An uncontrollable shiver ran down my back; my pulse beat faster; I was afraid.

We reached my rooms. The accustomed sight of Tania, my maid, waiting for me, somewhat quieted me. I undressed, took a bath and, putting on a dressing-gown, returned to Dmitri.

He stood by the mantelpiece, silently smoking. Gathering my feet under me I sat in an arm-chair and waited. I did not want to begin the conversation. I wanted him to speak first.

THE GRAND DUKE DMITRI

Brother of the Grand Duchess Marie

So I sat there watching his slightest movement. Oh! what would I not have given to have been able to help him at that moment. It was as if his eyes were fixed inwardly upon some terrible spectacle, from which he could not turn away. And I sensed also in his attitude a heart-struck disappointment; he sat contending with horrifying disillusionment on the border of despair.

What a stupendous responsibility he had undertaken; what doubt and struggle must have attended each step! And now the turn of events seemed not to justify it. The excitement was over; the effects had miscarried. My mind seemed now to enter into his and to follow his thought. And it now seemed to me no longer possible to ask him even one question. I did not want to know any more; I was afraid of what I might hear; I was afraid that I too would be unable throughout all my life ever to turn my gaze away from the terrible spectacle which my imagination depicted.

And we were silent. Thus, until today, although fourteen years have elapsed, we have never touched upon the events of that dreadful night. Frightened, finally crushed by this phantom that was rising between us against our will, we sought to break the silence. With difficulty turning his thoughts, Dmitri began to speak of irrelevant matters. Politics furnished us a vast theme. The impressions I brought from the provinces corresponded to his. Thunder clouds darkened every horizon.

Dmitri had, at different times, spent several months at the Emperor's headquarters in Mogilev, each time becoming more and more persuaded of the hopelessness of the situation. The Emperor, he said, did not in the least realize the terrible abyss gaping wider and wider under his feet. No words could, it seemed, arouse him to the danger that threatened his country and his dynasty. The blindness and obstinacy of the Empress had removed from his court the last trustworthy people; deceit surrounded her and her husband. They had, it appeared, no knowledge of the condemnation which now had become loud, general, open. The Duma was openly all but rebellious; deputies made speeches in which they freely attacked the order of things at the court. Even in high society the possibilities of a *coup d'état* at the court were discussed with talk of banishing the Empress, or of demanding that the Emperor send her to the Crimea, where she could not exercise her influence upon the course of events.

All this, however, said Dmitri, was nothing but feeble, impotent chatter. No one wanted to undertake anything. People had become small; no one ever thought of the obligations of Russia to the Allies, or of maintaining Russian dignity in the eyes of all the world. He did not say so, but from the way in which he spoke I understood, I think, why he had taken part in the murder of Rasputin. He hoped not only to rid Russia of a monster that was weakening her at her very heart, but also to give a new impulse to events, to have done with helpless drifting and hysterical chatter; to urge action, by example of action, all in one decisive stroke.

Little by little as we talked his tensity lessened; gradually he grew calmer and I felt that for these hours at least his thoughts had been diverted from the nightmare which had been pursuing him. We talked for hours. We spoke of ourselves, our life, our future. We both were still so young; the war had changed everything; and there was no telling what the future would bring.

It was after six o'clock in the morning that Dmitri, throwing his last cigarette into the ashes of the fireplace, rose and wearily stretched himself. Now in my turn I went with him to his room and bidding him good-night returned to my apartment.

Outside it was still night. I went to bed and only then noticed the familiar pain under the shoulder-blade, and the usual portents of a fever. Next day I woke with a terrible headache and all the symptoms of a returning attack of pleurisy. I arose, however, and dressed. Lunch was served in

Dmitri's rooms where he was waiting for me with Felix Yusupov, his fellow-conspirator, and one of our uncles, the Grand Duke Nicholas.

Lunch passed with comparative animation. When coffee was served some of our cousins came to visit Dmitri and I drew Yusupov into another room for a private talk.

From his first words I understood that his attitude towards the committed deed was quite different from that of Dmitri. He was intoxicated by the importance of the part that he had played, and saw in it a great political future. I did not ask him for any details, for I knew that the plotters had given one another their word of honour never to divulge what had happened that night.

Yet, in spite of his self-satisfaction and an outward assurance, there was in his words some anxiety both as to his own fate and Dmitri's.

Nothing new had happened since the previous day. The intentions of the court, he said, remained impenetrable, but, he added, the wrath of the Empress seemed directed chiefly upon Dmitri; she was enraged by what she called and believed to be Dmitri's ingratitude in relation to her and to the Emperor, and accused him of nothing less than treason.

Rasputin's corpse had been transported to Tsarskoie-Selo and buried at night in the park on a spot that she chose herself. The slightest details of the transportation of the body and of the funeral were public property and for some strange reason the sorrow of the Empress, quite natural from the point of view of existing conditions, seemed to affect people in a greater and more dreadful degree than the former muffled, even scandalous gossip. Her open manifestation of grief showed clearly how strong and irrefutable was her devotion to Rasputin. In this devotion, now outraged, lay, said Yusupov, our chief danger. There was nothing to do now but wait; justification was becoming merely verbal, impotent; the facts spoke for themselves. A great deal depended upon the Emperor; it was he who was expected to act.

This uncertainty affected Dmitri quite differently than it did Yusupov. The popularity that his name enjoyed gave him no satisfaction; on the contrary, it frightened him; and he also was frightened by the gathering consequences of the murder, so entirely opposite to those he had expected.

Yusupov spoke at length, yet not without nervousness, of his absolute assurance that neither of them would be touched. He believed in his lucky star and counted upon the protection of public opinion. Against that opinion, he held, the court would never proceed openly.

ii

THAT afternoon, around three o'clock, Laiming came to say that General Maximovich wanted to speak to Dmitri on the telephone. After a short conversation Dmitri returned, and told us that Maximovich asked him to come immediately as he had an important and urgent order to transmit.

We silently exchanged glances. The lightning had flashed. But we did not yet know where the bolt had struck.

Pale to the very lips, Dmitri ordered his car and left, accompanied by General Laiming. Yusupov and I remained alone. Our anxiety was so great that we could not even speak of it. Yusupov had now lost all his self-assurance. To still in a measure my own apprehensions I sat down at the piano and began to play the accompaniment of a gipsy song. Felix, leaning against the top of the instrument, sang in a low tone. My fingers shook.

Half an hour passed. Finally behind us the door flew open. I started and turned round. Dmitri stood on the threshold, grasping the handle of the door. It seemed to me that his features had changed almost beyond recognition. Felix and I looked at him in silence, not daring to say a word. Dmitri, leaving the door, advanced into the room.

"I have received the order to leave tonight for the Persian front, accompanied by the aide-de-camp of the Emperor appointed to watch me. During the trip I will have no right to see or correspond with anyone. My exact destination is not yet known," he told us in an impassive voice, making an effort to remain calm.

"You, Felix, are exiled to your estate in Kursk Province. The chief of police will let us know later as to the time of departure of our trains."

Dmitri threw his cap upon the divan and began pacing the room. We were crestfallen. It was not the question of the punishment which at first glance seemed very mild, as much as that of the influence which it might have upon the further course of events. All Russia was watching to see what would be the reaction of the court to the death of Rasputin, and its attitude towards his assassins. Here was the answer; how would it be received now; would this be the final touch that would let loose all passions, break all barriers down?

The persecution of the assassins, although quite legal in its essence, would nevertheless signify to the public the excessive devotion of the Empress to the memory of Rasputin, confirming the worst rumours of his influence, and demonstrate anew the helpless passivity of the Emperor.

What, moreover, would become of Dmitri? His exile to the remote Persian front carried with it an evident element of risk. Here, in Petrograd, he was comparatively safe from any attempts on the part of Rasputin's partisans, but who knew what could happen to him so far away and under unknown conditions? His disappearance would not be difficult to arrange; the traces could easily be hidden.

These were my thoughts; and if they seem, as here set down, disordered, so were they then. For a week we had been living, all of us, between the ghost of the murdered man on one side and the fear of a general collapse on the other. Never in my life, either before or since, have I been so assailed by a complete sense of catastrophe. Here, together with my fear for a loved one, there was a fixed foreboding of something final and inevitable, the immensity of which I could vaguely sense but not conceive.

"Father must be told," I said finally. "Do you want me to call him up?"

"Yes, do," replied Dmitri.

I rose and went into the telephone room. Just outside of it in a small corridor, leading to the back entrance, stood the sentinel charged to watch telephone communications. I was connected with Tsarskoie-Selo, and Princess Paley, who had answered the call, went to fetch my father. Dmitri, who had followed me, took the receiver from my hand and stood waiting.

"It is I, Father," he said a few seconds later, "I wanted to tell you . . ."

Here he faltered and thrusting the receiver into my hand, made a helpless gesture with his hand and left the room.

"Hello," said in the distance the low, calm voice of my father.

"Now it is I, Marie," I said, trembling all over.

"Oh, it is you. I did not know that you had already come from Pskov. When are you coming to see us?"

"Father, everything is . . . not all right here," I said, not knowing how to begin, and swallowing the tears which were choking me.

"What has happened," asked his voice, in which now sounded a note of alarm, "Dmitri . . ."

"Yes, Father . . ."

"But tell me what has happened? . . ."

"General Maximovich has just told him by order of the Emperor that he is to be exiled to the Persian front. He must leave tonight accompanied by an aide-de-camp of the Emperor.

During the trip he is not permitted to see or to write to anyone." Tears prevented me from continuing. There was no answer from the other side.

"Hello . . ."

"Yes, I am here," I heard the changed voice of my father. "Ask Dmitri whether he wants me to come; I can leave in the car right away. . . ."

I turned to Dmitri who had returned and repeated my father's question.

"No, no! it is not necessary. I do not want to disturb him. Saying good-bye to him would be too hard. I have caused him enough sorrow as it is."

"Father, Dmitri is afraid to disturb you, he begs . . ."

Dmitri took the telephone from my hand:

"Father, I beg you, don't come, I have been a source of such care and anxiety to you."

Our father's health was far from robust. We both knew that the events of the last days had greatly upset him. Dmitri could not say any more. Again he handed me the receiver.

"It is I again, Father. . . ."

"Tomorrow, as soon as you can, you are to come to us, do you hear me?"

"All right, I'll come," I replied.

After that Dmitri said a few more words and hung up the receiver. It was their last conversation; they never saw each other again.

iii

WE returned to the drawing-room. The report of Dmitri's and Yusupov's exile spread with inexplicable speed. The telephone rang ceaselessly, and many people came for exact information. But Dmitri wanted to see only those closest to him, and Laiming undertook to speak for him to the others.

Among the visitors were officers who offered to hide Dmitri in town; others offered to start an uprising in his name.

To all such proposals he listened with deep agitation and some bitterness, begging his too zealous champions not to complicate the situation. He would, he said, obey the orders of the Emperor with resignation and absolute submission. All that he had sought in joining the plot against Rasputin was to uphold the throne, and he did not now intend to reverse that attitude.

Later in the day, Dmitri was told that Count Kutaysov, the Emperor's aide-de-camp appointed to accompany him to the Caucasus, had come to see him. Extremely agitated, the Count entered. Then ensued a painful scene. Indignant, distressed by the commission entrusted to him, he saw himself almost a jailer, and he did not even try to hide his feelings before Dmitri, who in the end was obliged to calm him.

To complete the picture of the attitude that day taken by the officers of the Guards, let me add this one detail: Kutaysov's assignment made upon his brother-officers so revolting an impression that upon his return from the Persian front, they were ready to evict him from the regiment, and were only with great difficulty dissuaded from taking this action. Calmly considered, such an attitude bordered upon plain insurrection; but everyone was at that time so off balance that such talk was not in the least surprising.

Around six that evening the chief of police was announced. He told Dmitri that everything was ready for his departure. A special train would leave the Nicholas station about midnight. Dmitri would be accompanied by Kutaysov and Laiming, who had asked special permission. No one was to be allowed to see them off at the station.

Yusupov was to leave earlier, under escort of one of the officers of the Corps des Pages.

The chief of police departed; Dmitri went to pack. I remained alone, utterly distraught and bewildered. The old, solid construction upon which we had established our lives, from which we saw the world and thought we knew it—the whole meaning of our existence—had vanished. What had led us to this chaos? Who had freed these dark, mysterious forces of destruction? Where was justice? What was wise? On whose side was truth, on Dmitri's, or on the side of Tsarskoie-Selo, where an unbalanced woman reigned in solitude?

I found no answers to these questions. But I wanted to have faith in the future. Bowing before my brother's rash act and its consequences, I wanted to believe that his monstrous self-sacrifice would not be in vain.

Forgetting himself, he had stepped between the people and the imperial couple; he had sought to save his sovereigns in spite of themselves. Would they ever be able to realize that?

My thoughts shifted to Tsarskoie-Selo. I imagined the Empress bent over the bed of her son, suddenly taken ill. Rasputin had repeated, endlessly: "So long as I live, the Tsarevich will live." What could her feelings be towards those who had taken from her the only source of her hope? And in spite of my hostility towards her at that moment, my heart perceived her torture.

These thoughts were replaced unaccountably by others. I experienced a kind of patriotic uplift, altogether youthful, lighthearted, improvident. An end must be made to all that was taking place in Russia, to all that was leading the country to destruction, to a regime which to all appearances had outlived itself.

But what of Dmitri? What considerations, what influences had sent him to the Persian front? How long was my brother's exile to last? Who would protect him from the vengeance of Rasputin's partisans?

Dmitri, having packed, returned, and for the hundredth time we weighed and discussed circumstances of his departure. It seemed now that the only person who could have any influence with the Emperor was his mother. All other members of the family had exhausted every means of persuasion. We decided that I would spend two or three days in Tsarskoie-Selo and then go to Kiev where Marie Feodorovna, the Emperor's mother, lived at that time, supervising the work of the Red Cross. On my way I was to stop in Moscow to see Aunt Ella.

I wished passionately to continue the work begun by Dmitri, and I knew that it would lighten his exile and make it less hopeless to feel that someone was working constantly in his behalf.

We dined, speaking of other matters, trying not to linger among the thoughts which tormented us. After dinner a young captain, the teacher of the officers' course at the Corps des Pages, came to conduct Yusupov to the station. We all descended to the vestibule to see him off. The captain, in full fighting outfit, waited, somewhat embarrassed, on the top landing.

Felix put on his grey soldier's coat and bade us good-bye. We embraced. Followed by the captain, Felix went down the stairs, and the outside door shut behind him with a heavy slam.

We returned upstairs. Dmitri began to look over his papers in the drawers of his desk. He drew forth and thoughtfully examined several large photographs of a very pretty woman, hesitating as to which he would take with him; but they were all much too large and, with a sigh, he thrust them back into the drawer. Having finished with the contents of his desk his hands strayed, half consciously, touching for the last time long-familiar objects lying all around him. His glance rested finally upon a portrait in water-colours of our mother, in a black leather frame standing in front of him behind the inkpot. Then he arose and slowly made the round of the room. I silently followed his movements and the trend of his thoughts. We both knew that he would never see these things again.

Someone knocked at the door. It was my brother's valet with a small, square box of unpainted wood.

"Your Highness, this has just been brought for you," he said, as if embarrassed.

"Give it to me; what is it?" said Dmitri.

"That's just it; I don't know what it is. I won't give it to you. I only brought it to show you; there might be something dangerous in it. . . ."

"A bomb?" laughed Dmitri. "Give it to me, I'll look."

The valet cautiously handed him the box.

"Don't shake it, Your Highness, it might explode. . . ."

We examined it carefully on all sides. Dmitri took a penknife and placed the blade under the top.

"No, no, Your Highness, don't do it yourself, in the name of God," the servant begged him fearfully. "Let me open it."

Dmitri shook the box at his ear and, ascertaining that it could contain nothing terrible, gave it back. The valet left and returned a few minutes later still more embarrassed. The top had been taken off; on the bottom of the box, carefully packed with cotton-wool and tissue paper, gleamed the blue enamel of a Serbian order. This little incident distracted us for a while.

The hour of departure approached inexorably. I decided, in spite of the prohibition, to go to the station to see my brother off. Two of our uncles, the Grand Dukes Nicholas and Alexander had promised to join us. They came a few minutes before midnight, but left us for the while alone.

Now it was time to go. Dmitri threw a last glance upon all he left behind him, patted the soft red hair of his favourite dog, and put on his coat. All the members of the household were assembled in the vestibule. It brought vividly to mind the many farewells that had marked our lives, so heart-rending and so alike.

Most of the servants wept quietly. Dmitri's aide sobbed loudly and his tears dropped onto his coat front. We went down the stairs and entered the car.

The door shut. We rolled through the night down deserted streets. At the station we noticed that the entire square in front of it had been cleared and was surrounded by the police. The chief of police himself opened the door of our car, but made no protest at my presence or at that of our uncles who had come in another car.

We followed him silently through the imperial rooms to the platform. It was bitterly cold. The wind chased the dry, fine snow along the boards. A train stood before us—an engine and three carriages. Along the length of the train and in a semicircle about us, tall gendarmes formed a close cordon. Apart from that, the station was deserted.

The unusual setting, the complete stillness, the empty, half-lit station made a picture both curious and tragic. We huddled together, waiting.

The station master, excited, was keeping close to Dmitri, apparently wanting, yet not daring, to speak to him.

Finally making up his mind, he asked permission to say a word. I learned later that he offered to put the train on a side track after it had left the station, which would make it easy for Dmitri to leave the carriage and escape.

His escort now asked my brother to enter the carriage. We embraced and crossed each other. He turned from me and boarded the train, which began to move slowly. For a long time I could see through my tears Dmitri's white-gloved hand waving his cap.

I was no longer able to think or move independently. Someone's hand took me under the elbow and led me away. I came to myself only in the car, almost home, where Mme. Laiming was waiting for me.

I remained alone with her that night in the immense, abandoned house, and we talked until dawn, going over and over the same ground. Next morning I noticed that the sentinels were still at their posts, guarding apartments now empty. For some reason they had been forgotten. I had great difficulty in reaching the office of the commander and having the guard removed.

I began to plan a course of action and at once discovered that from many upon whose help and support I had the right to count I could expect nothing. Their high-sounding phrases had all been uttered. The object of their solicitude had van-

COUNTESS HOHENFELSEN

Later Princess Paley, with "Volodia" and "Natasha"

ished. It was over. Not knowing from where the wind might next blow, they retired to their corners. I was as one in quarantine.

There were however others more bold. The President of the Duma, Rodzianko, was one of these. We had a long talk. In the afternoon I went to Tsarskoie-Selo.

My father waited for me in his study. He was tired and worn. We kissed, and, leaning back in his deep chair, he asked me, with an attempt at calmness, to tell him in detail about the previous day and Dmitri's departure. He said that after his telephone conversation with my brother he had written a note to the Emperor, asking for an immediate interview. But under some pretext or other the Emperor had refused to receive him.

iv

HERE I must go back to the time when my father, who had already heard at Headquarters about the death of Rasputin, learned from his wife, who met him at the station, that Dmitri was one of the murderers.

The shock was terrific. My father wished immediately to go to Dmitri in Petrograd, but his wife, Princess Paley, fearing for his health, dissuaded him.

At home he called up Dmitri, intending to summon him to Tsarskoie-Selo. But he was already arrested, and they decided that my father would come to lunch the next day.

That same evening my father asked for an interview with the Emperor. After some hesitation he was received but only for a few minutes and only after having been made to wait forty minutes in the reception room.

The Emperor was very curt; he wished not to discuss the case, he said.

Next day at noon my father went to Dmitri. As soon as the door of Dmitri's room had closed behind him, my father, not approaching his son, asked the question which had been tormenting him.

"Can you swear to me that there is no blood on your hands?"

Dmitri raised his hand, crossed himself in front of the ikon hanging in the corner, and replied: "I swear by the name of my mother."

The rest of their conversation is unknown to me.

Two days later, when the rumour spread that the Empress was demanding a court martial for both Dmitri and Yusupov, they saw each other again, and Dmitri gave Father a letter which he begged him to transmit to the Emperor.

In this letter my brother said that as soon as proceedings were instituted there would be examinations and he would be asked for his motive in lifting his hand against Rasputin. But as they had all taken oath not to give any explanations he, Dmitri, proposed to refuse to give any answer, and later to shoot himself. He felt that by such an act he would justify himself in the eyes of the Emperor. I do not know if this letter ever reached the sovereign.

My father saw much more clearly than we, the young ones, the seriousness of the situation. His attitude to what had happened was circumspect and entirely without enthusiasm. He acknowledged that Dmitri and Yusupov had been impelled by a patriotic motive, but contended that their action had been dangerous and thoughtless from many points of view. The deed, as he saw it, only deepened the abyss separating the imperial family from Russia, and the assassination which Yusupov had planned and in which Dmitri participated, even if only in name, was, in my father's opinion, both futile and hideous.

He felt that Yusupov possessed sufficient means to permit him to choose another and more adequate way of getting rid of Rasputin, and blamed Yusupov for involving Dmitri in a deed that would bring such ugly notoriety.

My father felt, moreover, that the Empress, under the influence of her recent sorrow, would become more conservative and reactionary in her viewpoint, and would still more decidedly oppose the slightest concession to public opinion.

No advice, he feared, would now have any effect. Both she and the Emperor, now completely estranged from everybody, received Rasputin's partisans exclusively. His shadow hovered over his victims, still inspiring their thoughts and intentions.

At one time, by request of some of the members of the family, my father took upon himself to tell the Emperor what he thought of the situation, and had tried to depict the picture in its actual lines and colours, unadorned. But the Emperor, in spite of the respect he bore his only living uncle and the son of Alexander II, was mistrustful. He insisted on seeing the picture in quite another light—the more flattering light diffused by the selfish and scheming partisans of a degraded court. It was hopeless.

V

THAT day was Christmas Eve. As in former years a beautiful Christmas tree was set in the ballroom and decorated for my half-sisters, still quite small.

My father interrupted our sorrowful conversation. It was time now, he said, to think of the children; they were impatiently expecting their holiday. We went upstairs to the dining-room, where my stepmother, surrounded by children of both her first and present marriage, was pouring out tea.

The gathering was odd. The elder sister of Princess Paley, L. V. Golovina, and one of her daughters were sincere and fanatic partisans of Rasputin, and so was my stepmother's eldest son, A. E. Pistolkors, married to Mme. Vyrubova's sister. One of the Princess's daughters, Marianne Zarnikau, was on the contrary very friendly with Dmitri and so found herself in the opposite camp. And here were all these people, only a few days after the murder of Rasputin, assembled at the same table with the father and the sister of one of the plotters against his life. The atmosphere was strained and gloomy to the utmost; my stepmother offered in vain new subjects of conversation; all were politely uninterested. My poor little half-sisters, sensing in the air a mood in no way festive, anxiously scanned the faces around them. Finally, to put an end to this painful scene, my father rose to light the Christmas tree.

Next day I went to see my aunt, the Grand Duchess Marie. Intelligent, full of energy and enterprise, she did not enjoy the favour of a court afraid of her independence and rather sharp tongue.

She was the only Grand Duchess of that time who liked and knew how to entertain; she gathered around her not only the local élite, but also the diplomats and the foreigners coming to Petrograd. They respected her intelligence and were attracted by her charm.

She received me this time with even more than her usual kindness and announced herself with characteristic vehemence completely on the side of Dmitri.

The distribution of punishment, she said, had been utterly unjust, and had aroused widespread indignation. On Dmitri alone, the least guilty, had been visited the only sentence of any consequence. Yusupov was simply exiled to his estate; the others enjoyed impunity.

No one of us was now able to penetrate into the palace, so she had thought that we should draw up a family petition asking the Emperor to pardon Dmitri, or at least to mitigate the severity of the sentence.

I took to this proposal with enthusiasm. We drew up then and there a rough draft which I was to show to my father. But first, on my way, I stopped to see her eldest son, the Grand Duke Cyril; both he and his wife had always been very fond of Dmitri. They were still more vehement in their condemnation of the court's attitude. I returned to Tsarskoie-Selo. All that day, ignoring my pleurisy and a considerable fever, I had been driving in an open car, and the weather was very cold.

When I got back to Tsarskoie-Selo I found to my surprise,

and that of my family, a thick envelope addressed in the hand of the Empress and brought by a courier.

Opening it I found a letter and a small wooden ikon of the miraculous apparition of the Virgin Mary. I do not remember the exact wording of the letter but I remember its meaning. The Empress wished to show me that in her thoughts she entirely separated me from Dmitri and assured me of her unchanged feelings.

Immediately I wrote an answer, curt and polite. I said that I could not take a different point of view from that of my brother; neither could I stand apart from him, even if by doing so her affection was lost to me.

In the evening I spoke to my father and his wife about the project of the letter to the Emperor and showed them the rough draft. My father did not manifest the enthusiasm that I had expected. But he did not greatly object, feeling that such a petition would at least indicate a certain solidarity of the family.

My stepmother and I polished the text, copied it, and sent it to the Grand Duchess Marie, who had it printed. Signatures were gathered. Our grandmother, the Queen of Greece, headed the list. Then our petition was taken to the Alexander Palace. It was returned very shortly, addressed to my father, and on the top of the page the Emperor had written: "No one is permitted to engage in murders. I am surprised that you addressed yourself to me. Nicholas."

The Grand Duchess Marie, instead of keeping silent about the annotation of the Emperor, angrily showed it to everyone. Very soon the entire town knew by heart the short sentence that stood at the top of that page.

Immediately after Christmas I left for Moscow and found Aunt Ella much more *au courant* than I had expected. From the beginning of Rasputin's influence at the court she had, she told me, many a time warned her sister, the Empress, against taking him too much into her confidence and becoming too dependent on him. At first the Empress paid no attention to her words, but as Rasputin's importance grew in her eyes, she began to feel more and more prejudiced against those who brought such warnings.

When Rasputin's influence passed from the sphere of the household into that of politics, my aunt, seeing in this a still greater danger, decided this time to carry her warning directly to the Emperor. But again her advice was scorned. The relations between the sisters, until then very friendly and intimate, gradually cooled and the Empress soon began to feel oppressed by my aunt's presence.

In spite of this disagreement in principle they continued to see each other. Aunt Ella went almost as often as before to Tsarskoie-Selo, paying no attention to her increasingly cold reception. This, she said, she had preferred to the alternative—abandoning her sister at so crucial and unpromising a time.

Before deciding upon participation in the plot, Dmitri had paid Aunt Ella a visit in Moscow. He talked with her until he felt that he had a clear idea of the Empress's mental condition. It was only after that, having convinced himself that there was little hope of a normal *dénouement*, that he decided to join with those few men who were ready to bring this *dénouement* about.

My aunt clearly realized all the complications that were arising in connexion with the death of Rasputin, but she was so happy at his disappearance that she could not condemn the murderers. To her, Rasputin had been a living and active personification of evil; and she felt that Providence had chosen Dmitri and Felix to perform judgment upon him.

She told me the details of her last trip to Tsarskoie-Selo, some rumours of which had already reached us in Petrograd. After seeing Dmitri and pondering the situation from all sides, she had determined to make a last attempt to influence the imperial couple.

The Emperor was absent when she arrived in Tsarskoie-Selo.

THE EMPRESS WITH HER SON

She had from her sister the Empress a frigid welcome, and her representation of the sombre, rebellious mood of Moscow, and of the need of immediate change, led to a painful scene.

The next morning she received from the Empress a short note asking her to leave. Their opinions, the Empress wrote, so greatly differed that it would never be possible for them to agree. She added that although the Emperor had returned, he was so busy that he could not find time for the talk my aunt had requested.

My aunt returned to Moscow, greatly depressed. A few days after that Rasputin was killed. Not knowing any of the details my aunt sent Dmitri an enthusiastic and probably incautious wire which was brought to the attention of the Empress. As a result, she had been accused of complicity.

And now, in spite of her devotion to her sister and of all her Christian feelings, my aunt's patience was at an end.

Nervous enthusiasm reigned in Moscow; the inhabitants, considering Dmitri as their own, boasted of his deed. I left there that same day and went on to Kiev. The Dowager Empress, who since our childhood had always been fond of Dmitri and myself, received me with her habitual warmth. She listened attentively to what I had to say, but I understood very quickly that it was altogether useless to count upon any interference from her.

All arguments had long ago been exhausted; besides, there existed subjects which were never touched upon by the mother or the son. In their conversations, everything that concerned the young Empress was carefully avoided.

After this, there remained nothing else for me to do, no one to whom I might turn.

Completely worn out, I fell ill, yet before leaving Kiev I managed to see the Grand Duke Alexander, at that time in charge of aviation there. I remember that we had an interesting conversation on political matters, and he showed me a detailed project that he had worked out for the organization of a responsible Cabinet, in accordance with the demands of the moment and the needs of the country. He was planning to propose it to the Emperor as extremely liberal, yet in full accord with the dignity of power.

I reached Tsarskoie-Selo altogether sick and shattered. My father tried to keep me at his side, but as soon as I was able to leave my bed, I decided to return to the hospital, where work was waiting for me, work in which I might find a diversion for my thoughts.

vi

MEANTIME, my brother had been received with open arms at the small frontier post to which he had finally been assigned. He had been followed on his journey by a number of Rasputin's partisans, intent on avenging the death of their powerful benefactor, but these men had been apprehended and turned back, and his new comrades, General Laiming assured me, watched over him vigilantly.

The death of Rasputin had changed not at all the frame of mind at court. On the contrary, the Empress saw treason all around her and trusted only the people Rasputin had recommended. Revolution was in the air. Two months later, when it came, Dmitri was still at the Caucasus front. The punishment that had been meted out to him saved his life.

During these fourteen years there has been much said and written about Rasputin. No contemporary historical figure aroused such an interest as this peculiar, sly, adroit peasant. The details of his death have been known now for a long time, the causes and consequences of his position at the Russian court have been examined and studied from all sides. But my brother is still true to his given word, true to himself; no one has ever heard from him the description of what happened that night between the 16th and 17th of December, in the Yusupov palace; and it is doubtful that anyone ever will.

PART THREE

ESCAPE

CHAPTER XXIV

UPHEAVAL

I RETURNED to Pskov one cold winter morning early in 1917. It was still dark. The city for many months so familiar to me, now seemed strange, alien; and I myself looked on everything with different eyes.

Uncertainty hung in the air. Faces, till then open and trusting, had become dark and impenetrable. People's eyes avoided me.

I went to work again, but I had no longer my former strength or zeal; something seemed to have been broken within me. The simple and natural relations with the personnel began to change; soon I was being avoided. Our wounded, until then always meek and quiet, were no longer the simple-minded patient men of the beginning of the war. Conversations in the wards grew louder, complaints were heard of the care, of the food. An occasional patient became utterly unmanageable.

One day I was helping to bandage a succession of lightly wounded men, just in from the front. The patients, entering, were distributed among the tables. I had already bandaged an endless number when a short, unpleasant-looking soldier fell to my lot. He was wounded in his right thumb. I placed him on a stool in front of me and taking off the top layer of the bandage patiently began to soak the part of the dirty bandage which had dried to the wound. He fidgeted, muttering under his breath.

I began to take off the wet bandage. Suddenly he jumped up and struck me hard on the chest. I was thrown back but for some reason did not fall. He stood there in the middle of the room, glaring in all directions.

Everyone seemed turned to stone; the first to recover was the doctor who was working with us; he grabbed the man by the collar and dragged him to the other side of the room. That same day we transferred the poor wretch to another hospital.

ii

ABOUT March 8th we heard vague rumours of hunger riots in Petrograd. In Pskov everything was still quiet. On the morning of the tenth, I drove to the station to see my uncle, the Grand Duke George, who was passing through. Crossing the car tracks too rapidly, my driver bounced me against the roof of the car, violently bumping my head. He turned but, as I seemed unhurt, he drove on. After a while I felt drops on my forehead. Lifting my hand I touched it and saw blood upon my white woollen glove. When the car stopped at the station, the military commander, who had come to meet me and had opened the door of the car, started, and exclaimed:

"Are you wounded, Your Highness?"

Only later did I understand why the blood on my face had struck him so forcibly.

In my Uncle George's car, his doctor dressed my head, and we had tea. My uncle seemed to ascribe no great importance to the disorders in the capital. I returned to the hospital with little news for my personnel, who awaited me with some impatience.

Next day, reports were more definite and alarming. And I noticed somewhat curious, distraught glances when I entered the dining-room to take my usual place at the head of the table. It was clear, also, throughout the hospital that the trend of conversation changed at my approach.

On March 13th, the thunderbolt fell. We received direct report about the shooting in the streets of Petrograd. The Volyn regiment, followed by others, had mutinied, gone out into the streets and joined the crowd. Several buildings were set on fire. Prisons were opened and the prisoners set free. The fortress of SS. Peter and Paul was stormed. The Duma, dissolved by a ukase issued a few days previously, had assembled on its own initiative in the Tavrichesky Palace and had formed a committee to serve as mediator between the government and the rioting population.

All reports that reached us were incomplete, disjointed. Nothing was known about the Emperor, where he was, what he was doing, or what he intended to do; this was a bad sign. From time to time General Ruzsky sent his aide-de-camp to see me either with some new information or simply with the desire of reassuring me.

The wounded, especially those who could move about, gathered in groups and loudly discussed the situation. Discipline, upheld of late with such difficulty, perceptibly relaxed.

Towards evening on March 14th I was told that the Emperor had unexpectedly arrived in Pskov. It became known later that he had been stopped at the station of Dno on his way from Headquarters to Tsarskoie-Selo. Two members of the Duma, Guchkov and Shulgin, were coming from Petrograd to meet him there; they had been commissioned to ask the Emperor to abdicate in favour of the Tsarevich.

It was only then that I actually understood what was happening and comprehended the meaning of the word "revolution." Until then it had for me the same significance as the word "death" has for a child. I knew that there had been a revolution in France; I had read of its causes and of its consequences; moreover, I had realized that we were headed towards a like catastrophe, yet when it did actually happen, my eyes still were blinded by the age-old, terrible, and useless illusions.

Revolutions existed in history, books were written about them, and lectures given: they were complicated phenomena, scientific, remote. While here, the riot of a week ago had turned out to be a real revolution and the shadow of death actually threatened all of us who were of the ruling caste.

I remember that not for a second did I really believe in the possibility of the Emperor's abdication. His conduct throughout the past months indicated that now more than ever he was trying—in accordance with his ideas—to preserve the inviolability of power. He could not surrender. He still was the Tsar; he still had faithful servants whose ancestors had for generations served the Russian Emperors, who owed everything to the throne; they could not desert him. And there still were troops, generals, the clergy. . . . In Petrograd it was only a mob that was rioting and a garrison, consisting of worthless men, grown lazy, who did not want to go to the front.

I did not go to the station to meet the Emperor; the events of December still stood too vividly between us. In spite of the dreadful reality, personal grievances still held my imagination in their grip—insignificant grievances in comparison with the immensity of the catastrophe then befalling us; but, alas! it was human to feel them.

About nine in the evening my informant returned with further news. The Emperor was already in Pskov; the members of the Duma had arrived and were in his car, in conference. The mutiny in Petrograd was in full swing.

Through Ruzsky's headquarters, in direct telegraphic connexion with the capital, my friend promised to keep me informed of all that was happening.

Long, weary hours of waiting followed. The evening passed, the night began. I sat in Father Michael's room; Tishin had also come. We were silent; everything had been talked over long ago. The last scene of the drama was perhaps being enacted at the station that very minute. . . .

Finally, at two o'clock in the morning came word: General Ruzsky requested me to come to Headquarters. I threw on a coat and hurried through the yard and the quiet garden to the house of the Commander-in-Chief.

In the vestibule, orderlies sat and stood; it was stifling; a

PSKOV

The Pechersky Monastery

lamp was smoking. The door into the study was open, and I entered.

Ruzsky, sickly pale, with sunken eyes, seemed to have aged during the last few hours; he rose heavily and came in silence towards me. We looked at each other. I did not dare to ask the question. Grasping with both hands his leather belt Ruzsky straightened his tired, stooped shoulders with difficulty, and said:

"The Emperor abdicated tonight both for himself and for the Tsarevich, in favour of the Grand Duke Michael."

He averted his eyes from my face. I stood unable to move. It seemed as if a morsel of flesh had been torn from me.

"The decision of the Emperor to abdicate for the Tsarevich caught us unawares. No one had expected him to take that step. It will have immeasurable consequences," continued Ruzsky, gradually becoming more animated, and beginning to pace the room.

In spite of the heat of the room I was shivering; and his words, although I could hear them distinctly, seemed to come from afar. Mechanically I looked around for an arm-chair and sat down.

"I am glad to be able to tell you what has happened tonight. I do not know what the further development of events will be, nor what judgment history will pass on them; but I can swear by all that is most sacred to me that neither I nor any of those present are guilty of this step. As you know, two days had already been lost; no one knew where the Emperor was and not a single order had been received from him in Petrograd. Before his arrival I talked all the evening on the direct wire with the President of the Duma. Anarchy reigns in Petrograd, the Tavrichesky Palace is inundated by the insurgent troops, the work of the Duma committee is taking place under the most adverse surroundings, with the continual interference of the members of the Soviet of Soldier and Peasant Deputies. Apparently, confusion is supreme. The Soviet demands the immediate establishment of a republic. The committee, however, considers that a change in the form of government is at this moment too risky."

He turned his eyes towards me, then away, and went on:

"Monarchy must be preserved. Yet some concession seems to be necessary. While the power had not been completely snatched away from the Emperor, he should have voluntarily abdicated in favour of the Tsarevich, having previously sanctioned the executive committee of the Duma which by this would have become the new responsible Cabinet. They feel there that succession, juridical as well as dynastical, should be preserved."

Still I said nothing. Ruzsky continued:

"After the Emperor's arrival at Pskov, I spent my time between the station where the imperial train was staying and my office, from which I could communicate with Petrograd by telephone. I was present in the Emperor's carriage during the interview between him and the deputies from the Duma. The text of the abdication had been composed at Headquarters in Mogilev and sent on here by wire. The draft spoke of the Emperor's abdication in favour of his son, with the Grand Duke Michael as regent. But in the meantime the Emperor had conceived a different idea, and the text of the manifesto was altered accordingly. Completely dumbfounded by its contents, we tried to persuade, to exhort, but it was impossible to move the Emperor. He was very calm, as he usually is. . . ."

I listened numbly. It is strange that I should recall, when I hardly listened, so many of his very words and intonations:

"It seems that before leaving Mogilev the Emperor had a talk with the court physician, Prof. Fedorov, about the health of the Tsarevich, and becoming definitely convinced that the disease was incurable, decided to abdicate for him also. Strictly speaking, such a decision is illegal, but is explained by the fact that he could not be separated from his son. No one knows what will happen now. Before abdicating the Emperor signed a ukase dismissing the old Cabinet and naming Prince Lvov Prime Minister and Grand Duke Nicholas as Commander-in Chief of the army. We must await now what the Grand Duke Michael will say. . . ."

I rose. My place was now by the side of the Emperor; I thought of going immediately to the station. He was Tsar no longer. He was alone.

"I am going to the station," I said.

A short pause ensued.

"The Emperor has already gone back to Mogilev," replied Ruzsky.

The room whirled, it seemed, around me; or was it the whole world? Gently, Ruzsky took my arm and led me back to my chair.

Then he began to tell the details of the conference, to describe the expressions of the faces, to recollect various gestures. Little by little I recovered and plied him with questions until the entire picture, so tragic and terrible in its simplicity, stood vividly before my eyes.

The last representative of a dynasty which had occupied the Russian throne for three hundred years had presented the frightened deputies with a sheet of paper upon which the text had been typewritten—and this paper was his final act, the final expression of his autocratic will.

My brain refused to accept the simplicity of such a *dénouement;* it seemed quite natural to me to expect a miracle at that moment. I would not have been surprised had the lightning struck, or an earthquake occurred. It was an historical death and subconsciously I expected it to be followed by signs—as after the death of the Saviour upon the Cross.

Neither could I accept the thought that all hope was lost; although lately the regime had not been what it should; still, in my opinion, it formed a natural part of my country; I could not imagine Russia without a dynasty. It would be like a body without a head. . . .

Comforting thoughts flashed through my mind and I shared them with Ruzsky, wishing, longing to hear a confirmation. The old man looked pensively at me; he did not want to deprive me of my hope, yet he could not encourage my illusions.

"The Grand Duke Michael has never taken much interest in state affairs. The responsibility may frighten him, as well as the people who are now at the helm. It is very difficult, almost impossible, to form a correct estimate of the situation in Petrograd, viewing it from Pskov.

"The tone of the President of the Duma bespoke confusion bordering on helplessness. The situation changes from hour to hour. The cautious, wise men are in the minority. The question is, Will they take some definite line? Anyway, tomorrow I shall order a Te Deum in the cathedral after which will be read the manifesto of the Emperor's abdication and of the ascension to the throne of the Grand Duke Michael. It may have a calming effect."

On this we separated. It was already four o'clock. The aides took me back to the hospital. I went up the dark stairway and stumbled into my room.

iii

LATER that morning Ruzsky sent a messenger to advise me to go to the cathedral for the Te Deum. Revolutionary excitement was, he said, spreading in Pskov; it would be well for me to appear in public, so that it could not be said that in the face of new conditions I was sulking.

I did not argue; it was all the same to me. I don't remember who went with me.

The square and the cathedral were crowded. In the crowd were many soldiers, their breasts adorned with red ribbons, their faces excited.

Entering the church I placed myself behind Ruzsky; someone thrust into my hand a red bow. I glanced at it unseeingly and found it tightly gripped in my glove when I returned home.

The clergy, in their glittering, golden chasubles, came into the centre of the church. The service began. But the mood was not devout; the habitual solemnity of the occasion was altogether absent. Almost no one seemed to be attending to the service. It was the same old Te Deum, but all the atmosphere was changed, new. It proceeded, a thing in itself; all the congregation were thinking and feeling by themselves, apart, and all seemed eager for the end of a needless performance, so that they could take up business more agreeable.

Their faces did not manifest any particular joy, nor even agitation; they were only curious. After the manifesto had been read and after the prayer for the prolongation of the days of the new Tsar and the new government had been offered, I pushed my way through the crowd to the church steps.

Until now, way for our passage had always been cleared by the police, but today the police were absent. The crowd took obvious pleasure in pushing the old general, the officers of his Headquarters, and myself, and sought whenever possible not to yield an inch. There was, however, as yet no real provocation in their attitude. Eyes stared at me with cold curiosity and were ill rewarded, for my face was stiff, my eyes dry and empty, and my body seemed to be made of stone. I descended the church steps, entered the car, and was driven home.

By evening disorders started in the city. Crowds of unruly soldiers roamed the streets, and prisoners were freed from the jail.

Within our walls this roused perceptible reactions. Our wounded no longer straightened up when addressed by the doctors, they began strolling along the corridors in their underwear and smoking, both of which were forbidden. Those who were seated now rose no longer when I passed; and I heard at first timid jokes, then rude remarks. Although it was now disagreeable for me to go through the wards I nevertheless did so twice a day on my way to and from the dining-room. After the first day the doctors asked me not to come to the bandaging-room any more. To this I agreed. I saw that this was no longer my hospital. My child was no longer mine; little by little, it was being torn away from me, and there was nothing that I could do about it.

On the morning of March 17th, rumours as to the abdication of the Grand Duke Michael, which had been circulating about town since the day previous, were officially confirmed. About that time, also, the famous Order No. 1 reached us. Issued by the Soviet of Soldier and Peasant Deputies, without the knowledge of the Provisional Government, it established Soviets throughout the army, abolished the disciplinary subordination of the soldiers to the officers and the familiar appellation "thou" used by the officers when speaking to the soldiers.

Order No. 1 increased, naturally, the general ferment and disintegration. At the front soldiers began to maim, torture, and kill their officers. I was myself, evidently, an officer, and my situation was becoming dangerous. Only two doors separated my rooms from the hospital. One was, moreover, a glass door. There was no place for me to hide and no chance for me to slip away. We had in the hospital at that time about three hundred lightly wounded soldiers who could move about quite easily and eighty orderlies of whose attitude I could not be certain.

When I had investigated the mismanagement and reorganized the hospital, I had taken these orderlies in hand, and although I had no official right to do so, I had nevertheless disciplined them, as need arose, ever since. Recently I had appointed as head orderly Tikonov, a Moscow workman, painter by trade, and a very intelligent man. He read everything he could get hold of, discussed with some self-assurance all possible subjects and never touched a drop of alcohol. Towards his superiors he held himself always in an attitude of independent self-respect. He had socialistic leanings and the doctors had not approved my choice, but I knew him well and trusted him. Now, however, I had to resort to guesswork altogether when I tried to figure how the turbulent events of recent days had affected him.

I was soon to learn. On the very morning that the famous Order No. I was issued, the orderly appointed to the dining-room of the personnel came to see me. He was also a workman, a small, agile Lett, very efficient and one of my favourites. In his hand he held a pack of group photographs—our orderlies, with me in the centre, taken a few days previously.

"Your Highness, allow me to ask you to sign these with your name; the comrades desire it very much," he said, smiling broadly and placing the photographs upon the table in front of me. "Also Tikonov has asked me to tell you not to come alone to the dining-room; we both shall accompany you," he added, continuing to smile.

"All right," said I, asking no explanations, and began to sign the photographs. "Listen to what I want to tell you. We have lived here more than two years together and you all are like my own children. I cannot begin right away to use 'you' instead of 'thou.' Do you understand?"

"Yes, I do. Well, call us as you like, we have always been satisfied with your treatment," he replied, and bending over kissed my hand which was holding the pen.

I told Tishin, who came to ask me not to pass through the hospital, what had happened; now I could not refuse to go into the dining-room. A few minutes before dinner there was a knock at the door.

"Come in," said I. Tikonov stood on the threshold. I looked into his face; it seemed changed to me, morose, hard. Doubt stirred for a second in my heart.

"Come, Your Highness; dinner is served," he said simply. I rose and followed him. The Lett was waiting outside. From that day on until my departure, those two accompanied me twice a day into the dining-room and back.

But in spite of everything, and of all my wavering hopes that such insane conditions would not endure, it became each day plainer that for me to remain in the hospital was only to invite disaster. Only a few days later, for instance, a crowd of drunken soldiers in the town square publicly beat up the General commanding the Pskov garrison and threw him into the river.

This same crowd suddenly remembered me. The husband of one of my nurses, for whom I had obtained a clerkship at Headquarters, told some of his comrades to try to divert the mob's attention and rushed to the hospital to warn me.

I dressed and accompanied by Tishin went through the garden into the Headquarters where I was met by Ruzsky's aides. But even there I could not feel entirely safe. The crowd, not finding me in the hospital, would in the end have discovered my whereabouts. The little group of officers could not have defended me, even if they had wanted to. However, nothing happened this time, for the crowd, although they set out for the hospital, never reached it. In some form or other, such incidents occurred several times.

To stay virtually a prisoner in my own hospital under such conditions was senseless. I went to see Ruzsky and was amazed by his harassed, exhausted appearance. The situation at the front, he told me, was going from bad to worse. The soldiers dealt with their officers with increasing ferocity. Soviets had been organized in all the units, discipline had almost completely disappeared, and the soldiers were deserting their positions in crowds, taking arms and ammunition with them, and attacking trains. Guchkov, the War Minister of the Provisional Government, had made the round of the Northern Front, trying with his speeches to re-establish in the army the fighting mood, but it was all perfectly futile.

As to my departure, the general said that I would have to

wait a few days; the trains were so overcrowded with soldiers running away from the front. If, as he hoped, this flood soon would stop, then I could go. He would let me know in time to get ready.

Leaving Ruzsky's study I came out into the vestibule where several Ural Cossacks—who served as bodyguard to the Commander-in-Chief—were warming my coat by the stove. They offered to accompany me to the hospital. Such an attitude both surprised and moved me.

It was by no means the general attitude. On all sides, all that related to the old regime was being trampled under foot with revolutionary contempt. The Emperor had been abandoned with surprising easiness by everyone, beginning with his courtiers and ending with the clergy. There was something terrifying in this easiness, expressing, as it did, not only contempt for tradition, but the utter absence of any conscious attitude towards the future. The intelligentsia, now at the helm, had nothing concrete to offer for what they had destroyed, and the people appeared to distrust this new caste just as they had the castes preceding it.

The new rulers felt that distrust and wavered before it. They who had not expected to encounter a beast in the people found themselves from the very first in the grip of a beast whom they could not control. All that remained was words. Flaming generalities, fluent demagoguery, fiery speeches; the air was rank with them, endlessly arising; and at that time, words still produced an effect upon the superficial Russian imagination.

Amid all this turmoil I felt myself entirely lost. A feeling of complete helplessness never left me; it seemed as though I was thrown into waves which might swallow me up at any moment; the people floating upon the wreck laughed at my efforts and were ready at any convenient moment to put an end to me. They did not seem to notice that all the time the waves were rising higher and that they themselves were in mortal danger.

On March 21st, following the reading of the manifesto of the Provisional Government, the oath of allegiance to the new order was taken by the soldiers of the hospital, just as in all military units. I did not have enough courage that day to enter the church, but I remember wandering in its vicinity and hearing from afar the words of the Te Deum and of the manifesto.

No one needed me any longer; I seemed to have become an enemy of the people—of my own countrymen—to whom I had given all my strength. To them, I was worse than a stranger; they no longer reckoned with me.

The chief physician, with whom we had never been on good terms, sent the indignant Zandina to ask me when I intended to leave Pskov; he was, he said, expecting his wife and wanted to put her in my room. It was his revenge, and my heart contracted painfully. This doctor's hostile attitude towards me could at any time reach Father Michael, and I decided before it was too late to send him, with the monk who served him, to a friend of his in Kiev. Father Michael, Tishin, and I were going through difficult hours. They knew that they were now impotent to protect me; and we felt, all three of us, that we were living through the last days of our friendship.

Father Michael was the first to leave. Then Ruzsky sent word that I should get ready. I began packing my ikons, my negatives, my drawings, my papers. All that I collected with such love seemed now unnecessary but precious rubbish. My former life lay dead. The one I faced would be a fight for mere existence and an adaptation to this fight.

I made for the last time the round of my favourite churches and spots together with Tishin and Zandina, saying good-bye to Pskov, where I had spent many happy months; I also wandered into the cathedral. Looking at the shrines containing the relics of the Pskov princes, I thought how they too had participated in history and, having played their part, were also relegated to the past.

All the personnel came to see me off at the station, even the chief physician. A crowd had gathered on the platform. The nurses kissed my hand as in former days. The train presented an alarming spectacle. Everywhere, on the roofs, on the platforms, even on the buffers, sat soldiers with their sacks and rifles. The corridors were overflowing with people. The railway authorities, impotent in the face of the grey mass flooding every crack, penetrating everywhere like a swarm of locusts, tried in vain to establish some order. To board a train and travel in such conditions was far from safe, but I had no choice.

Zandina had insisted on going with me as far as Petrograd to protect me. She and my dog and I finally got into the carriage somehow and took our seats in a compartment which Headquarters had secured with great difficulty as for their own use. The staff officer, having closed the door after us, secured it with a seal which the military commander of the Petrograd station was to break. This seal was our only protection.

When the train began moving, and first the people on the platform, then the city, disappeared from view, my nerves gave way completely. For a long time I could not stop my tears. I was painfully sorry for everything, for Pskov, for the past, for myself, and no matter how I tried I could not in the least imagine what the future would be.

We arrived safely in Petrograd although the train was many hours late. The seal was broken by an aide of the commander. No one met me at the station. The imperial rooms, through which I usually passed, were locked. A footman from the house, no longer wearing his livery, was waiting for me in the street and, instead of the car, there was a hired, ancient brougham, drawn by two faded white horses. Wearily I climbed the high step into the coach and sat upon the faded, sunken seat. A thick, musty smell enveloped me. We started. Everything around seemed alien and terrifying. The streets were deserted and quiet. The Sergeievsky Palace resembled a mausoleum.

Only two weeks had passed since the beginning of the revolution, yet they seemed like years.

CHAPTER XXV

SHELTER

THE day following my arrival I watched, from the window of the drawing-room looking out on the Neva, a procession which had been arranged to honour the victims of the revolution. The ceremony was civil. For the first time the clergy did not participate in a Russian affair of state. And this parade of mourning served another purpose; it was a display of power on the part of the new government.

Astounded, I watched the pageant that, with the utmost order and ceremony, slowly unfolded itself. Here was old Russia expressing in forms curiously modified its past, glorious and tragic, and its hope for a better future.

Paléologue, the French Ambassador, in the memoirs that he has written of his days in Russia, remarks with his usual penetration that the dignity of the revolutionary celebrations can be explained only by the Russian genius—and weakness—for an outward, theatrical display of every emotion. The present ceremony, although a funeral, bespoke joy and relief that the great change had come. This mood, strange to me, permeated all Petrograd. In Pskov, where the military predominated, the governing mood had been one of perplexity and anxiety.

But Petrograd rejoiced. The statesmen of the former regime were under lock in state buildings or in prisons; the newspapers sang laudatory hymns to the revolution and freedom and reviled the past with an astounding fury. Pamphlets with caricatures of the Tsars and with despicable and libellous hints and accusations were sold in the streets. Altogether new expressions became the fashion; the language was suddenly enriched with foreign words, imported to express more forcibly the enthusiasm of the moment.

But the practical life of the city had, in spite of all this revolutionary enthusiasm, become sluggish and colourless. The streets were carelessly cleaned. Crowds of idle, dissolute soldiers and sailors wandered continually about, while the well-dressed people who owned carriages and cars hid away in their homes. Police were not to be seen. Things ran themselves, and very badly.

Even those of our servants who had been in our service for many years, sometimes even for generations, were influenced by the new currents. They began to present demands, form committees. Few remained faithful to the masters who had in all times taken care of them, pensioned them in their old age, nursed them when they had been sick, and sent their children to school.

Petrograd frightened me. I removed to Tsarskoie-Selo and joined my father. As usual, he remained calm. The trend of events cut him to the heart, but he displayed no impatience and did not blame the revolutionaries. It was all, he said, the result of the terrible blindness of the past regime.

I learned less from him than from others of the family the part he had played in the drama of the last days of the reign. He had sought by all possible means to save the situation. On March 13th, he had determined at any cost to see the Empress. Since the death of Rasputin all relations between our house and the Alexander Palace had been broken off, and he was somewhat at a loss as to how to proceed. But the Empress solved this difficulty by suddenly sending for him.

He went to the palace. She received him sternly, and accused all the imperial family, headed by him, of trying wrongly to influence the Emperor and of being insufficiently devoted to the throne.

More than ever before, she opposed the idea of concessions. She was certain, and said that she had proofs, that throughout the country the people were on the side of the Tsar. The imperial family, the aristocracy, and the members of the Duma had the audacity to think otherwise, but they were mistaken, as would soon be shown. My father found it necessary to remind her that all that he had personally undertaken had been with the purpose of dispelling illusions which constituted, in effect, a fool's paradise. She said that the Emperor was expected back the next morning.

Father arose early and went to the station but to his confusion the train did not arrive. Alarmed, he returned home after having waited for a long time. Later in the day came the report that the train had not been allowed to come through to Tsarskoie-Selo.

Every minute now was precious. My father composed a manifesto, granting the constitution, and sent it to the Alexander Palace, imploring the Empress to sign it. She refused.

So my father signed it himself and sent it to Petrograd to be signed by the elder Grand Dukes, after which it was delivered to the Duma, where eventually it came into the hands of Milyukov. Together with the manifesto my father sent a private letter addressed to Rodzianko, the President of the Duma, asking him to do everything in his power to protect the person of the Emperor.

At four in the morning of March 16th, the new revolutionary commander of Tsarskoie-Selo knocked at my father's house and announced the abdication of the Emperor, both for himself and for the Tsarevich, in favour of the Grand Duke Michael.

In the morning my father went again to see the Empress. Incredible as it may seem, she did not know of the abdication. No one had found the courage to impart this news to her and my father was obliged to do it. She took the blow with remarkable steadiness, speaking with the utmost self-possession of her children, then sick with measles, and of the possibility of leaving with them for the Crimea.

That same day the Grand Duke Michael abdicated also, and in the evening the commanders of the reserve units stationed in Tsarskoie-Selo gathered in my father's house for a conference. They decided, in view of the impossibility of acting otherwise, to submit to the will of the Emperor Nicholas II, expressed in the manifesto of the abdication, and to recognize the Provisional Government.

In laying down his power, the Emperor had insisted that Russia fulfil her obligations to the Allies and carry on the war, at any sacrifice, to a victorious conclusion. The Empress had finally received this word from him, together with more personal messages, that evening. He was in Mogilev, and was transferring command of the armies to General Alexeiev, Chief of Headquarters; his mother, he added, was to come to see him there.

Leaving the palace, my father addressed from the steps a crowd of soldiers who had gathered in the yard. He asked them not to disturb by noisy demonstrations their former Empress and her sick children. The soldiers took his words good-naturedly and promised to be considerate. My father's appearance and his sonorous, imposing voice made an impression, which, however, soon evaporated; for the next day certain of their number wandering under the palace windows took pains to be overheard in vulgar and insulting remarks about their former sovereigns.

On April 4th, in consequence of the rumour that General Ivanov was approaching Tsarskoie-Selo with five hundred cavaliers of the Order of St. George, it was decided to place the Empress and her children under arrest in the Alexander Palace. Of this she was informed by General Kornilov, the new Commander-in-Chief of the Petrograd district.

Next day, late in the evening, the Empress again summoned my father to the Alexander Palace. Guchkov, the Minister of War of the Provisional Government, and General Kornilov were making the rounds of the Tsarskoie-Selo garrison and had asked her to receive them. The Empress had not thought it wise to refuse, but she did not wish to stand alone in this ordeal, so she asked my father to be present. She comported herself, my father told me, with outward calm, in the presence of these envoys of revolution, and spoke to them with cold dignity.

What, they asked, could they do for her? She asked two things, first, freedom for her arrested attendants, guilty only of devotion to her; second, that the new government continue to supply with all necessary equipment the hospitals she had organized in Tsarskoie-Selo. For herself, she added, she asked nothing.

As the conference ended, my father came out into the corridor with Guchkov and Kornilov and asked them to remonstrate with the soldiers appointed to guard the arrested Empress; their behaviour was shameful. Both Guchkov and Kornilov promised to do all in their power, but this was very little. No one dared to order the soldiers about. Oratory and cajolery had to be used instead; and words had become cheap.

Father spoke sadly of the changed appearance of the Alexander Palace. It was, he said, all but unrecognizable. Few of the court remained; some had been arrested; others had fled, or stood apart, afraid to arouse the suspicion of the new rulers by their devotion to the old. In these wide corridors, covered with thick soft carpets, where formerly efficient, silent servants glided noiselessly, throngs of soldiers now reeled, with coats unbuttoned, in muddy shoes, caps on the side of their heads, unshaved, often drunk, and always noisy.

ii

At my father's home there still reigned a certain atmosphere of inward warmth and comfort that made it seem doubly a refuge from surrounding chaos and uncertainty. It was a state of mind, rather than an expression of any actuality. My father, who was fifty-seven years old at the time, endured with a remarkable serenity the loss of associations and the repudiation of standards long dear to him; and he met those material deprivations, which began already to intrude upon us, with a patience and resignation that cut me to the heart.

Our everyday life had changed very little. We still followed the order established by years of habit, but in many ways our life became quieter. We were now in such a position as to make friendship with us compromising for others. Anyone who called at our house or at the homes of any other members of the former imperial family was liable to find himself afterwards in difficulties. Those who did come found it best to invest their call with mystery; the farewell call of the French Ambassador Paléologue was, for instance, carefully veiled. But my father preferred not to place his friends in awkward positions, so we saw fewer and fewer people.

I missed my work and could not help regretting my idleness. Two weeks after my departure from Pskov, Dr. Tishin came to see me, charged by the hospital orderlies with an astonishing commission. They had formed their own Soviet and had passed a resolution asking me to return to Pskov and to reassume full authority over the hospital. I refused, but in spite of everything, I was, I remember, flattered by their request, which even today I do not know how to explain.

Tishin said that the hospital and personnel had changed completely; no one was any longer interested in the work. They quarrelled constantly; every day more nurses requested transfer, or walked out. This confusion within reflected only feebly the wilder confusion without. The whole city of Pskov, Tishin told me, was plunging into revolutionary disorder.

Even at Tsarskoie, everything around us changed with vertiginous speed. We followed with painful interest each new change and reversal, and sought endlessly to foretell our future. Our horizon was cramped. We could see little. Each new day gave the lie to our hopes and conjectures of the day previous.

Yet still we lived, and hoped. In spite of the revolution, in spite of the insults which we encountered at every step, we still believed in the traditional Russian ideal, believed in the Russian soul. A brief dose of reality would, we imagined, quickly drive out of the heads of the people their enthusiasm for bungling amateur government; things would readjust themselves.

Meanwhile one heard less and less about the government. The Soviet of the Soldier and Peasant Deputies every day clamoured louder and more often. The intelligentsia, who had so warmly welcomed the revolution, sought desperately now to conceal with catchwords, speeches, and sounding manifestoes, its complete incapacity to govern.

Like ourselves, they also had their ideals, cherished their illusions, believed in them. They thought that they could expect from the masses, so suddenly freed, a conscious response, a rational co-operation. The inspired speeches of Kerensky, then a Radical minister in the new Cabinet, were an expression of this belief, and so was the struggle of the government and of the generals to continue the war and carry out our obligations to the Allies. All was futile. The country was in the power of soldiers under arms. There were several millions of them, and they did not want to fight.

The Emperor, having returned to his family, lived with them under arrest in the Alexander Palace, constantly subjected to unnecessary mortifications and cruel insults. The people surrounding this once royal family took pleasure in humiliating them. They had been completely torn off from us, and no one from the outside world was permitted to see them. Their former voluntary solitude was now replaced by solitude enforced; and they struggled patiently, one heard, to obey all the orders—often contradictory, and usually altogether senseless—of the new government.

Sometimes one could catch a glimpse of them from afar.

Every day after lunch the Emperor came into the garden with the children and, under the supervision of many guards, cut the ice and cleared the snow. The place for this performance was usually chosen near the fence of the park and the inhabitants of Tsarskoie-Selo, especially those of the lower classes, gathered on the other side to stare and jeer. Remarks always rude and sometimes obscene flew about, while the Emperor continued his modest work, very calmly, as though he heard nothing.

My stepmother sometimes joined this crowd and would return weeping at what she had seen and heard. What hurt her most was not so much the crowd's hostility towards this monarch who so recently was omnipotent, but the strange indifference and brutality with which these common people gathered to gaze at their former sovereign as if he were some rare animal in a cage. They spoke of him, she said, exactly as though he were a beast unable to hear or understand them.

Neither my father nor I went to look at this spectacle. I avoided driving by the park of the Alexander Palace. At the main gate, and at all the small ones, sentries lounged on benches or boxes, trying apparently to indicate by their untidy, dissolute appearance that they belonged to the revolutionary army.

My sympathy for the captive imperial family, especially for the Empress, was, I must confess, purely impersonal. I was sorry for them as I would have been for anyone in their position, but that was all. Deep within my heart had accumulated so much bitterness that even our past personal relations could not stir my heart in their behalf. It was too great, the price we now had to pay for their age-long narrow-mindedness and stubbornness.

Such feelings, even if they were shared by my family, were never openly discussed. It had all been considered long before; and now that the thing had happened, it was too painful to talk about. Moreover, in spite of the blows that the revolution

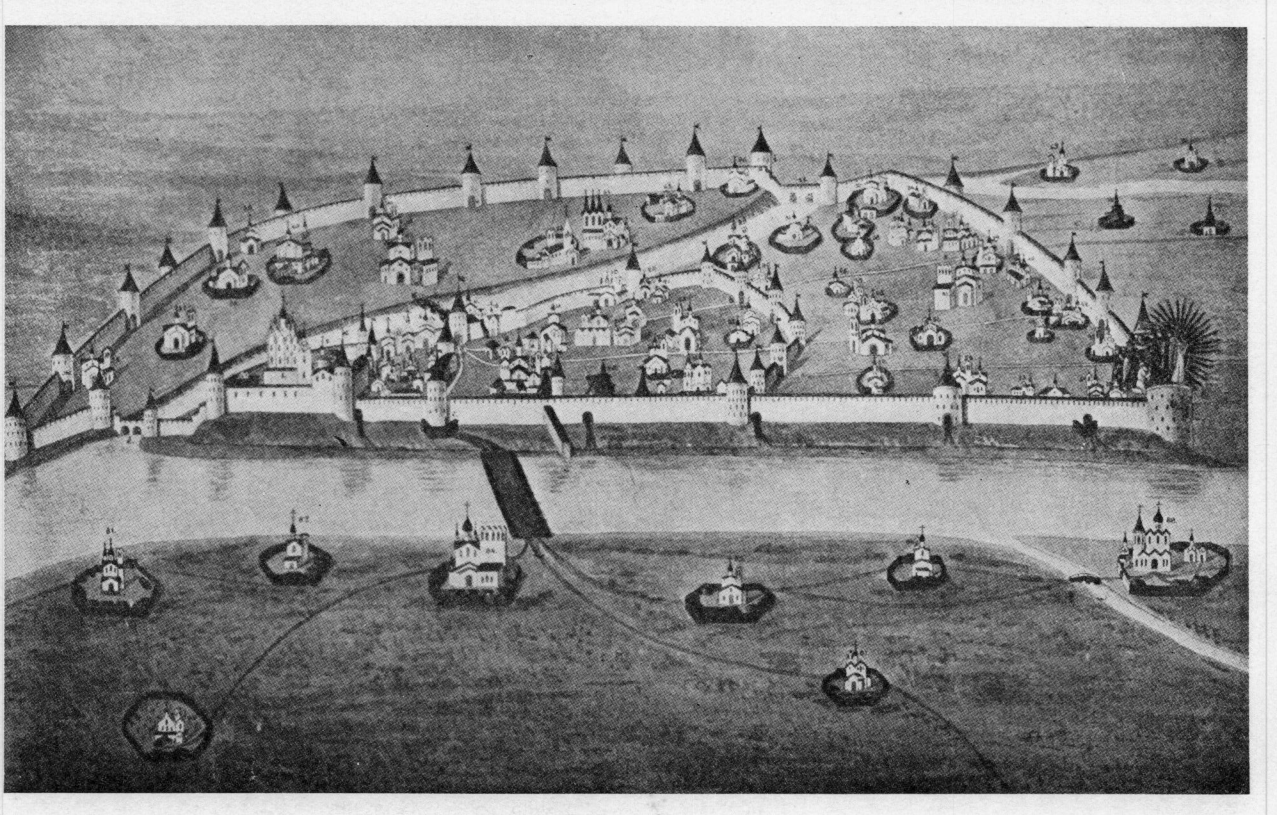

PSKOV IN 1581

From an Ikon

was dealing us, we had to recognize that we were all in a way guilty and responsible parties.

It seemed to me now, as it had in the past, that in our inadequate training and education lay the principal explanation of our downfall, and I saw now that this applied to all ranks in Russia, high and low. That same lack of a conscious attitude towards life, that same light-mindedness and superficiality with which we had faced the disintegration of the old, we now displayed even more markedly in trying to adjust ourselves to the new. We gave, as do children, a tremendous attention to trifles. For instance, an infantile lack of all sense of proportion was responsible for the hysterical decision of officious clergy to delete from the Psalms of David all lines containing the word, "king."

All that had formerly been honoured among us was now to be destroyed without a trace. Neither history, country, honour, nor duties existed any longer. Liberty was a new toy that fell into the hands of clumsy and dangerous grown-up children, only to be broken immediately by their rough hands. The revolution permitted, justified, and excused everything. The new rulers strove to attach to the word a special, sacred meaning, the meaning that made it a Sign from Heaven and a shield against all rational criticism. A remark of my father which was especially to the point characterizes the mood of that time. "There is no Russia any longer," he said. "There is a country called Revolution and this Revolution must be protected and saved at any price."

Holy Week came and then Easter. We celebrated at home. Slowly the joyless spring asserted its rights. In our house an appearance of peace still reigned, but around us every day brought new changes for the worse. Tsarskoie-Selo bore an entirely different appearance. Instead of the well-dressed people and the neat soldiers of the former garrison, the peaceful, clean little town was now inundated by unruly, dissolute soldiers of the reserves. The immense old park, in which there had usually worked a whole army of gardeners, now stood deserted. The streets had not been cleared of snow and when it began to melt there was no one to take care of the mess.

Later in the spring it was impossible to walk in the park alone. The soldiers, from whom there was no escape anywhere, had taken complete possession. They damaged statues, trampled the grass, broke the trees, and bathed naked in the ponds in plain sight of everybody.

In the Town Hall, which was separated from our garden by a canal, noisy conferences and meetings took place continually, lasting sometimes throughout the night and giving us a great deal of worry and anxiety. Drunken shouts, mixed with the sounds of the *Marseillaise*, laughter and abuse, drifted across the water with appalling clarity. When I happen now to hear the *Marseillaise*, I always connect with it the memory of those months.

This unattractive and often repulsive outward existence made me value still more dearly our family life. All that was left to us in this world was our tender love for one another, which grew deeper and more understanding every day. I remember how, in the evenings, sitting in my father's study listening to him read, I used to watch his face, his greying temples, the movement of his lips, the gestures of his hands. I drank in every detail, every intonation of his voice, saw the little vein throbbing at the side of his ear, observed the lines of his neck above the collar. Distant memories of my childhood, all connected with him and with my love for him, flashed through my mind, and it seemed to me that all the love I had known in my life centred around him and my brother. How dear he was to me! With what joy I greeted him every morning and with what tranquil satisfaction heard him speak. His conversation was as serene and as witty as ever. His mind overrode disaster. I valued every minute I spent with him and was grateful to fate for each new day.

iii

Most of my time I spent in the company of Volodia, my step-brother, whom I had learned to know well and to love during my trips home from the hospital.

Volodia was an extraordinary being, a living instrument of rare sensitiveness which could of itself produce sounds of startling melody and purity and create a world of bright images and harmonies. In years and experience he was still a child but his spirit had penetrated into regions reached only by a few. He had genius.

The first child of my father's second marriage, he confirmed the theory that exceptional children are born of a great and exceptional love. When he was still a baby there was something indefinable about him that set him apart from the others. When he was a child, in fact, I considered him a nuisance, affected, and priggish. But later I understood that he was simply a being older than his years lost in the milieu to which his age assigned him. His parents saw how different he was from the others and wisely did not try to shape him according to pattern as had been done with us. They allowed him comparative freedom to develop his unusual abilities. While still a child he wrote good verse and very fine plays, to be acted by his small sisters. He played the piano; he painted; and at a very early age astounded people by his extensive reading and his extraordinary memory.

Until he was sixteen, he shared my father's banishment in France. Then he was sent to Russia, with the Emperor's permission, and entered in the Corps des Pages, a military school. According to the family tradition he was to be an officer. There was nothing military in his character, but the years spent away from an adoring family, the contact with boys of his own age, and the discipline of the school did him a lot of good. He became more natural, simpler in his ways. Having formerly spoken Russian very badly, he quickly learned his mother-tongue and knew it better than many of those who had lived in Russia since childhood.

The many subjects studied at the Corps did not prevent him, even there, from developing his own abilities. At eighteen he brought out a first book of verse which made something of a stir. He wrote with equal facility in three languages, but preferred to publish his first works in Russian. Throughout his stay at the Corps he continued privately to school himself in painting and music. He was more than talented; one had the feeling that mysterious forces worked within him, driving him onward to inspirations inaccessible to ordinary humans and remote from all things mundane. In his later verses, which came out during the war and the revolution, contemporary events were not in the least reflected; his work, on the contrary, was permeated by a profound sense of peace and of spiritual equilibrium.

For a long time I had been following his development with increasing interest and trying to penetrate the workings of a mind so different from my own. We talked for hours, exchanging impressions, trying to express to each other our thoughts and feelings. Sometimes our conversations lasted till dawn. I remember once, during a beautiful white night, we opened wide the window of my bedroom. Climbing upon the wide sill, we waited for the sunrise and watched in silence the constantly changing nuances of the sky. My stepmother from her bedroom heard us talking and came to tell us to go to bed.

Volodia was passionately and tenderly attached to his family and especially to his mother, whom he adored. She repaid him in kind and understood him better than my father, whose psychology was more removed from those qualities which made Volodia extraordinary. Father regarded his writing as a divertisement and looked at him with a trace of amused condescension. Apparently Volodia was to him some curious kind of duckling that had hatched in an eagle's nest.

It was, I believe, in 1915 that Volodia left the Corps des Pages, and joined as an officer the regiment of Hussars of the Guards. He served in the war for several months, both in the regiment and at the headquarters of my father when the latter was commander of an army. But he had no aptitude for things military; he suffered, moreover, from weak lungs and did not bear up well under the hardships of the war. Several times he had to be sent home from the front with a high temperature and a serious cough and finally he was obliged to go to the Crimea for treatment. The climate of Northern Russia did not agree with him; he could not get used to it.

There dwelt, without any doubt, deep in his heart, a premonition of what was in store for him; yet this premonition provoked in him neither bitterness nor regrets, only a burning desire to perfect his mind and express it. During the last summer he wrote ceaselessly. Inspiration seemed never to forsake him. He would sit down at the typewriter and write, without pausing, verses that needed almost no correction. Yet in spite of this productivity and this purely mechanical way of writing, the quality of his verse improved continually. It seemed to me then that the speed of his work was somewhat overdone; I remember saying to him once that in pouring forth such torrents of new verse he gave himself no time to polish them.

He was then sitting at his desk, one hand propping his cheek while with the other he made notes upon the margins of the poems he had just finished. Having listened to my words he turned towards me his face, always pale, and smiled sadly and somewhat enigmatically.

"What I am writing now comes to me in a completely finished form; changes would only spoil the freshness of the inspiration. I must write. After I am twenty-one I shall not write any more. Everything that is in me must find its expression now; it will be too late afterwards. . . ."

So his work went on. To the pile at his elbow were added

new sheets, neatly typed, of sonorous rhymes. In his lighter moments, he made very good caricatures. There was a whole album of such drawings representing amusing episodes of our family life, and they were so witty and so to the point that you could not look at them without laughing.

At that time my stepsisters were still small girls who lived their own separate, childish life. They did not look alike, nor had they the same dispositions. The elder, Irene, was thin, pensive, and impressionable. She had regular features and resembled my father. The second, Natasha, was gay and animated, with a turned-up nose, plump, pink cheeks, and beautiful blond curls. My father bore towards these, his youngest children, a tenderness altogether particular; and they adored him.

I have never known how to treat children; I remember all too clearly my own childhood; and all those things which in the conduct of grown persons used to surprise and hurt me seem now curiously transferred to my own relations with children. Impulsively I tried to come closer to my little sisters, tried to show them that I understood them better than they thought, but it was all wasted effort. They were not afraid of me; it was not even that they distrusted me; but in their minds I belonged irrevocably to the category of the grown-ups. Only one thing ever united us overwhelmingly—our common, childish love for our father. This feeling is so lasting that even now our relations are mainly built upon our memories of him.

The girls revered their brother and greatly admired him. Volodia took advantage of this to make them carry out all his desires. In rehearsing them in the plays he wrote he worked them mercilessly for hours on end. Highly flattered by his attention his sisters endured patiently all his rudeness, his scolding, even his slaps. He often made them cry, yet they always took up a new play with the same enthusiasm and did not in the least appreciate it when I or some other grown-up tried to protect them from Volodia's arbitrary tyranny.

iv

In the beginning of the summer I went to Moscow. At that time everybody was advising everybody else as to the best way to hide jewels and property. Our money and bonds, which were at the Department of Appanages, had been confiscated at the very beginning of the revolution, and we only had the little that remained in private banks. I had also enough jewels to form in themselves a large capital and I had to think of some place to put them where they would be safe. A friend recommended the Moscow Loan Bank. I followed this advice and, taking my jewel cases, went to Moscow where I stopped at Aunt Ella's nunnery. I had not seen my aunt for several months. Nothing around her had changed, the atmosphere was still the same, but I was struck by her tired and ill appearance. She, who had always been on the go, now spent most of her time upon a wicker chaise-longue with a piece of embroidery or some knitting.

We talked at length of present events and of the causes that had brought them about. One evening when I was telling her about the life of the captive Emperor and his family, I added that if she wished to send them a letter I might find the means of having it delivered.

Her eyes turned hard and cold; her lips tightened. She replied somewhat sharply that she could not send a letter; she had nothing to say; she and her sister, the Empress, had long ago ceased to understand each other.

I kept silent. Nothing more was said but I clearly felt in her reply a reverberation of what had happened between them two months before the revolution, at the time of their last meeting. That had been the climax of my aunt's long effort to show her sister where false advisers and headstrong ignorance would lead her—and lead all Russia.

From time to time the alarm was sounded. The Soviet of

the Soldier and Peasant Deputies was acquiring greater and greater power and, since the beginning of the summer, especially since the arrival of Lenin, the overthrow of the weak Provisional Government was to be expected at any moment. The day for the uprising had more than once been set and many people were said to have exact information about the movements and intentions of the Bolsheviks. We lived on rumours or warnings of the most diverse character, sent to us by well-wishers, often unknown, whose zeal exaggerated and even distorted the facts.

Once in the beginning of July, late at night, when we had been long asleep, there was a knock at my door. Waking, I saw upon the threshold of my bedroom Marianne Zarnikau, one of my stepmother's daughters by her first marriage. She explained that we must immediately dress and go to Petrograd. She had come from there in an automobile to fetch us. According to information which had come to her the uprising of the Bolsheviks was set for the next day, and it was among their plans to go with armoured cars to Tsarskoie-Selo and tear away from the Provisional Government the Emperor and all his family.

Marianne and her husband had driven all the way to Tsarskoie-Selo to warn us. We dressed and drove to Petrograd. But that time nothing happened and we returned to Tsarskoie-Selo the next day. The plan of the Bolsheviks to overthrow the Government had failed. Lenin and Trotsky went to Kronstadt where, since the beginning of the revolution, the most lawless elements had gathered. Several brutal murders had already been committed in that locality, but we still had a few more weeks of comparative peace.

CHAPTER XXVI

LOVE

VOLODIA had several friends who came to see him. Oftener than the others came Aleck Putiatin, the youngest son of Prince Michael Sergeievich Putiatin, the commander of the palaces in Tsarskoie-Selo. His eldest brother Sergey, who served in the Fourth Regiment of the Sharpshooters, sometimes came with him. He was a splendid officer, twice wounded, and cited for heroism in action. He came fairly often to our house; I had known him since childhood; but during the war I saw him but seldom. He spent almost all his time at the front and I in Pskov, and our leaves did not correspond.

Only once, I think, we found ourselves in Tsarskoie-Selo at the same time. It was in winter. Some friends gave a dinner followed by a sleigh ride at night in the park, and Putiatin and I found ourselves in the same sleigh. A light flirtation began between us, and a week later, when I had returned to Pskov he surprised me by appearing at the hospital on the way to his regiment. He brought an immense package of jellies as a gift from my stepmother—and as an excuse for seeing me; for this attractive and agreeable young man was endowed with an almost insurmountable shyness. Until then, I had seen him alone only once, and we were completely at a loss how to begin our conversation.

Many months passed. The revolution which brought me to the comparative refuge of Tsarskoie-Selo brought him there also from the front, where—because of his father's situation at court—his position had become dangerous. And now that we were both refugees, in a manner of speaking, at Tsarskoie, he came often to see me at my father's house. Our relations adjusted themselves; our mutual shyness disappeared; we were definitely attracted to each other.

Feelings that I had never before experienced stirred in the depths of my heart. In spite of the revolution, in spite of all the uncertainty, all the anxiety, our unused youth, our fresh mental forces, leaped to claim their due. Spring was upon us, carrying along living floods of new joy. Above all else, one wanted happiness, one wanted to take from life everything that was left for life to give. Our very realization of the peril, of the indefiniteness of our situation, our constant personal danger, contributed to the awakening of these feelings and set them aglow. Thus, at the collapse of our old world, we dared upon its wreck to seize at a new chance of happiness, to live a new life.

I gave myself entirely over to the strange new delight of being really in love. Hesitating to invite him too often to Tsarskoie-Selo, I began going to Petrograd to receive him in my apartment in the palace on the Neva.

These trips I made entirely alone, a new experience, as I had never until then travelled unaccompanied. Before, even for the short trip from Petrograd to Tsarskoie or back, the imperial rooms were opened for us and a special compartment or even a whole carriage was assigned to our use. Now, I had to buy my own ticket and take a place in the train together with the rest of the people, most of whom refused to conform themselves to class distinctions. Upon the velvet seats of a first-class carriage I travelled side by side with soldiers who carried their rifles loaded and smoked a villainous cheap tobacco, being careful to blow it in the direction of their neighbours, the hateful bourgeois.

A certain risk was involved in these trips. Once in summer when the Bolsheviks were trying out their strength, I came into Petrograd when it was in a state of ferment. Everything that we owned in the way of a vehicle had long ago been requisitioned and there was not a single cab in waiting at the station; I had to walk. As soon as I came out from the station on to the square, I sensed that something was wrong; I had by that time become used in a certain degree to recognize by intuition the mood of a street. Where trouble was brewing, those streets would be deserted, and the whole vicinity would seem tense, hushed, holding its breath.

So it was now. I had to walk to the Neva. On the way I met almost no one. I heard distant shots and the bark of machine guns. I cannot say that the walk gave me any special pleasure and I was glad when I reached the gates of the house safely.

That evening Putiatin accompanied me back to Tsarskoie-Selo. Nothing, however, would have prevented me from making these trips, and my family, who knew about the disorders expected in Petrograd, received me upon my return with offhand questions and no particular anxiety.

This was in no sense surprising. We had become accustomed to living from day to day amid constant alarms, true and false. We knew that we lived only on sufferance, that our lives hung in the balance between the whims and expediencies of contending factions. The danger was so obvious and so constant that we ended by pretending not to notice it. Otherwise, life would have been unbearable—and one had to live.

But my father one day broke through all such pretences.

"No one," he said, "can possibly tell what will happen to us. We may be obliged to part or we may be parted by force. I am old; Dmitri is far away. You must find yourself a good man and marry him; then I would feel easy about you."

This last he repeated, half teasingly, when he began to note the frequency of Putiatin's visits; and then one day he said to me quite seriously:

"Listen, if you like Putiatin, I consider that you should marry him."

Our own minds were already decided. With my father's

approval, we became engaged early in August and decided not to postpone the marriage but set the date for one of the first days of September. For the first time in my life I was truly in love, and very happy.

ii

On all sides one heard rumours of the government's intention to remove the imperial family from Tsarskoie-Selo. Tsarskoie had become a centre of Bolshevist activity; the government feared for the safety of its former rulers and proposed to transfer them to the Crimea—this was but one of the rumours; also, many other things were said. In reality, the Soviet was afraid that the Allies might aid the Emperor and his family to leave Russia.

Europe, however, showed but small concern for the fate of her former mighty ally; she was busy with her own affairs. Having hastened to recognize the Provisional Government at once, she had been sending missions and diplomats to greet the revolution, hoping always to receive better support from a democratic order than from the former autocracy. But Russia could not help any longer. She could not, it seemed, even help herself. Striving to retain power as long as possible, Kerensky made greater and greater concessions to the Bolsheviks.

On August 12th, at which time the Emperor, the Empress, and the children had spent five months under arrest in their palace, they were sent, with a few of their former attendants and servants, to Tobolsk in Siberia. No one was permitted to bid them good-bye except the Grand Duke Michael, brother of the Tsar, who was admitted only for a few minutes.

Their departure was accompanied by humiliations similar to those which had accompanied their life under arrest. They were told the night before to hold themselves ready for departure and were kept waiting, dressed, almost all night. Their departure left us with painful impressions, but we had no definite intimation of the tragedy that would put an end to their exile.

A month before my marriage I moved to Petrograd, to the Neva, in order to prepare some things. On one of the last days of August, Putiatin and I went to Tsarskoie-Selo for lunch. In a pouring rain, we took a cab from the station.

Coming to my father's house I noticed that the immense grilled entrance gates, which usually stood wide open, were closed. A second glance showed the house surrounded by sentries.

Chilled to the heart with fear, I jumped from the cab and, followed by Putiatin, began pacing along the grille, trying to peep into the windows of the house and see someone.

But there was no one to be seen anywhere; the yard was empty, the house looked as if everybody were dead. The only thing that we succeeded in finding out was the number upon the soldiers' shoulder straps.

Putiatin knew the commander of the regiment to which the sentinels belonged. Not knowing what else to do, we went to the barracks. This was not especially safe, for had the soldiers recognized me there might have been trouble, but we never thought of that.

Even there, we did not learn very much. The commander of the regiment could only tell us that thus far my father and his family had not been taken away; they were under arrest in their home by order of Kerensky.

I was somewhat calmed by the realization that my father was still in his own house. But the situation was none the less threatening. This arrest, I saw, marked us out. Until now, no one had touched us; in the general turmoil we had escaped attention. Now that we had been drawn by this act into the focus of public notice, it was likely that the consequences would go beyond mere arrest.

Still, I hoped. Misunderstandings constantly occurred these days. Not infrequently these arrests were unauthorized. On our way back to Petrograd I determined to take a desperate chance and appeal to the government direct.

I telephoned the Winter Palace where the new government held its sittings. A member of the Cabinet, M. I. Tereschenko, came to the telephone; I spoke with him. His manner was kindly; he said that he would come to see me as soon as he could.

Shortly after he came into my drawing-room. It was my first meeting with a man taking an active part in the new regime. I hardly know what I had expected him to be, but I was greatly surprised, I remember, by his irreproachable appearance and manners. He listened to me with great attention, and promised to find out the cause of the arrest and to do everything possible to have the order withdrawn.

In spite of his amiability and all his promises, I never heard from him again. Distressed, distracted, not knowing that the Provisional Government was living its last days and that Kerensky himself was of little importance in the eyes of the Soviet, I struck out more or less blindly in another direction.

I determined first of all to see my father. The first step was to get a permit. Several devoted friends undertook to help me and after long hours of waiting in various Headquarters, the permit was attained.

Written for Citizeness Romanova, it gave me the right to a half-hour interview with the former Grand Duke Paul Romanov, in the presence of the officer of the guard.

Armed with this paper I went to Tsarskoie-Selo. Putiatin went with me. At the gates to our back yard, to all appearances an admission post, I showed my pass to the officer of the guard, summoned by the soldiers. The young officer read the paper, looked at me silently, and motioned to the soldiers to open the gate.

Putiatin remained in the street. I followed the officer who led me to the well-known way. We crossed the yard and, turning the corner of the house, came to the veranda. I heard voices.

A few steps ahead, with his back to me, was my father, talking to the girls. Near by, facing me, stood a soldier with a rifle. A little further, my stepmother was walking with Volodia. I could not speak. Volodia was the first to see me.

"Marisha!" he cried, running towards me. Everybody turned, and the joy on my father's face was such as would have rewarded me for any torture.

We went into the house still accompanied by the officer. Tea was served in the dining-room. It was not like the teas which we used to have. There were now no cakes, no delicious buns, no butter. The bread that we ate was black, and we had no cream for our tea. But the joyous atmosphere, it seemed to me in my excitement, was the same as of old.

The officer sat at the table with us. My stepmother offered him a cup of tea. He placed it in front of him and began, with obvious embarrassment, to stir it, evidently trying not to listen to our conversation. Having sat thus for some moments in silence, not knowing in what direction to look, he suddenly jumped up and rushed out of the room.

I stayed almost an hour. Having finished our tea, we went into the drawing-room. There the officer came for me and escorted me back to the street. Thanks to his kindly attitude we had the chance of discussing the situation. It was decided that I should try to see Kerensky and obtain from him the withdrawal of the arrest. Only a few days remained until my marriage, and we wanted to be together that day.

CHAPTER XXVII

KERENSKY

AFTER repeated difficulties and many approaches, I was finally told that Kerensky could receive me only late in the evening, around eleven o'clock.

I took a cab and went to the Winter Palace. A young aide-de-camp was waiting for me at the entrance. I mounted with him the wide, stone stairway now stripped of its rugs and curiously bare. We had to give way at every step to groups of ragged soldiers who were going continually back and forth.

We reached the apartments of Emperor Alexander III. In the ballroom through which I passed people were gathered, a great number of them, but I seemed to be moving in a dream and the faces were blurred. I only noticed that at my entrance into the room all conversation stopped.

My guide led me to the high mahogany doors. There we halted. He went in alone to announce me and a moment later opened the door, motioned me to enter, turned, and left.

I stood before Kerensky. In spite of my agitation I looked at him carefully and now remember every detail of his appearance. He was of a medium height, with a face broadening towards the cheek bones and a large, narrow mouth; his hair was cut *en brosse*. He wore riding breeches, high boots, and a dark brown coat of military cut without shoulder straps. He held his left hand, somewhat unnaturally, within his coat, in a Napoleonic position, while he extended his right hand to me. Having greeted me, he indicated an arm-chair standing beside a massive mahogany desk.

I sat down. He took his place behind the desk and, leaning back, beat a tattoo with his right hand on the papers. The

KERENSKY

corners of Alexander III's large study were plunged in darkness, only a few lamps lighted the centre of the room and the desk. There was dampness in the room, and the smell of mustiness, as it had been closed and not aired for a long time.

"You wanted to see me. What can I do for you?" he asked, looking me over with indifference; he knew perfectly well why I had come.

"Alexander Fedorovich," I began nervously, feeling that my voice did not sound right, "for reasons unknown to us, my father and his family have been arrested. . . ."

"Yet you are his daughter and you are free, as you see," he interrupted, smiling wryly. "There is a reason. Your stepmother and her son have spoken disrespectfully of the Provisional Government."

It was true that about three weeks before the arrest Volodia had anonymously written satirical verses about Kerensky himself. The name was not mentioned but the picture was drawn so accurately that everybody recognized him. And these verses my stepmother had been so thoughtless as to circulate privately, far and wide; it was even said that someone had placed a copy upon Kerensky's desk in the Winter Palace.

"Besides, there are other reasons which I cannot disclose to you," he continued.

It was useless to argue. I decided to turn to the sentimental part of my programme. It was upon this that I had counted the most.

"In a few days," I said, "I am to marry. My fiancé is Prince Putiatin," I added, hoping that so democratic a choice on my part might soften my judge.

"Yes. I am informed. He is an officer of the Fourth Regiment of Sharpshooters." Kerensky uttered with such contempt the name of that crack regiment of the Guards that I understood how widely my tactics had miscarried, and continued with still less confidence:

"You can understand my desire to see my father and his family at my wedding."

"Do you also insist upon having your stepmother?" he asked, with more than a touch of mockery.

"Why, of course," I replied. "It is natural that on such a day I should like to have around all those dear to me. Please, Alexander Fedorovich, arrange it so that the arrest be withdrawn by that time. . . ."

"But do you know what the soldiers on guard would tell me, were they to learn that I had freed your father for such a reason? They would say that when their daughters married they were not permitted to go home for a visit, let alone being freed from arrest."

He drew in his breath, looked past my eyes to the top of my head and added in a patronizing tone: "However, I will try to do everything I can. But I do not promise anything . . . we shall see. . . ." His voice trailed off. He became fidgety. It was plain that he wanted to end the conversation. I was almost wild with despair. All the fine speeches and plans that I had rehearsed so carefully had rushed out of my head completely.

"For God's sake, Alexander Fedorovich," I cried, "give the order at once! You know that everything depends upon you alone. You are going away tonight and there is no one to whom I can turn while you are gone. My father is no longer a young man; his health is not good; he has experienced so much anxiety, so much grief. He was so pleased with my marriage and he wanted so much to be there . . ." I continued, rapidly losing all self-possession.

Evidently amused by my confusion, Kerensky smiled and rose. The interview was ended. I rose also.

"I tell you that I will do all I can; but you know yourself how busy I am. . . . I will take care of it. . . . I will give orders. . . ."

In reality, there was almost nothing that he could do without the Soviet, but I did not know that then.

I shook his hand and muttered some parting words. My efforts had been wholly unsuccessful. I could not, I knew, expect from my visit the least result. Besides the grief that I felt at this failure, I was deeply mortified. That I should have found no more adequate words, that I should have pleaded and stammered and lost my wits in Kerensky's presence, that I should not only have failed my father, but have also given Kerensky occasion to laugh at me!

Again I passed through the rooms filled with people, whose glances weighed heavily upon me. I descended the wide staircase and came out into the street. As I trudged heavily away from the Winter Palace, its empty, dark windows seemed to gaze down at me morosely, mockingly. But even before I had reached home I had other plans.

Direct attack had availed me nothing; very well, then, I would try the indirect.

Upon inquiry, I learned that Kuzmin, Kerensky's new assistant, enjoyed the confidence of both Kerensky and of the Soviet. A socialist and former political exile, he was acting at that time as a mediator between the Kerensky government and the Bolsheviks.

I decided to act through him and attack, as it were, on both fronts at once. But first it was necessary to meet him and preferably not in an official atmosphere.

Certain of my friends who had the necessary connexions undertook to arrange this meeting. This they soon accomplished, and very adroitly. They gave a dinner to which they invited among others Kuzmin and myself.

Kuzmin was among the guests awaiting my arrival. He was in uniform but there was nothing military in his carriage. He was thin and pale with narrow shoulders and a narrow head. His hair was thin and of an indefinite colour; it was impossible to guess his age. He stood embarrassed among the guests and seemed throughout the dinner hardly more at ease. But there were enough people to permit the conversation to flow easily, and I could see in his attitude nothing hostile.

Purposely, he was not placed beside me at dinner. When we rose from the table and scattered about the rooms, I watched for an opportune time to begin my conversation. Finally the moment came. Small tables were placed in the dining-room; an excellent string orchestra began to play, and our host who sat with me at one of the tables drew Kuzmin into our conversation. After a few words our host excused himself and rose, leaving Kuzmin and myself alone.

We were both embarrassed. So as not to be silent, I said something inconsequential and fumbled for my cigarette case in my bag. The case was empty. Kuzmin reached for his somewhat awkwardly, offered me a cigarette, and gave me a light.

When we both were smoking, the ice seemed to melt. We talked. Now that our rôles were reversed; now that, at any moment, his former fate could quite readily befall me and mine, it seemed quite natural that I should ask him about Siberia and his life in penal servitude.

It was the first time that I had ever talked with a convict. He spoke without bitterness, with a smile. He told of organizing an uprising somewhere on the border of Russia, of proclaiming a republic there, of being hunted and caught. He spoke of the prison where convicts at hard labour waited to be sent to Siberia, of the chains, of the endless Siberian days.

I listened. When he finished speaking about himself, he questioned me. I had at least some idea of the life of Siberian convicts through Russian literature, which describes with a special love the dark existence in those far prisons, but these poor political exiles, I now learned, had not the remotest idea of what we were like. Oh, yes, they had an idea—they thought that we were beasts in the image of man. We could not, they thought, have any human feelings, nor act humanly.

With candid frankness and childish simplicity Kuzmin asked

me the strangest questions. I began to tell him about myself, about the atmosphere in which I had been brought up, about my work during the war, my conversations with the peasants. He listened intently, hands folded on the table, head bent. It was now his turn to hear for the first time in his life something contrary to all that had been taught him since childhood. Much of what I said was evidently incomprehensible to him and he asked more detailed explanations. Finally, when I had spoken of my life at the front and at Pskov, he raised his head and asked:

"Is it possible that the Romanovs love Russia?"

"Yes, they do; they have loved and will continue to love her always, no matter what happens," I replied, not suspecting how often I would in the future have cause to remember this sentence.

The way was paved. Now I could speak of my father. And that night, bidding Kuzmin good-bye, I felt that I had accomplished something by talking with him.

My father was not set free by the day of my wedding, but I now felt less anxious about his fate. And I was not mistaken; a few days later the guards were removed from his home.

CHAPTER XXVIII

CHAOS

A STORM was gathering over Petrograd and its stupid rulers. The great Russian patriot General Kornilov, seeing that the Kerensky faction with its wordy vacillation and its constant concession to the Bolsheviks, could lead Russia only to ruin, decided to demand more decisive measures in regard to the army.

Kerensky at first pretended to consent and co-operate, but suddenly changed front and betrayed Kornilov. Thus he hoped, it seems, to maintain the good-will of the Bolsheviks; in reality, he only facilitated their full victory. The bold action of General Kornilov was the last act of the sort before complete darkness and chaos descended upon my country.

My wedding coincided with this time. Since now it was certain that my father could not be present, we decided to celebrate it in Pavlovsk, where my grandmother, the Queen of Greece, was living. Caught in Russia by the revolution, she had stayed on with her nephews.

Pavlovsk had been at one time the favourite residence of the Emperor Paul I. It was only a few miles from Tsarskoie-Selo. The palace and the park surrounding it had passed into the hands of a collateral branch of the imperial family. They were now in the possession of Prince John, married to the Princess Helen of Serbia with whom I had gone to the front.

Our wedding was set for the nineteenth of September. Two days before, rumours began to circulate as to General Kornilov's proposed *coup d'état*. These rumours were so insistent that the soldiers, who had by this time exceeded themselves in brazen disregard for discipline, began to wonder whether they had not better be good; at any rate, the forces around Tsarskoie visibly smartened up and pulled themselves together for those few days.

The Kornilov *coup* had no monarchical aims, but we all hoped and longed for its success, for we felt that it might save Russia from utter anarchy and perhaps afford us a greater degree of personal safety.

But all such hopes proved fruitless. At the last moment, when everything was ready and the success of the enterprise seemed guaranteed, Kerensky disclosed the whole plot to the Soviet. One of the participants shot himself; all the others, together with Kornilov, were arrested.

On the eve of my wedding it was impossible to determine what turn the events would take. Kornilov was almost at the gates of Petrograd. Civil war seemed inevitable. Alarm was in the air when, on the morning of the nineteenth, accompanied by the faithful Mlle. Hélène, who carried my wedding dress in a box, I took the train from Petrograd to Pavlovsk. That little town, we had heard, was in turmoil, and it seemed quite probable that we might find ourselves in the fighting zone. From time to time, indeed, we did hear the dull rumblings of a not so distant cannonade; but Pavlovsk, when we reached it, seemed calm and peaceful. It was a beautiful autumn day; the vast park glittered with amber and gold, contrasting brilliantly against a clear, cold sky.

My dear grandmother, the Queen of Greece, met me that day with particular tenderness. After a light lunch Princess Helen took me to my rooms. Mlle. Hélène drew from the box the grey satin dress, the grey lace cap, and the rest of my wedding costume, and helped me to dress. When I was ready, Prince John came in and blessed me with an ikon. In this, he took the place of my father whose absence I felt keenly. With tears in her eyes, my grandmother also blessed me. Then on Prince John's arm I went to the private chapel of the palace where Putiatin was waiting for me.

There were only a few guests, all very grave. During the service we involuntarily lent an ear to the outside sounds, as though waiting for something to happen. Unknown to us Kornilov's plan had already come to nothing; the curtain had already fallen.

After the ceremony we had tea and even sipped champagne, a rarity in those days. Friends had succeeded in securing for me and my husband another permit to see my father; we went almost immediately to Tsarskoie-Selo. My father and his family were at this time still under arrest, but in spite of the soldiers standing guard at the gates and of the peculiar atmosphere created by such a situation, a festive spirit reigned in the house; the gates were opened to permit us to drive directly to the entrance, my stepmother and the girls wore light dresses, Volodia gestured and shouted, and my father radiated happiness. Oh, how touching this joy, especially at such a time, seemed to me. Yet how terribly my heart bled inwardly, in the knowledge of all that might, at any moment, befall my father and all who bore his name.

There could be, of course, no question of a honeymoon voyage. We returned that same evening to the Neva and settled for the time being in my usual apartment. We had no longer the money to maintain this immense building. General Laiming had offers, and was already in negotiation with buyers. As soon as the sale was made, we would have to seek a new home.

Meantime, we started to live our own small, happy life—a life submerged, so to speak, and yet forgetful of the sea of sorrows and anxieties which surrounded us. My father had now been released from arrest; we went often to Tsarskoie-Selo. Sometimes we visited friends in town and occasionally saw a play.

The Bolshevist *coup d'état* was expected any moment. As far as I could see, everyone was ready to welcome it; no one believed any longer in the Provisional Government. Kerensky had become odious by his continual speechmaking, his mania for grandeur, his posturing towards the Radical elements, his falseness. Moreover, no one ever thought that the Bolsheviks could keep the reins for more than two or three months; their rule would arouse, it was believed, a powerful reaction; and after that the least that could happen would be a dictatorship.

By dreams thus deluded, with no real intimation of what was in store for us, we never gave a thought to the idea of leaving Russia. Besides, how could we? The war was still going on on the Western front; we could not imagine ourselves abandoning our country in time of war. Involuntarily we still linked ourselves with her fate. And had not the Emperor refused to leave Russia at the beginning of the revolution although he still had the possibility of doing so?

ii

THE Radicals of the extreme left grew constantly stronger and more energetic. It was said that once in power they would carry out their programme and nationalize private property. Evidently, in this procedure they would begin with us. But even if they would confiscate all the money in the banks, we would still have our jewels. Mine were in a state bank in Moscow. I thought that it would be wiser to take them from there before it was too late; it would be safer, I thought, for me to hide them at home.

We decided therefore to go to Moscow and take the jewels from the bank, and to see Aunt Ella, who had not met my husband. Taking very few things with us, we left at the end of October. In Moscow we stopped in the house of the Yusupovs, near the Nicholas station.

The first two or three days we did not go to the bank but stayed at home with my aunt or paid visits to my husband's parents, who were also staying in Moscow with friends.

The town seemed peaceful. Finally on October 30th, we

decided to go to the bank for the jewels. We rose early and set off.

As he opened the gates for us the old janitor said:

"Something's wrong in town. It strikes me that the Bolsheviks are up to something today. Maybe you shouldn't go out; it pays, nowadays, to be careful."

He was right; there was in the air of the town something altogether peculiar. That curious sense of imminence to chaos acquired since the revolution, warned us that something was going to happen; as we walked, my heart contracted painfully.

But the streets were still deserted. We took the first cab we came upon and drove towards the centre of the city. At first we met small groups, then crowds of armed soldiers. Their faces expressed the same silly excitement that I had noticed before.

As we turned into the Tverskaya our cab was stopped by a post of soldiers who barred the way with their rifles. We made a detour. Then, somewhere in the distance we heard shots in quick succession, like the beating of a drum. People ran down the street and there were soldiers again, gathering in groups, running. At the corner of the side street on which the bank was located, we dismissed our cab, preferring to walk. The driver, lashing the horse, set it at a gallop and quickly disappeared from view.

Some men were carrying two stretchers towards us; the stretchers were empty. A man in a dark, shabby overcoat was lying at my feet, sprawling awkwardly, his head and shoulders upon the sidewalk, his body on the street. And still I did not quite understand what it was all about.

Suddenly a volley broke from unseen rifles towards the end of the side street, leading into the Tverskaya. Putiatin and I did not even exchange a glance. We hurried towards the bank. The door was locked and bolted. At a complete loss, we stopped and looked at each other. What now?

The excitement in the street was swiftly increasing. The

shooting, sometimes distant, sometimes quite near by, was almost incessant. All the cabs had quite naturally disappeared; and it would have been now, in any event, quite out of the question for us to drive through the town. Where were we to go and how?

Putiatin did not know Moscow at all. I had forgotten most of it during the years of my absence. Still, we could not remain standing there; the shooting was coming closer; we had to move.

A small crowd had rushed into our street from the Tverskaya, as though pursued. In their continued rush they now carried us with them. Putiatin, afraid that we might lose each other, clutched me tightly under the arm. Together with the crowd we ran along, half pushed and half dragged, to a street running parallel to the Tverskaya.

Here trucks rumbled noisily by, filled with armed soldiers. These soldiers stood crowded closely together, shooting at random, as the trucks bounced them up and down on the cobblestones. Bullets whizzed above our heads and smashed through the lower windows of the houses. The shattered window-panes fell clattering to the ground.

Occasionally, one of the crowd would suddenly sit down in a heap, or fall with an awkward throwing gesture of the arms. I did not turn around or look at them. For the second time in my life I was experiencing mortal fear.

We sneaked from one side street into another, avoiding the larger thoroughfares, rushing like rats from corner to corner. As far as possible we tried going in the direction of that part of town where my husband's people lived. The Yusupovs' house was so far away as to be out of the question.

By noon we were only at the Grand Opera. Now shells were bursting over the city; we could hear the explosions and the deafening roar when they hit. In one of the side streets adjoining the Theatre Square we had to remain for a long time. Shooting was going on on all sides, all exits were blocked.

Then suddenly, probably from the square, a file of soldiers swung quickly into our street. It was steep going; they bent forward as they marched uphill towards us. As they marched we could see them reloading their rifles.

A short distance from us they halted, exchanged matter-of-fact glances, deployed and, lifting their rifles, took aim.

The small crowd of people, amidst whom we were first flattened in terror to the wall, now seeing no hope in that, with the black muzzles of those rifles still steadily upon them, all of one accord lay down flat.

I remained standing. I could not lie down in front of the rifles of these men. I preferred to take what was coming on my feet. My head did not work; I did not think, yet I could not lie down.

After a first volley came a second. I heard a bullet hit the wall just above my head, then two others. I was still alive. I do not remember how nor where the soldiers went; I do not remember what was going on around me. I remember only that I turned around and saw upon the bright yellow plaster of the house three deep holes and around them white circles where the lime was knocked off. Two of them almost merged into one, the third farther off.

What happened afterwards remains in my memory as a continuous nightmare. The details of all the hours we spent that day in the streets of Moscow are enveloped in a fog permeated by a feeling of inexpressible horror and despair. People ran past me; they fell, rose, or remained lying; cries and moans were intermingled with the roar of shots and the exploding of shells, while a thick, vile-smelling dust stood in the air. My head had been crammed with so many impressions that it now refused to register; my mind was dulled. We reached the old Putiatins only after five in the afternoon, having spent the entire day, since nine that morning, in the streets.

I do not remember how and when we returned to the Yusupovs' house. I only know that throughout the next day the cannonade did not stop, mingling with the sound of church-bells, which made it, somehow, the more distressing. The servants had barricaded all entrances from the street; throughout that night and the day following we lived in expectation of an armed attack.

Fortunately, however, the house was located on the edge of town and the bands that pillaged the houses and apartments in the centre did not reach us.

On the night of the second day there was an alarm. We were not asleep, of course. Suddenly in the stillness that had settled on the city with the coming of the night we heard a trampling of heavy boots, then a knocking at the door with butt-ends. These sounds coming from the street echoed distinctly through the whole house. We listened with hushed breath. I could not move. But the lights were all extinguished, the house was surrounded from the street by a thick wall and the marauders apparently did not know the locality, nor realize whose house this was. After tramping for a while along the wall they decided to go away, but not without sending a few shots in the direction of the house. Their bullets hit the wall.

Thus passed two, three, days. The shooting did not cease. We were cut off from everything. The servants were afraid to go out to get provisions. When such supplies as we had in the house, and which we used very carefully, were completely exhausted, we were obliged to take counsel and consider our situation.

Only a short street and a wide square separated us from the Nicholas station. It seemed that the best thing to do would be to go forth, attracting as little attention as possible, and attempt to return to Petrograd.

My husband's orderly was with us in Moscow. He volunteered to go that evening, under the shelter of darkness, to the station and find out whether there was any train service. In his grey soldier's coat he would attract, he felt, no particular attention. I remember how anxiously we saw him go forth. He returned shortly with the information that there were some trains to Petrograd; he had also learned that to all appearances the Bolshevist uprising had succeeded, though the losses were great. A great many buildings, he added, had been damaged, the Kremlin worst of all.

We decided to pack our things and go to the station. It was quite late when we left the house and, accompanied by the orderly and the janitor, who carried our suitcases, proceeded along the street plunged in complete darkness. The square was like an inkpot. But we did not meet anyone, and reached the station safely.

It presented an extraordinary spectacle. People were sitting or lying all over it, their luggage or bundles piled up by their side. Many had been sitting there for three days without eating, without changing their position. The air was thick and close from human exhalations. Talks, arguments, abuse, rose in a hubbub.

In the crowd were many wounded, tied up with all sorts of rags. Here and there sneaked suspicious-looking soldiers, and beggars in indescribable tatters loitered about.

We were unable to learn anything except that the Bolsheviks had been victorious over the troops loyal to the Provisional Government; nor could we learn whether anything had happened in Petrograd.

Finally, after endless inquiries and waiting, we discovered the time of departure of the train for Petrograd. It seemed strange beyond belief that there still existed such things as trains. And when we actually got into a carriage, my astonishment knew no bounds. For it was an ordinary, clean, old-fashioned first-class sleeping-car with a polite conductor, electricity, polished mirrors and doors, and clean bed-linen.

We reached Petrograd safely, if not on time. Everything there seemed quiet. We drove home to the Neva. The minute I was in the house I rushed upstairs to the Laimings to find out what had happened during our absence.

At my entrance they both fell a step backwards as if they were seeing a ghost. In Petrograd, as in Moscow, the Bolshevist uprising had succeeded. Kerensky had fled, the members of the Provisional Government had disappeared, but the troops loyal to them had engaged the Bolsheviks in several bloody combats. In this fighting the heaviest losses had been sustained by the Women Battalions and by the youths who were defending the Winter Palace.

Petrograd appeared to have had no reports of what had happened in Moscow, and the Laimings could tell me nothing about conditions at Tsarskoie-Selo.

We made inquiries and learned that the passenger service between Petrograd and Tsarskoie-Selo had been discontinued. That terrified me. I had to know at any cost what was happening there. I could not go myself, so again we dispatched the orderly, the only suitable person in this world of grey soldiers' coats.

He remained absent the entire day. Upon his return he came into my room, and, with that imperturbability which so often distinguishes people of his mentality, announced:

"I am to tell you that everything is all right and that the Grand Duke Paul was taken away to the Smolny Institute two days ago."

I was benumbed with terrror. Further questions were useless. He did not know anything more and could add to his message not the slightest detail.

iii

Although the Bolsheviks had made as yet no official pronouncements, their intentions, expressed since the beginning of the revolution, were perfectly evident. "Death to the aristocrats." Now anything could happen. We were entirely in their power and nothing but chance could help us.

The thought that my father might already be their victim chilled me to the heart. I was frantic, impotent; all I could do, that night, was to wait, and this waiting was painful beyond words.

Next day I sent the orderly again to Tsarskoie and he brought me this time more reassuring news. He had heard, he said, that my father was to be set free that day from the Smolny. In the expectation of this, my stepmother, Volodia, and the girls had left for Petrograd; the house in Tsarskoie-Selo was empty. The orderly did not, however, know where they would stay in Petrograd, and all attempts to locate them proved useless.

Another day passed, then Volodia came to see us. My father, he said, had been for the moment set free only on the condition that he would not leave Petrograd until he had received special permission to do so.

For this reason my stepmother, the Princess Paley, had decided for the time being to settle in one of the back apartments of my father's house on the quay.

The Bolsheviks, Volodia said, had intended to imprison Father in the Fortress of SS. Peter and Paul, but word came of this in advance from a devoted retainer, who learned of it from a conversation overheard in the Soviet of Tsarskoie-Selo. The warning came to Princess Paley. Utterly terrified, she rushed at once to the Soviet, where, with the energy and persistence inherent in her, she did not desist until the decision was revoked.

My father spent three days in Smolny. Then he was told that he would be transferred to the fortress. He understood perfectly how such an imprisonment might end.

This time, however, the storm passed us by. My father was placed, as I have said, on parole with his family in Petrograd. They lived thus for two weeks and then received permission to return to Tsarskoie-Selo accompanied by a sailor, a member of the Petrograd Soviet.

While my father and his family were in Petrograd I saw them often. When they went back to Tsarskoie I saw them

TSAR AND TSAREVITCH

Nicholas II with his son

scarcely at all; it was nearly impossible under existing conditions to make the trip. I had discovered, moreover, upon returning from Moscow that I was expecting a child; this, in the circumstances, disturbed me greatly.

Life became every day more unstable, more alarming. The Bolsheviks issued decrees demolishing everything and hastened to carry out their programme. We stood, all of us, at the edge of a precipice, and I especially feared for my father. Several searches were made in his house in Tsarskoie by members of the local Soviet, men in soldiers' uniforms, with foreign names and alien, un-Russian faces. They looked for and confiscated firearms, which were now prohibited in private homes.

Discovering my father's immense and very valuable wine cellar, the Soviet sent men to destroy it. Throughout an entire night they carried out bottles and smashed them. The wine burst forth in a torrent. The air was saturated with vinous vapours. The whole population came at a run and, paying no heed to the threatening shouts of the Soviet representatives, gathered into pails the snow saturated with wine, drew with cups the flowing rivulets, or drank lying flat on the ground and pressing their lips to the snow. Everybody was drunk—the members of the Soviet who were smashing the bottles and the people surrounding the house. Throughout the night the drunken uproar continued. Shouts and abuse filled the house, the yard, the adjoining streets. No one in the house slept that night; it seemed as if every minute the free debauch would end in some terrible violence, but this time the crowd was too drunk to close in and kill.

iv

WHILE we lived on the Neva I continually expected a search, which, strangely enough, never took place although the conditions were most suitable. Since early in the war the second floor of the palace had been occupied by a hospital, organized by the English. About fifty Russian orderlies lived in the basement and knew perfectly well the layout of the rooms.

Almost every evening we could hear them at actual orgies, the sounds reaching us through the pipes of the antiquated heating system. We could hear distinctly the drawing of corks, and conversations becoming more and more menacing as tongues were loosened.

Once, late in the evening, our old butler, who had been in the house before we were born, came to warn me not to go to bed that night. The orderlies had had more to drink than usual and were in a particularly violent mood. They threatened to make the round of the house, hoping to find wine. The old butler, who alone of all our numerous personnel had remained wholly loyal to us, hid as well as he could both the wine and the silver. But nothing happened; the orderlies got too drunk to come upstairs for loot; I mention it only as an example of that constant uncertainty, that constant expectation of some possible and generally indefinite misfortune, in which we lived.

Thus, for a long time I found myself threatened with unpleasantness on the part of that same orderly who used to be a footman in our house and whom I had sent to Dmitri with a letter after the death of Rasputin. I had with great difficulty secured the position of orderly in my hospital for this man, after having learned that he was sick at the front and could not stand the life in the trenches. In the hospital he had so completely forgotten the obligations of military service and complained so outrageously at comparatively easy work that I had often to reprimand him and finally, for some outstanding negligence, ordered him put under arrest for twenty-four hours.

After the revolution, following the general example, he left his work and returned to Petrograd with his wife, who was at one time my maid in Pskov. Either she or her husband continually came to me with the threat to betray me to the Soviet on some pretext or other, this in revenge for the well-deserved punishment I had laid upon him. The majority of our servants who had been with us for a great many years and had lived in the house with their families, had now become dangerous enemies ready to do us any mischief that they felt would satisfy or enrich them or gratify the new rulers. We could not feel safe even in the privacy of our rooms. Malevolent eyes and ears watched our every move, listened to our every word, seemed even to read our thoughts. And it was impossible to dismiss any of them; for the servants had formed their own house Soviet and elected a chairman. They continually sent their delegates to General Laiming, demanding this or that, knowing perfectly well all the time that there was no longer any money to satisfy their claims. The sale of the house appeared to be the only way to put an end to all this. General Laiming awaited with impatience the moment when he could liquidate everything.

And our experiences were only a small illustration of what was going on around us.

Those days cannot be described in words. All the words that related to our former life had no longer any meaning; and no words, old or new, could express the chaos which now surrounded our slightest thought and act. Tongues were helpless; thought, bounded by our now impotent speech, was dulled. My nerves were taut; I trembled continually for the fate of my dear ones. The slightest noise seemed suspicious, a knock at the door brought to mind, with the swiftness of lightning, painfully distinct pictures of what would follow after a possible search. I imagined a crowd of soldiers behind the door, cruel faces, hands fumbling all over, coarse words, brutal touches. I imagined an arrest, the leaving of the house and the walking along the street surrounded by menacing bayonets, the incarceration without food, first in some cold and damp basement filled with rats, then in the fortress, then . . .

What is the use of speaking of it now, when the thought of death comes only once in a long while? Yet one had to live then as well as now. So new habits were established; each calm moment seemed precious in quite a different way; bare existence seemed in itself to attain a high and special value.

Owing to the war and the simpler habits I had acquired, I did not suffer greatly from the material shortages that speedily grew worse. My upbringing had been such, however, that in spite of all its deficiencies, I was able to maintain an outward appearance of poise and balance. Only once, as I remember it now, did the impression of the moment prove stronger than my former training.

One evening at the very beginning of the Bolshevist rule, my husband and I decided to go to the ballet. I had never before been in the Imperial Theatres otherwise than through a private entrance and in the imperial box, and I found it interesting to view the house from orchestra seats, as a private individual. We bought our tickets and went. At that time no one ever thought of dressing for the theatre so we went as we were.

We arrived when the spectacle had already begun. During the first interval we went into the foyer. The theatre was crowded by people from all walks of life. I remember that from the beginning I was shocked by the contrast between the well-known music and performance and the unusual, odd appearance of the house.

On our way back to our seats I looked up—it must have been for the first time—and saw the box on the right side of the stage which from time immemorial had been occupied by the imperial family. Framed by the heavy silk draperies, in the arm-chairs with the gilded backs, there now sat several sailors, their caps on their dishevelled heads and with them their ladies in woollen, coloured kerchiefs. All things considered, there was nothing unusual in this sight, but nevertheless it affected me powerfully. My sight grew dim; I felt myself about to fall, and groped for the hand of my husband, who was walking beside me. Beyond that, I remember nothing. I came to myself after a thirty-minute fainting spell, the first and the last in my life, lying upon the hard oilcloth couch of the theatre's infirmary. The strange face of a doctor was bending over me and the room was filled with people who must have come to stare. My teeth chattered; I was shivering all over. Putiatin wrapped me in a blanket and took me home, and I recovered only the next day.

V

As the house on the Neva was being sold, we took a small furnished apartment on the Sergievskaya street and moved in. The former large staff of servants was replaced by a cook and a maid and by the orderly, who volunteered to stay for a while. Everybody had less and less money. The delivery of food was falling rapidly into disorganization and prices soared. Food was distributed only by cards, and was of poor quality. Speculation was in full swing; with money, one could buy a great many things, but it was precisely money that we lacked. There were times when we had so little in our pockets that we wondered how we would live the next day.

We were not long alone in our new apartment. My husband's parents, who had spent several months in Moscow, were obliged to leave there and return to Petrograd. They came to live with us, and Princess Putiatina took it upon herself to run the household, which was becoming more and more difficult as months went by. Since the beginning of winter we had had only horse meat and even that quite seldom. One could buy white bread at an extravagant price but this was illegal and the penalty in the event of discovery might be very large. So we bought buckwheat flour. The black bread, rationed on cards in smaller and smaller quantities, was made of flour at first mixed with bran and later simply with sawdust; it was not only unsavoury but dangerous for the health. There was no sugar; we used saccharine. In winter we ate mostly cabbage and potatoes. Sometimes, as a special treat, my husband's mother prepared cakes of coffee grounds.

Although I had never been fond of sweets I suffered now for the lack of sugar. Conversations between people meeting in the street or with friends who came to call usually revolved around food. Addresses of speculators were exchanged, recipes were given for the preparation of dishes of the most extraordinary and unexpected products, and a home-made roll, brought as a present, caused more pleasure than a valuable piece of jewellery. I shall never forget the joy I experienced from a box of food sent by the Swedish royal family, who had heard of my half-starved existence; I remember to its smallest detail everything it contained and the state of almost sacred exaltation with which we unpacked it.

When the cold weather set in we began to feel also the lack of fuel. All the windows in the apartment under us had been broken. As a result, our floor was icy, and we could heat only one room. My feet, frostbitten during the war, were so exposed to the cold that terrible sores opened on the soles, and for a long time I could not put my shoes on; I had to go out even into the streets wearing felt slippers.

Banks were nationalized; our private deposits confiscated. In order to live, people began little by little to sell their things. The old Putiatins had succeeded, before private property belonging to the imperial family was finally confiscated, in taking my diamonds from the bank in Moscow. My mother-in-law made a sort of jacket which she wore under her dress; into this she sewed the greater part of the jewels. The tiaras, which it was impossible to flatten, she tucked in the crowns of her hats. As we needed money at that time we were obliged to sell some of the things—a difficult procedure; first, because there were no buyers; second, because we feared to attract attention. So only the small pieces were sold.

The rest of the jewels we decided to keep in the house. Although this was very risky, there was nothing else to do. The problem now was to hide them. Already we had learned that during searches, attention was mainly directed upon chimneys, curtains, upholstered seats, pillows, and mattresses. Avoiding all such places, we found others, some of which, I must say, spoke well for our ingenuity. I had, for instance, a diadem in an old setting, consisting of diamond rays strung on a wire. I bought a large bottle of office ink and emptied it out; then, having unstrung the rays, I dropped them to the bottom of the bottle and poured paraffin over them. The last step was to pour back the ink. Since a large label surrounded the bottle, it was all but impossible to make out its contents. It stood for months on my desk in full sight of everybody.

Other things we fastened in home-made paperweights; still others in empty cocoa tins; dipped afterwards in wax and provided with a wick, they appeared to be ends of large church candles. We adorned them with spirals of gold paper and sometimes lighted them before the ikons to divert the attention of the servants.

In winter, registrations of all sorts were introduced. Former officers, my husband in their number, were forced to clean streets. In order to receive a food card one had to have some profession or other, and to exercise the art of cunning.

Our lack of means and the attention that an idle life was bound to attract on the part of our new rulers turned our thoughts towards finding some suitable work. We decided to put into practice the artistic abilities that we all possessed in greater or less degree. My husband's father was a connoisseur of ikon painting and the entire family took up ikon painting and the colouring of wooden Easter eggs. I cannot remember now where we sold our wares and whether it was a profitable occupation. Besides, at Volodia's request, I began to translate from the English a very sentimental novel which had greatly impressed us both. It was called *The Rosary*. There were many verses in the text which Volodia wished especially to render. In the course of the winter I finished my part of the work but Volodia was not destined to do his.

But on the whole I led a rather idle existence. The constant danger, the increasing want and hardships were becoming to us habitual, almost natural, phenomena. The inert, shut-in life wore me down, bit into my nerves. Each new day seemed longer than the one before, duller, more intolerable. And these interminable, circling conversations, either on food, which we did not have, or on our former grandeur now over! Especially on the days when I was hungry—which was, I admit, more and more often—all such talk stirred in me an impotent, silent wrath.

During the war I had drifted from the old traditional viewpoints; I saw many things in a new light, but I was still unable to shape conclusions from a constant point of view. Even now my views were puzzled, intuitional, pointless. All I could do was to keep silent. But I did know enough, hearing these discussions of the causes which had brought us to the conditions under which we were now slowly perishing, to be amazed by the superficiality and narrow-mindedness of opinions that were expressed. I could not accept the idea that some insignificant political personality such as Kerensky or Rodzianko was responsible for changes so catastrophic and profound. They had not sown this bitter crop; the beginning lay far back—in the soil, so to speak, upon which such personalities could be born, exist, thrive.

My still untrained mind sought among all the chatter to beat its way back into the very depths of these mysterious and incalculable causes and motives which had brought us all to ruin. What fatal flaw in the Russian character, what absence of balance and control, could have led to the gradual maturing of the new, monstrous order now ruling the country? I could not answer these questions, I could approach them only in thought. There seemed to be no answer to them, and I do not know that there is today.

CHAPTER XXIX

MASSACRE

BY the beginning of 1918 the Bolshevist anti-militaristic propaganda and the reluctance of our peasants to go on fighting had attained such proportions that Russia reeled towards a shabby and makeshift peace.

Negotiations were begun between the Soviet government and Germany. At the beginning of January, Trotsky announced full demobilization in spite of the fact that the treaty had not yet been signed.

The remains of the army, in complete disorganization, abandoned the front—which had collapsed long before—and, devastating everything on their way, returned home. Here, joining with the rest of the villagers, they burned and wrecked the estates, pillaging and destroying furniture, art collections, and libraries, torturing and killing the landowners and even wiping out, wantonly, valuable herds of breeding cattle.

The Germans, naturally, took advantage of the situation. Towards the end of February they made a lightning advance which brought them so near Petrograd that the Allied embassies and missions were obliged to leave hurriedly. By the end of February the Germans were before Narva, and the Bolsheviks, badly frightened, agreed to all demands and signed the proffered treaty of peace.

The actual signing was on March 3rd. The Allied embassies returned to Petrograd for a while, but left it definitely in the beginning of April. Their departure was a cruel blow to us. Their presence in Petrograd had served as a guarantee that somewhere civilization still existed, and perhaps even protection. No one of us had left Russia while the war was going on.

And now we were definitely abandoned to the dubious mercy of our new rulers.

In the middle of March, Uritsky, who was at the head of the terrible Cheka, issued a decree making obligatory the registration of all the men belonging to the house of Romanov. Again the Princess Paley succeeded in saving my father from the ordeal. She personally presented to the Cheka a certificate of his illness and the Bolsheviks, after submitting him to an examination by their doctors, released him from the registration.

But Volodia and my uncles and cousins who lived in Petrograd or its vicinity were obliged to appear at the Cheka where they were listed and told that they were to be sent into exile.

On the ground that he did not bear the name of Romanov, Princess Paley did her utmost to save Volodia from the claws of the Cheka, but all her efforts failed. Volodia was summoned to a personal interview with Uritsky, who gave him the chance to disown once and for all his father and all the Romanovs. The reply Volodia made tended in no way to mitigate his fate.

Two weeks later Volodia, together with the three sons of the late Grand Duke Constantine, John, Constantine, and Igor, and the Grand Duke Serge—who during the war was Commander-in-Chief of the Artillery—were exiled to Viatka. We never saw any of them again. At the end of April they were all transferred, first to Ekaterinburg and then to Alopaievsk where later they were joined by Aunt Ella, exiled by the Bolsheviks from Moscow.

My aunt had never become reconciled to the thought that the wife of my father—fully pardoned and re-established in his rights by the Emperor—had received an official, although morganatic, title and was recognized by everybody, beginning with the court. The hostile feeling that she bore Princess Paley she transferred to my father's children by his second marriage.

But fate devised it so that the last months she and Volodia spent upon this earth they spent together in an atmosphere of intimacy which brought them close and taught them to appreciate one another. By their long and intolerably agonizing death they sealed this friendship which was a great comfort to both of them during the time of incredible suffering which fell to their lot.

My father did not live to know of this. But he and his wife were distraught beyond words by the separation from their son. A tremendous weight seemed to hang over all of us. Princess Paley blamed herself bitterly for not having sent Volodia abroad when it was still possible.

Each time I went to my father's house at Tsarskoie-Selo, I noticed some change for the worse. Little by little he was obliged to deprive himself of everything. This in spite of the constant solicitude and energy of Princess Paley to procure for him at least a shadow of that comfort to which he was accustomed. From the beginning of the winter it became evident that there would not be enough of the petroleum used for the central heating, and many of the rooms were closed. As my father suffered periodically from an ulcer in the stomach, he was on a diet and it was with tremendous difficulty and at the price of great sacrifices that the provisions for it were procured. In January, in spite of all precautions, the fuel gave out, and my father with his family had to move into the house of my cousin Boris, also located in Tsarskoie-Selo, where the stoves could be heated with wood.

The local Soviet and its constantly changing members were continually blackmailing my father under some pretext or other for the purposes of personal material gain. Finally, the new government nationalized and took his house and its valuable collections, registering it as a museum.

By spring I could no longer stand it in the city. We took a cottage in Pavlovsk, not far from my father, and organized our life as best we could. We planted vegetables, and I took care of them myself, watering them in the morning and at night. We bought a goat; it was impossible to get any cow milk.

I was to be confined in the beginning of July and a week

before that a trained nurse was to come to live with us. It was also arranged that the doctor who had been in charge of the case from the start would come to Pavlovsk at the first call.

One evening, about three weeks before the appointed time, I was watering the vegetable garden, as was my custom. I was doing it barefooted in order to save my stockings and shoes; and I remember that my two large watering-pots seemed that day especially heavy.

The watering finished, I went into the house. Suddenly I felt a suspicious pain in my back. My husband had just returned from Petrograd where he had gone on business, and my mother-in-law, who had gone for the whole day to Tsarskoie-Selo, had not yet returned. My husband tried several times to telephone to Petrograd in order to summon the doctor or the trained nurse, but in vain. In the twilight of a white northern night we sat upstairs in my bedroom and waited. My pains grew worse.

Finally my mother-in-law returned from Tsarskoie-Selo. She saw at once how things were; there was no time to lose. She dispatched Aleck, my brother-in-law, to bring some local midwife if possible. Two hours passed. My mother-in-law, with the help of old Tania, prepared the room and the bed and set some water boiling. Between attacks I paced the room. My brother's favourite dog, which I was taking care of since his departure, feeling an unusual stir in the house, hid under the dressing-table. They tried to chase him away, but he persisted in returning, trembling all over, never taking his eyes off me; and when anyone approached him, he growled.

At last the bell rang. It was Aleck with the local midwife, whom he had roused from her bed. He did not dare tell her where he was taking her, afraid that she might refuse to come and assist a new little bourgeois into the world. She brought everything that was needed and proved very efficient. Without asking questions she quickly changed into her white smock and, rolling up her sleeves, set to work. Less than an hour later I heard the cry of the newly born baby, and I could hardly believe that everything was over.

The night pressed white and brilliant at the window. A little over twenty-five years before, a similar midwife, hastily summoned, had attended my mother at Ilinskoie. She had died giving birth to Dmitri.

Ten days later I was up and the christening was celebrated. My father and my husband's grandmother were to be godfather and godmother to the newly born boy, whose arrival gave my father his last joy. My mother-in-law succeeded in preparing a real feast and we tried at least for these few hours to shake off the cares and anxieties that beset us. I think I never saw my father in such a gay mood as he was that day of the child's christening.

How could we know that on this same day, almost at that same hour, hundreds and hundreds of miles away, in a small Siberian town, Volodia, Aunt Ella, and their companions in exile were ending their earthly existence in hideous suffering? The Bolsheviks threw them that day down an old, unused mineshaft, then shot at them and threw stones upon them. Some were killed at once; others lived for days and died partly of wounds, partly of starvation.

Of all this we, of course, knew nothing on that day of my baby's christening. And, mercifully, we could not know that this newborn child itself was fated not to live long. He died when hardly a year old.

When our guests were taking their leave, I came out to the porch to see my father off. Instead of a splendid car, there waited for him an ancient, shabby carriage, unearthed goodness knows from where, and drawn by a workhorse, formerly used in the garden. The gardener, dressed in a costume that had nothing whatsoever in common with livery, acted as coachman. My father, who had been wearing civilian clothes for a long time, wore this day an old tweed cape. He took his seat in this extraordinary vehicle with such simplicity as made it all seem perfectly natural; as if he had never been accustomed to anything else. The gardener shook the reins and urged the horse on. The carriage, squeaking and swaying, began to move. For a long time I looked after the slowly moving carriage. My father's broad shoulders with the cape drawn over them and his neck under the dark hat are for ever stamped in my memory.

About that time came vague reports of the assassination of the Tsar and his family, but we refused to believe them. Also there came from Siberia unverified rumours of the escape of a group of our relatives who were in Alopaievsk; among them, Volodia. Poor Princess Paley was beside herself with joy at this news but my father was silent, rightly attaching little faith to such talk. Letters from Volodia, which came quite frequently, had ceased since July; his fate was unknown; but my father never learned of his death.

ii

Many months later, when the armies of Admiral Kolchak had occupied Siberia, there was an inquiry; and I received, in London, various small belongings of Volodia's—a two-fold leather frame with pictures of his parents, a small pocketbook with some paper money that smelled mouldy, as though long buried in damp earth, and a few yellowed letters from home. This together with official photographs of the corpses as they were carried out of the mine. Aunt Ella's and Volodia's bodies were found, we were told, side by side. The bodies, seven in all, were placed in coffins and sent to the Orthodox Mission at Peking. Still later, Aunt Ella's brother and sister took her coffin, together with that of a nun who had perished with her, to Jerusalem where now in the Holy City she lies buried.

The Bolsheviks, feeling their strength more and more, turned their attention towards the cultured part of the population. They first drew up a deliberate programme of butchery, directed against all who had in some way participated in the old regime. The fate of the Putiatin brothers distressed me terribly. Our turn might come now at any time. Desperately, we started making plans for an escape.

My only reluctance was at the thought of separation from my father, but he urged us by all the means in his power to go through with our plan.

It was vague, this plan, and appeared almost hopeless. In spite of the Brest-Litovsk peace treaty, South Russia, including Kiev, was now occupied by the Germans, who were drawing from these provinces, rich in wheat, enough supplies and cattle to feed their own starving country. Moreover, in the places under their control they had established order.

Under the protection and with the aid of these same Germans a local government had been organized in Little Russia, now called Ukraine. At the head of this government was a former general of the Russian Army, by name Skoropadsky. We decided to try to make our way to Ukraine. It was still our hope not to have to leave Russia, but simply to live for a while in the south, awaiting better days.

Most important of all was procuring the necessary documents. The shortest trip now required innumerable permits and identification papers. There could be no question of travelling with false passports. Although I now lived under the name of my husband, the Putiatins were known all over Russia, and their name did not give any protection.

The deeper we penetrated into the details of our project, the more difficult, even impossible, it seemed. In the end we decided that the safest way to go would be without any documents at all.

All preparations for our departure were enshrouded in mystery. I and the two brothers were to be the first to go; the old Putiatins with our little son would follow us as soon as we arrived in Kiev and found a place to live.

We decided to take with us only as much luggage as could

be carried by hand. Everything had to be packed in three suit-cases. My jewels, concealed in the bottle, the jewelled paper-weight, and the candles had been sent to Sweden, when the opportunity had presented itself some time previously. I now sold some small pieces to provide us with money for the trip, and besides this, I sewed into my stays and my hat two or three brooches. My travelling attire consisted of an old, worn-out dress and a raincoat. During the last years I was best known in Russia in the uniform of a war nurse and I hoped that I would not be recognized in civilian clothes.

We received a permit of departure from the local Soviet and at the last moment decided to ask the Swedish Legation for a paper that would identify me to the Germans in case of necessity. This paper we concealed in a piece of soap; thus also we hid a part of our money and secreted the rest in penholders made specially for this purpose. Everything was ready.

On the eve of our departure we went to Tsarskoie-Selo to bid my father and his family good-bye. It was a beautiful summer day. The house in which my father now lived was almost completely hidden in the green of the trees; on the lawns, in the high grass, daisies lifted their white heads; grasshoppers whirred lustily, and yellow butterflies fluttered here and there. The leave which we had come to take, all the mortal anxieties surrounding us, seemed in the light of this summer day a monstrous unreality, the fantasy of a sick imagination.

We sat down to tea. For some time now no one of us had made plans for the future or spoken of it. To do so was futile; one simply did not know. Now at this last meal not a word was said about any hope of reunion, even in a distant future. My father only remarked casually, when the conversation turned to Dmitri, that I should give him, if I ever saw him again, the greeting and the blessing of his father.

The conversation flagged, everybody felt uncomfortable. It was getting late; time to go, yet I could not muster the courage to say good-bye. At last it could not be postponed any

THE IMPERIAL FAMILY

The Emperor, the Tsarevitch, and the four Grand Duchesses visiting a Cossack regiment

longer. Trying not to think, not to recognize the probable finality of the separation, we rose from the table and embraced each other. We tried to find words to express our feelings and could not.

In silence my father went ahead of us to the door and led us into the garden. Once again we kissed and blessed each other in silence. My father stood in front of the house, smiling as he looked at us, and I continued to turn round until the path hid him from sight. I think that my father realized that we saw each other for the last time. I tried to push this thought from my heart, but it was breaking.

On July 20th, we went to Petrograd and took a train for Orsha, which served at that time as the frontier between Soviet Russia and the more southern region occupied by the Germans. The first-class carriage in which we travelled was in comparatively good order although the small compartment for two was now occupied by four; my husband, his brother Aleck, myself, and an unknown gentleman.

Before the train started, my husband pushed into the hand of the conductor a small sum of money and this saved us from great trouble which could well have ended tragically. The few friends who came to see us off informed us with great dismay that orders were circulating through town for the mass arrest of officers, all of whom were being sent, it was said, to Kronstadt to be dealt with by the sailors. And it is strange, but it was precisely from that day that there began the arrests, tortures, and executions which plunged Russia into an ocean of suffering and blood and which have lasted for these many long years.

CHAPTER XXX

FLIGHT

THE train moved slowly, stopping often. At almost every stop, detachments of armed soldiers boarded the carriages, entering the compartments and verifying the documents of the passengers. The flight from Northern Russia, where conditions were growing steadily worse, had already begun.

As I have said, we had no documents; we trembled, therefore, every time the train stopped. But our conductor, as soon as the soldiers appeared in the carriage, was always by the door; and he always found some reason for preventing them from entering. Sometimes it was a sick woman whom no one should disturb; sometimes it was military engineers going to their posts. My heart beating frantically, I listened to the heavy steps and the loud conversations in the corridor, expecting every time that the explanations of the conductor would be disregarded; but this did not happen. On the way we learned that forty sailors were travelling on the same train, sent by the Soviet of Petrograd to verify documents in Orsha, as there were too many people passing over the frontier without permits.

We spent two nights and one day on the train and arrived in Orsha early on the morning of August 4th. So far everything had gone off smoothly, but the hardest and most dangerous part was ahead of us.

Alighting, I saw the sailors jumping down from their carriage; they were armed to the teeth and loaded with ammunition belts. Upon the advice of one of our Petrograd well-wishers we were to go in Orsha to a Jewish office, the owner of which secretly dispatched travellers without passports over the frontier. My husband and Aleck went to check our suitcases. I waited on the platform. It was then that two soldiers approached me and asked for my documents. My heart froze.

"My husband has them," I replied, trying to appear indifferent. "He went to town on business. I do not know how long he will be," I added, in case they wished to wait. Undecided, the soldiers consulted each other. They could well have arrested me and taken me with them. But for some reason they decided not to do so, nor even to await the return of my husband. They had barely left my side when he and Aleck came back.

I understood perfectly well what I had escaped. We might never have seen each other again.

Leaving the station, we went in search of the Jewish office. It proved to be a small store at the edge of town. My husband went in alone.

The negotiations lasted a long time; one had to approach carefully the real cause of the visit, but when my husband came out I saw at once that he had failed.

When he heard that we had no documents, the owner of the store positively refused to help us, and neither arguments nor the promise of a payment could shake his decision. He said that during the last days the frontier was guarded far more vigilantly; that, without papers, we had now no chance.

This staggered us. The Jew was our only hope. We were at a loss to know what to do.

Disappointed to the point of anguish, we retraced our steps and set out to find lodgings.

The only decent hotel in town was overcrowded; we could not stay there. Besides, some of the sailors who had come on the same train with us were standing about. In the hotel, if we can call it that, we were given addresses of several private houses where rooms were rented to travellers; but after looking them over we decided against entering any of them. It seemed wiser to spend the night in the open than to put oneself in the hands of the owners of those houses.

So here we were without shelter, without documents, in a strange town, overcrowded by refugees of all sorts—refugees among whom, we learned, typhus and dysentery were raging. Moreover, we were likely at any minute to be apprehended by the Bolshevist patrols verifying documents.

Often in such cases, one comes to a heroic decision, and ours, like so many such, was a forced one. We could not remain in Orsha; neither could we return to Petrograd. We had no choice; all that remained was to put everything on one card.

I proposed to my companions that we go straight to the frontier and try our luck there. They agreed. We engaged a cab, went to the station for our suitcases and then our driver took us to the frontier gates just outside the town. How plainly I remember the rough, dusty road under a scorching sun and the endless carts filled with Ukrainian refugees, peasants returning home.

We had no definite plan of action, no clear idea of what we should do. Each one of us realized that we were voluntarily walking straight into the lion's den.

Our driver, making his way with difficulty between the carts and the pedestrians, finally stopped and pointed to a fence blocking the road. This, he said, was the frontier.

We alighted. On the left by the side of the road was a low, unpainted wooden shed; on its threshold, in the open door and occupying it entirely, stood a huge man wearing a smart soldier's uniform—a khaki shirt of fine cloth without straps, and new, shiny boots.

In one hand he held a long whip, the thin leather ends of which curled on the floor at his feet like live snakes. His cap was pushed back and a lock of dark hair escaped from it and fell on his forehead. His shaven, fat face expressed complete self-satisfaction. This man had nothing in common with the soldier whom I had learned to know so well during the war and to whom I was accustomed; I did not know where he belonged, or how to handle him.

But it was too late now to hesitate, he had already noticed us and, without changing his position, was watching us approach the shed.

Indecision or confusion would ruin everything. I boldly walked up to him. But even now I did not know what to say. Raising his eyebrows, and without bending his head, he gave me a mocking glance.

"What do you want?" he said, following me.

"Listen," I began, and paused until I had perfect control of myself and of the intonations of my voice. "Early this mornings my relatives crossed the frontier. Our train was late and we have not had time to obtain our papers. I am afraid that our relatives may get so far ahead of us that we will not be able to catch up with them. Yet I must see them before they cross the German frontier. Let us pass. We will come back after seeing them and will then attend to our papers."

"That is quite impossible," he replied. "To cross the frontier one should have a permit of the local Soviet of Orsha. Do you have it? And what about the Ukrainian visa?"

"But I am telling you that we have not had time to get our papers," I returned, trying to express natural agitation. "That's just it. Our relatives have our Ukrainian visas with them." I invented while talking.

"Show me your identification papers and the documents given you at the place you came from."

My husband took from his pocket the paper issued by the Pavlovsk Soviet. The representative of authority, upon whom our fate depended, took it into his hands and studied it. Our name was indistinctly written; this was the decisive moment. Fortunately his attention was attracted mainly by the seals, the profusion of which seemed to satisfy him.

"Hm," he mumbled, transferring his glance from the seals to us, "still, I cannot let you pass."

"Oh, Lord, but this is *terrible!*" I wailed, entering more and more into my part. "What are we going to do? If we don't get our visas, then we must begin all over again. Do you want us to go back to Petrograd?"

"I don't care what you do; but I can't let you pass without the permit," said the man somewhat impatiently.

By this time I had firmly decided not to surrender. Come what might, we had to get on the other side of the Bolshevist fence. Our whole future, our life, depended on it.

"Listen!"—I suddenly took a tremendous risk. "Don't you see the droshky there? We have all our luggage on it and my husband's brother will remain with it until we return. And we have no money." Saying this I opened my old handbag under his very nose. It contained only a worn cigarette case and a handkerchief. The piece of soap in which was concealed the paper from the Swedish Legation was at that time in the pocket of my raincoat and seemed to burn my side. The penholders containing the money were in my husband's pockets. What if this soldier suddenly took a notion to search us?

Yet I noticed that my last arguments appeared to have some effect on him; he was undecided. I became still more convincing. My eloquence rendered him silent. Finally, looking around and convincing himself that we were alone he suddenly said:

"All right, go on."

I did not even answer, so great was my surprise; with one step, my husband and I moved towards a door.

"This way," he said, pointing to another doorway. We passed through a second room where emaciated officials still wearing the old custom-house uniforms glanced at us curiously.

In a moment, we were on the other side of the Bolshevist fence. Before us lay a stretch of no man's land, perhaps a quarter of a mile wide, separating us from the German side.

For some reason unknown to us, both the frontiers were closed at this time. The Ukrainian refugees whom we had passed on the road gathered on this narrow strip of land into an immense and compact crowd. It was evident that they had been there for a long time. Hungry-looking peasants in rags apathetically surrounded carts loaded with their belongings and drawn by horses ready to drop from starvation. Mangy cows and sheep stood about with drooping heads too worn out to graze. On some of the carts, amid piles of rags, children were lying, exhausted and weakened by hunger or disease; they looked like skeletons. Never in my life had I seen a more pitiful gathering of people and animals.

We pushed our way through the crowd. It paid not the slightest attention to us. We came to the German fence, solidly built of boards, between which one could see barbed wire.

The wide strong gates were locked. Behind them stood two German soldiers in helmets.

We came close to the fence and peered through. Officers in grey uniforms walked calmly to and fro or stood in groups. So short a while ago we had fought against these men, and now I was forced to ask their protection against my own people.

I took the soap from my pocket and, slitting it open with a penknife, took out the paper which identified me—our only document! I noticed that one of the officers, apparently on duty, was pacing to and fro at the gates. He was so close to us that I could speak to him. Yet some time passed before I mustered my courage. Finally, remembering with difficulty my forgotten German, I called:

"Please, couldn't you come to the fence? I must speak to you."

He did not hear me; I had to repeat the sentence. He stopped and peered attentively at the fence trying to discover whence came this voice. His face under the steel helmet was young and pleasant. He approached the fence. I spoke with greater boldness.

"Owing to a stroke of luck, we have succeeded in passing the Bolshevist frontier, but we have no papers, no passport, no permit of departure, no Ukrainian visa. If you refuse to let us in we shall have to return to the Bolsheviks. My husband and his brother are with me; they are both officers of the Guards. The Bolsheviks have just begun to persecute officers and we cannot remain in Russia. In the name of God, let us in."

The officer coming close to the boards deliberately looked us over. I saw at once that he had grasped the situation.

"You are an officer of the Guards?" he asked, glancing at my husband. "And where is your brother? I don't see him."

"We were obliged to leave him on the other side with our things," I replied, for my husband spoke no German.

"I really don't know what to do with you." The officer smiled irresolutely. Then, rolling into a tube my paper from the Swedish Legation, I pushed it through the boards. He took it, read, and silently scanned my face. Our eyes met.

"Open the gates," he ordered the guards.

The soldiers obeyed. The key clicked loudly once, twice, there was the sound of a drawn bolt, and both folds of the gate swung wide open. We entered. It was just as terrifying, just as simple, and just as wonderful as a miracle.

On this side of the fence even the air seemed lighter. Everything was different here, from the expression on the people's faces to the cleanly swept grounds and the neat custom house that stood at the roadside. We were now in the camp of our enemies.

No one paid any attention to us when we entered. Our officer, striking his boots with his whip, spoke to us as to old acquaintances. The fact that he had saved our lives bound us to him by strong ties. He was full of solicitude, yet not so much as hinted about what he read in my paper.

I asked his advice. Weighing our situation, he offered to take us to the Ukrainian commissar who, in his opinion, would grant us a visa, without which we could neither remain here nor continue our trip.

But the word "commissar" terrified me; it seemed to personify all the horror that we had gone through during the past year. I positively refused to appear before the Ukrainian commissar and no arguments could move me.

I preferred, I said, to deal with the Germans and asked to be sent to the local commander. The officer finally acquiesced to my demand, shrugging his shoulders good-naturedly.

"But I assure you, you are making a mistake, a great mistake," he added, turning us over, under receipt, to a short soldier.

We went with this soldier along the dusty road, and in spite of our thirst and hunger—we had not eaten since morning—we could not help wondering at the order surrounding us; we had grown so unaccustomed to it.

The way was long; it took us about an hour. Finally we reached a field on which were several wooden huts, painted a khaki colour. Our guard told us that this was the office of the commander; he would, he added, find out when the commander could receive us.

He was gone a very long time. Upon a trampled field stood or walked men in grey uniforms.

Orderlies continually went in and out of the building. Efficient, unhurried organization was everywhere noticeable.

Our soldier came out of the barrack and, without explaining the cause, told us that we must wait. We sat down on the shaft of an unharnessed wagon near by. I looked around and my thoughts began to take shape. Escaping the Bolsheviks we had now come to a country where the Germans ruled, yet still it was Russia. Oh, Lord!

Time passed. The sun, which had been mercilessly scorching us since morning, hung now immobile over our heads. Our mouths were dry, our arms and feet felt heavy. On the field in front of the building the same quiet activity went on; grey uniforms passed back and forth; the door of the barrack continually slammed. Our guard was gravely concerned with a small, badly smelling cigar at which he avidly puffed a few times, then, extinguishing it, hid it carefully in his pocket only to take it out again a few minutes later to make a new attempt.

It was strangely quiet. One could hardly believe in all this stillness; it seemed as though any minute machine guns would begin to rattle or cannon to roar.

Thus several more hours went by. From time to time, our soldier, at my insistent requests, would go to the hut to see if the commander would receive us, but usually he left us reluctantly as though afraid that we might run away, and returned without having attained the least result.

From time to time my husband or I would get up and walk up and down the lawn. The hours dragged on endlessly. Finally even the sun grew tired and began slowly to glide to the horizon. We did not believe that the commander intended to see us. But just when we had lost all hope, the soldier made signs for us to follow him. We had decided that my husband would go to this interview alone. The commander, we had been told, spoke Russian. Soldier might better speak with soldier, without a woman by. I was to join the parley only as a last resort.

My husband went into the barrack. I remained alone with our guardian. A short while later my husband returned. My presence, he said, was necessary; the commander refused to give us a pass across the frontier without the visa of the Ukrainian commissar.

I went with my husband to the commander. We entered an empty, badly aired room smelling of paint and heated wood. Behind an unpainted table sat two or three officers with tired faces. One of them rose and came to us. I saw at once that it would be impossible to induce this man to change his mind. His expression was cold and haughty. I addressed him in Russian and tried none the less to move him. He listened to me with indifference and repeated what he had told my husband. Without the Ukrainian commissar he could not do anything. That was final.

We left. A desperate lethargy seemed to envelop me. Our situation was now, it seemed, completely hopeless.

We trudged in the direction of the frontier. All that remained was to return to Orsha, to the Bolsheviks. I could hardly walk. All hope had abandoned me, yet I did not care; I was too tired.

The sun was setting. I walked leaning on my husband's arm and stumbling at almost every step.

It was nearly dark when we reached the German outpost. Suddenly a familiar figure appeared from the darkness—it was the German officer, our rescuer. He understood at once that we had failed.

"You were wrong not to listen to me," he laughed. "A good thing for you I'm on duty again. Wait here, I think that the Ukrainian commissar has not gone away. This time you will not refuse to talk to him?" He turned to me. "But you can hardly stand," he exclaimed. "Probably you haven't eaten for a long time. Come into our guardhouse; we might find something for you to eat." As he took me under the arm I was actually reeling; my head swam; my eyes were dim.

"Give me some water," was all I could say.

I do not remember how I reached the small porch of the house. I was sitting upon a bench under wooden eaves, and as one in a dream I heard someone open a bottle of soda water. The sizzling liquid filled the glass which was handed me. I groped for it and drank avidly and then ate with the same avidity a bar of chocolate that was offered me. Very soon strength flowed back into me, and my husband, having in his turn appeased his hunger, went to talk to the commissar, who had just arrived.

Another miracle. He proved to be the nephew of someone we had known well and for a long time. We could tell him everything and as if by a magic wand the situation changed.

The commissar gave my husband a pass and a visa for the unfortunate Aleck, who had been waiting the whole day, with the suitcases, at the Bolshevist frontier gate. Two soldiers were dispatched with my husband to bring the luggage. I stayed on the porch of the little house and the commissar and our rescuer tried to keep my thoughts diverted while my husband was on the Bolshevist side.

Shortly afterwards my husband returned safely with Aleck. Soldiers carried the suitcases. The Bolsheviks must have forgotten our morning promise and had not appeared to recognize my husband. The pass and the Ukrainian visa had satisfied them. Even the custom examination passed off quite smoothly; my husband had succeeded in slipping into the hands of the miserable officials a few kerenki—paper money of the smaller denominations, issued by Kerensky—and was permitted to go after the most superficial inspection.

Now that we were safe, we had to think of where to go. The next train for Kiev did not leave until the day following. The Ukrainian commissar offered us for the night his carriage which stood on a siding near by. He conducted us there and had dinner sent us from the German officers' mess. In my whole life I have never eaten anything better than the thin bean soup splashing at the bottom of those enamel pans.

Sitting opposite each other on the torn velvet seats of the carriage we laughed and laughed. A tremendous weight had rolled off our shoulders. Life seemed beautiful as after a mortal disease. We were as happy to be together as if we had not seen each other for an eternity. Thus ended August 4th, my saint's day.

ii

Excitement and happiness kept us awake late, and when we put out the light we still could not sleep, but for a different reason. If the Bolsheviks had shown us mercy this could not be said of the insect inhabitants of the carriage. Next day there was not an unblemished spot on my body.

In the morning we received the visit of the commissar. He was greatly agitated by the reports from the other side. The sailors who had arrived on the same train with us had that night made the rounds of the hotel and the rooms rented to travellers. Many of those whose papers and visas were in order had been delayed indefinitely in Orsha while additional information was sent for, and those who had no documents had been arrested and put in the local jail. We heard later that some of those arrested were returned to the towns whence they came, and others transferred to prisons in which they spent many years. From the very day of our escape the crossing of the frontier had been rendered almost impossible by the Bolsheviks.

Next day, while waiting for the train, we stayed in the commissar's carriage. He asked us not to come out; he was afraid of trouble should it become known that I was there. We submitted of course, but never found out what kind of trouble he was expecting, whether from the Bolsheviks or from the Germans.

At night we boarded a train that took us to Zhlobin; here we had to change for Kiev. The train consisted exclusively of carriages of the third and fourth class. It was crowded mostly by common people. With great difficulty we found room, if we can call it that, in a fourth-class carriage. (Formerly these fourth-class carriages were used for the transportation of prisoners only.) A passage ran from door to door along the windows while on the other side there were wooden-backed benches facing each other. Above the seats were two rows of shelves. On one of these shelves, close to us, we placed our suitcases, afraid to leave them out of our sight. We could only lie flat on our shelf; it pressed so closely upon an upper one. The carriage was hideously overcrowded; once we had climbed up, further movement was out of the question. Spreading our coats over the bare boards, we all three lay down. The carriage was wholly dark. Somehow I succeeded in extracting from one of the suitcases a candle that I had brought along in case of emergency and, sticking it into the cover of a neighbour's basket, I lighted it.

That made things better. The train began to move. It was close in the carriage; it smelt of people, and the noise of conversations rose in a constant hubbub. Someone was loudly arguing and a fight started. But we had, at least, a light.

Little by little the voices became subdued. Settling the best I could on my hard bed I drowsed. Suddenly I woke up from a terrific jolt and was thrown against the partition, striking my head. This jolt was followed by the squeak of brakes, a cracking and crunching of wood. The train stopped.

Undoubtedly one of the other carriages had run against ours, but it was impossible to gauge the extent of the wreck.

After a few moments of dead stillness, especially striking because it followed the clicking of the wheels and the deafening crash of the sudden stop, a panic broke out in the carriage. People surged in utter disorder to the exits, crying, moaning, crushing each other. Suddenly on the shelf above us, a bottle broke. A thin spray of transparent liquid began to drip between my head and the candle.

"Benzine!" shouted my husband. There was no time to lose; I stretched out my hand and with the palm mashed out the light. In the darkness the panic increased.

We remained on our shelf. There was no sense in climbing down. Through the dirty panes of the carriage windows flickered the lights of lanterns. Only when our carriage had emptied, did we climb down from our shelf and jump out upon the embankment.

Our carriage had indeed struck the next one, and one of its ends was broken to pieces. We went along the train to the engine, which stood apart, the train having been broken off from it. No one could explain what had happened.

The bustling and shouting continued for a long time. Finally we were told that we would have to abandon our carriage and move into another. Dragging our suitcases, we tried to find seats, but this was impossible. The train had already been overcrowded, and now the passengers of two broken carriages had to be squeezed in. While we were walking along the train I noticed that a carriage, somewhat cleaner than the others, had been assigned to German officers; this was announced by a notice in both languages. Having ascertained that we could not possibly get on the train any other way, we decided to thrust ourselves in there, hoping that we would not be run out.

I led the way. Hoisting myself to the platform I opened the carriage door and found myself in a large boarded compartment. A table stood in front of me; behind it was a long wooden couch. Several German officers were sitting on the couch, their coats unbuttoned. They were drinking and talking and laughing noisily. Their faces were red; it was plain that they were drunk.

I backed out, but it was too late; they had already seen me and greeted me with roars of laughter and compliments rather too outspoken.

Embarrassed, I explained with difficulty that my husband was with me and that we could find no place; our carriage had been wrecked. Although somewhat disappointed, they let us into one of the back compartments and, paying us no more attention, continued their revels until morning. Nevertheless our new abode, although made of board, seemed a palace to us after our fourth-class shelf.

iii

NEXT day, towards evening, we arrived at Zhlobin. We were struck by the outward appearance of the station; it had undergone almost no change, even the service was as it used to be.

Everybody was polite and cleanly dressed; people and things alike were in their places. Here also, for the first time in almost a year, we enjoyed real food. In the dining-room of our hotel stood a table of *hors d'œuvre*, overloaded with good things to eat. Plates piled high with white and black bread stood in front of each diner and in the soup, served steaming hot, floated large pieces of meat. The smell alone made one's mouth water. I cannot understand how we did not die that day from overeating.

In the few minutes that my husband was absent buying the train tickets, Aleck and I dispatched an entire sucking pig. This was only an appetizer; when my husband returned, we sat down to a dinner which would ordinarily have satisfied at least ten people.

It is difficult to express in words what we were experiencing that day! We were alive, out of danger. He who has not lived through such a moment does not know what it means actually to enjoy life.

Late that night we boarded the train which was to take us to Kiev. Still there was no end to our raptures. We were in a real first-class sleeping-car, where for the first time in all these days we could at last undress and wash. And how agreeable it was afterwards to stretch out on a soft couch between two crisp white sheets.

We arrived in Kiev next day. The city was so overcrowded that there was no room in any of the hotels, but this did not disturb us now. We knew that somehow we would find a place to live.

Our faith was justified. My husband met on the street an old acquaintance, who at once invited us to her house. And that day also, like a blind person who suddenly has seen the light, I rejoiced in everything. Everything seemed new and wonderful—the hairdresser's where my hair was washed and curled, the attractive confectioner's where, like a schoolgirl, I ate twelve pieces of pastry one after the other. Lord, what a day that was!

We moved with our suitcases to our friend's house. Next day, finding that there was an opportunity of sending a package to Petrograd, I bought a sack of white flour for my father. Later I learned that it had reached him.

Now began an unreal, camp-like life, in which was no stability, no real peace. Kiev had been saved by the Germans, yet it had at the same time been conquered by them. The Ukrainian government issued orders, made decisions, yet one knew always that its very existence depended on the Germans, who used it as a sort of mediator between the inhabitants and themselves.

The Germans behaved like conquerors, but without them the country would again have been in the power of the Bolsheviks. Both the refugees from Northern Russia and the higher classes of the local population who had gone through the horrors of the Bolshevist regime now relaxed in body and in spirit; here was food, gaiety, security; and yet one could not believe that it would last. A nervous tenseness was in the air. Fantastic rumours circulated. Suddenly, for instance, I heard on every side that my brother was in Kiev. He had been seen, I was assured here and there. I was even told the names of people who had met him. At first I laughed, but later the tales became so convincing that hope was born in my heart. I had been for many months without news from Dmitri; the times were such as to make possible the most incredible things.

I began to make inquiries which led me from source to source, until my meeting with Dmitri was all but arranged; then the whole thing collapsed, as one might have expected. Evidently some adventurer had been using my brother's name.

The hospitable house where we were stopping was already overcrowded with guests. At night every room was occupied, and the visitors continually changed. People came without warning, straight from the Bolsheviks, in rags, hungry, often without money. Often our hostess would meet friends on the streets and bring them home with her, as she had us. In her small dining-room we never sat down to table with fewer than fifteen or twenty.

Our plans were still very indefinite. We did not know what to do. I began to see, however, that we should not remain in Kiev too long. First of all, I did not feel quite at ease. The war was still going on in the West. The presence of our former enemies, their bearing, their tone, the farcical character of the political game, and the intrigues between them and the local administration—all this irritated me. And the instability of the situation was all too evident; it was impossible to maintain any illusions as to the future of the Ukraine. Having succeeded in escaping the Bolsheviks, it would now be stark madness to expose ourselves to new catastrophes. We should move on, farther south, nearer to the sea, to the frontier, and wait there.

We decided to go to Odessa where some close friends of mine had a house, to which they urged us to come.

The final impetus to our departure, however, was given by a rumour circulating about town which almost prostrated me. I was told that my father had been arrested again and this time imprisoned. Shortly afterwards this report was confirmed. From that day I no longer knew peace. From Petrograd came endless reports of the cruelties of the Bolsheviks. The era of arrests, executions, and tortures had now definitely begun. Throughout many long months my imagination painted dreadful, horrible pictures. I woke up at night and in mortal terror; it was as if, just at that moment, far away, the dreadful, ultimate thing was happening. There was now, I knew, no longer any doubt as to what the end would be; yet my heart was continually torn between hope and utter despair. The last word I received from my father was a pencilled note, written in prison, thanking me for the flour I had sent him.

It was not until I was a refugee in Rumania, months later, that the outcome became known to me. My father was arrested only ten days after our departure. He was confined in one of the state prisons where he remained six months, partly in the prison itself, partly, by reason of illness, in the prison infirmary.

Princess Paley exerted all her energies. It appeared towards the end that my father would be released. This was, in fact, definitely promised by the Bolsheviks; but on January 30, 1919, the very day that freedom was to have been granted him, he was suddenly taken from the prison, transferred to the Fortress of SS. Peter and Paul, and, without further torture, shot.

CHAPTER XXXI

LAST SALUTE

ALECK decided to stay in Kiev. My husband and I went on to Odessa, to the large villa of our friends there. Odessa was occupied by the Austrian troops but their presence was less noticeable than that of the Germans in Kiev. The Austrian general and the Russian military governor peacefully shared the power in the city. Before the arrival of the Austrian troops, Odessa had also been swept by a wave of Bolshevist cruelties, but for the time being life had settled into comparative order; and save for the high-crowned caps of the Austrian officers on the streets, one would have thought that everything was as it used to be.

Further travel was not as yet feasible. Almost all Rumania was in the hands of the Germans; besides, and still more important, we had almost no money. We had to wait. But the constant anxiety as to my father urged me to write to the Kings of Spain and Sweden and to the Queen of Rumania, who was at that time with her court in Jassy.

In Odessa we relaxed little by little from our anxieties, rested, recovered our health. The hospitality of our hosts was touching; they shared with us everything they had, and did their utmost to make our sojourn agreeable. We had some acquaintances in town and their number grew steadily as other friends came to Odessa. We saw each other frequently and led, all things considered, an existence that would have been most pleasant but for dark premonitions about my father and his family.

Success, meanwhile, was decidedly inclining to the side of the Allies. It could now be hoped that this terrible war would end. One heard more often and more insistently of growing discontent in Germany and Austria, and of internal political complications.

The peace in Odessa was merely outward; it could only be temporary and last as long as the town was occupied by the alien troops. At that, even the occupation could not prevent things happening from time to time that set the whole city trembling with fear.

The heat was terrible. Every morning the blinds were drawn, the shutters closed. Everyone rose early; everything was attended to before noon, and after lunch we rested.

One afternoon about four o'clock I was awakened by the dull noise of explosions. At first these explosions were at rare intervals, but soon they followed one upon another so rapidly that the air was filled with a dull incessant roar.

We all rushed into the garden. From there we saw an immense black cloud of smoke rising in waves at the northern part of the city. Someone went to telephone for information and was told that the ammunition stores situated at that edge of town were afire.

We had seen these stores; they stretched for miles. Towards evening the uproar increased considerably. From the roof of the house we saw a grandiose spectacle, a display of giant fireworks. A bright, immense flame licked the ground and, on the black background of the smoke, thousands of huge rockets rose high in the air, threading the sky with innumerable lines of fire.

Thus it continued throughout the entire night. The noise made sleep impossible. In the morning the air was saturated with the smell of burning wood and powder, and the smoke had screened the sun.

Ashes and bits of ammunition began to fall around the house. Then the big shells began to explode. Panic swept the city. The window-panes shook ceaselessly; some broke. The military governor of the town sent word to me that all the efforts to check the spreading of the fire had been fruitless. People rushed along the streets in every direction, some carrying pillows, others clothing, still others, perfectly useless objects. Frightened acquaintances continually rushed into our garden, bringing new panic-stricken rumours. The earth shook; there was now such an uproar in the air that we could hardly hear one another.

To instil calm in myself and in the others I placed a wicker chair on the terrace, took a book, and pretended to read. The military governor telephoned each half hour. He said that the main danger now threatened from the large stores of melinite which were buried deep in the ground, but which might explode any minute from the shaking of the earth.

I asked him whether it would not be better for us to go down into the port and, taking a boat, sail into the open. He replied that, should the melinite explode, a sort of earthquake would result and there might be nothing left of the city, while a tidal wave would rise in the sea, swallowing everything.

All the other ways out of town had been cut off. We were obliged to stay. The melinite had probably been dampened for it did not explode, and by evening the fires subsided. They had burned, on the whole, for almost thirty-six hours.

ii

By the end of October rumours as to the revolution in Germany and Austria had become quite definite. Two more mighty monarchies were on the eve of dissolution. My attitude towards these reports was divided, just as was my feeling towards the recent enemy who had temporarily rid part of Russia of the Bolsheviks. A change in the social order of Central Europe meant, doubtless, a near end of the war, but at the same time it retarded the possibility of re-establishing the monarchical principle in Russia. (At that time, I still could not imagine my country otherwise governed.)

As soon as the rumour of the revolution was confirmed, the Austrian troops went from Odessa. This took them only a few days. There was talk of Allied troops coming in, but no real sign of it; and our situation, meantime, was again dangerous. As was to be expected, the lawless and troublesome elements in town became active; robberies in the city assumed the character of an epidemic, while in the province organized armed bands threatened to reinstall Bolshevist rule. Moreover, an epidemic of Spanish "flu" raged in the city, and people died like flies. Our house was not wholly spared. Among the first to catch the disease were my husband and I.

Once, at the very beginning of November, when we were still in bed, an unknown Russian officer came to see me from Bessarabia, which at that time had already been annexed by Rumania. This officer had been sent by the chief of the Allied Intelligence Service in Rumania, a Canadian colonel by the name of Boyle, who was then either in Jassy or in Kishinev. This Colonel Boyle was almost a legendary person, and his fame spread along all the shores of the Black Sea. He enjoyed great influence at that time in Rumania, and by the use of that influence saved many Russians. He had heard from the Russian officers surrounding him of my presence in Odessa and, knowing how dangerous it was for us to stay there, he now sent word that he was ready to help.

I thanked him and answered that I would be ready to leave in about a week. Somehow I did not put much trust in the desire of a Canadian colonel to save us, but I was utterly mistaken. At the appointed time, to my great surprise, the officer returned. He brought me a letter from the Queen, my cousin, with an invitation to come to Rumania and announced that everything was ready for our departure. A Rumanian officer had come with him, who was also assigned to accompany us.

We were first to go to Kishinev where further instructions awaited us. Our preparations for departure soon were made. On the very eve of our departure a new wave of the "flu" swept the house; our host fell ill and I had another attack of fever.

But the trip could not be postponed. Bolshevism with its,

for us, inevitably fatal consequences was on the verge of reassuming control. Several small detachments of officers, volunteers from the White Army which was being organized on the Don, had already been sent to Odessa to protect the inhabitants and maintain order; and another such small detachment had been dispatched north to defend a large junction station, Razdelnaya, towards which were marching the bands of the Ukrainian adventurer and highwayman, Petlura.

We were assigned a special carriage in which we were to make the entire trip to Rumania. The two officers travelled with us and also an elderly maid, whom I had engaged a few days before our departure.

Everything went well for the first sixty or seventy miles. Then, reaching Razdelnaya, we plunged unexpectedly into an atmosphere of war.

It appeared that Petlura was much stronger than had been expected. His bands had crushed the small detachment of officers and forced them to retreat to Razdelnaya, this very town. Petlura pressed his advantage closely, and was still advancing.

The behaviour of this adventurer and his associates did not differ from that of the Bolsheviks. They burned and wrecked everything they could, tortured and killed.

Our train stood in the station a long while. Then it was announced that we could not proceed. There was no more water in the engine, and the water pipes at the station were out of order. Our carriage had stopped just in front of the platform, upon which thronged the officers of the detachment of volunteers. This gathering comprised the most varied faces imaginable and was dressed in all manner of clothes. The young White Army consisted of most diverse elements. It was united solely by the idea of active fighting against the Bolsheviks. I could not determine from their appearance anything of their sympathies and was far from sure as to what their attitude would be towards me when they found out who I was, and to where I was travelling.

Our Russian officer went in search of the commander of the detachment and brought him into the carriage. A courteous young colonel, he somewhat dispelled my doubts. He would be happy, he said, to give us the engine belonging to their troop train. To this I would not agree; I was afraid of depriving them of their only means of transportation. But the colonel assured me that water would soon be procured and that then they could use our engine. It would be too dangerous, he added, for us to delay that long our departure.

While the new engine was being attached to our carriage the colonel went out to the platform to give orders; when he returned he announced that he would not let us go without a guard.

I protested. First, his men did not inspire me with confidence; second, I would be taking them away from their direct duty. But the colonel held his ground. Our argument was ended by his announcement that it was he who was in charge here, and that he assumed all responsibility.

Several officers with machine guns were placed on the engine while two others stood guard at the doors of our carriage. When everything was ready the colonel came to ask for permission to start the train.

I thanked him and wished him luck. He kissed my hand and jumped down. The train began to move.

I stood by the window. Suddenly it was as though an electric current had passed through that crowd of volunteers. As one man they turned towards the car, straightened in line, and saluted.

I seemed for a moment glued to the spot, then, forgetting everything, without hat or coat, I rushed to the back platform of the old-fashioned carriage. Choking with emotion, the tears pouring down my cheeks, I shouted greetings and good wishes. They gathered at the end of the platform and removed their caps at the departing train. I stood there on the platform until faces could no longer be distinguished and figures had blurred into one grey spot.

That evening we came to Bendery, where the frontier of Bessarabia began. It was completely dark. The carriage was dimly lit by a few candles stuck here and there into empty bottles. It was cold. During the day my fever had increased. I was shivering; my cheeks were burning.

Before our arrival in Bendery I sent for our volunteer guards to thank them and to say good-bye to them, to say good-bye to Russia in their persons. Six men entered the car and filled it with their heavy winter clothing, their fur caps, the jingle of their soldiers' rifles. They brought with them the smell of the Russian fields in autumn, of the smoke of burning wood, of leather boots, and ammunition, of soldiers' coats. In the half-dark compartment, lit by a single candle, one could only discern their contours.

I was so agitated that I could not speak. These strangers, people I had never seen before, were closer to me now than my own kin; they were a part of my own being; they contained all that I was leaving.

Wishing to engrave their faces for ever in my memory, I took the candle from the table and lifted it up to each face in turn. The tiny yellow flame illumined for a second the heads of clipped hair, the faces, weatherbeaten and wearing heavy moustaches.

I wanted to say something significant to them so that they too would remember me for ever, but I could not utter a word; only tears, bitter tears and comfortless, rolled down my cheeks.

Thus I said good-bye to Russia.

INDEX